Easy as 1-2-3 Crochet™

Edited by Carol Alexander

HOUSE of
WHITE
BIRCHES
PUBLISHERS
SINCE 1947

Easy as 1-2-3 Crochet™

EDITOR Carol Alexander
ART DIRECTOR Brad Snow
PUBLISHING SERVICES DIRECTOR Brenda Gallmeyer

EDITORIAL ASSISTANT Beth Dietsch
ASSISTANT ART DIRECTOR Nick Pierce
COPY SUPERVISOR Michelle Beck
COPY EDITORS Kim English, Susanna Tobias
TECHNICAL EDITOR Agnes Russell

GRAPHIC ARTS SUPERVISOR Ronda Bechinski
GRAPHIC ARTISTS Jessi Butler, Minette Collins Smith
PRODUCTION ASSISTANTS Marj Morgan, Judy Neuenschwander

PHOTOGRAPHY Tammy Christian, Don Clark, Matthew Owen
PHOTO STYLIST Tammy M. Smith, Tammy Steiner

CHIEF EXECUTIVE OFFICER David McKee

BOOK MARKETING DIRECTOR Dwight Seward

Printed in China
First Printing 2008

Library of Congress Control Number: 2007922642
Hardcover ISBN: 978-1-59217-188-0
Softcover ISBN: 978-1-59217-189-7

Every effort has been made to ensure the accuracy and completeness of the instructions in this book. However, we cannot be responsible for human error or for the results when using materials other than those specified in the instructions, or for variations in individual work.

1 2 3 4 5 6 7 8 9

DRGbooks.com

A Note From the Editor

 "Quick and easy" doesn't have to mean dull and uninspired when it comes to your crochet projects. The enticing projects in *Easy as 1-2-3 Crochet* are loaded with lots of style and creative appeal to turn "simple" into sensational!

If you are a beginning crocheter, or if you have a friend or family member who wants to learn how to crochet, this book will be a great addition to your library. Many of the patterns are perfectly suited to new crocheters or those with just a little bit of stitching experience. Of course, we've also included a few patterns that are a bit more complex for those crocheters who really like to get their hooks going!

From fashionable accessories and stylish garments to chic home accents and adorable items for babies and kids, the patterns in *Easy as 1-2-3 Crochet* are sure to delight a variety of tastes and are perfect to make for almost any occasion. The projects are made with an enticing mix of yarns and threads that are fun to use and readily available in stores, catalogs and online.

All of us who worked together to bring you *Easy as 1-2-3 Crochet* wish you many relaxing and rewarding hours of enjoyable crochet with the appealing projects in this delightful book.

Carol Alexander

Contents

Accessories in a Snap

Fashion in a Flash

Great Gifts in a Dash

Wee Folk in a Wink

Home Accents
in a Hurry

General
Information

Accessories
in a Snap

This chapter features a variety
of fun, fanciful accessories,
including wraps, scarves, hats,
purses and more!

Hairpin Lace Shawl

DESIGN BY MARGRET WILLSON FOR CARON INTERNATIONAL

INTERMEDIATE

Finished Size

24 inches long x 50 inches
wide, excluding Fringe

Finished Garment Measurements

One size fits most

Gauge

Size M hook & hairpin lace loom & MC: 10 lps =
4 inches

Pattern Notes

Weave in loose ends as work progresses.
Join rounds with a slip stitch unless otherwise stated.
When working edging on hairpin lace strip, insert
hook from back to front through hairpin loops so
that all loops will twist in the same direction.

Materials

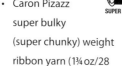

- Caron Pizazz
  super bulky
  (super chunky) weight
  ribbon yarn (1¾ oz/28
  yds/50g per ball):
    15 balls #0009 black tie
    (MC)
- Caron Glimmer super bulky
  (super chunky) weight yarn
  (1¾ oz/49 yds/50g per ball):
    4 balls #0020 black (A)
- Sizes K/10½/6.5mm and
  M/13/9mm crochet hooks
  or sizes needed to obtain
  gauge
- Hairpin lace loom
- Yarn needle

Hold specified number of loops together as one.

Special Stitch

Shell: (Sc, ch 3, sc) in indicated group of 3 lps.

Hairpin Lace Technique

1. With loom set at 3 inches, make a long slip knot
equal to half of the width of the loom, place slip knot
on left prong.
2. Replace bottom crossbar.
3. Bring the yarn around the RS of the loom to the back.
4. Insert hook through slip knot, yo and draw lp
through, ch 1.
5. Pass hook to back, between prongs, while turning
loom clockwise (right to left).
6. Insert hook through lp on left prong, yo and draw
lp through (2 lps on hook).

Hairpin Lace Illustration

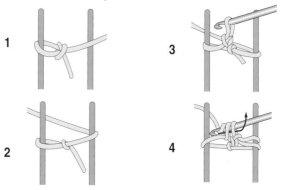

end, sc in end of last group, shell in spine, sc in end of next 3-lp group, rep from * around, ending with join in beg sc, fasten off.

Joining Strips 2–7

With size K hook and A, [sc in next 3-lp group of working Strip, ch 1, sc in corresponding ch-3 lp of previous Strip, ch 1, sc in same 3-lp group of working Strip] across edge, *working across end of working Strip as for previous Strip, sc in end of last of 3-lp group, shell in spine, sc in end of next 3-lp group held tog*, shell in each 3-lp group held tog across 2nd side of working Strip, rep from * to * across 2nd end of Strip, join in beg sc, fasten off.

Shawl Edging

Rnd 1: With size M hook, attach A in first ch-3 lp on long edge, *shell in each ch-3 lp across long edge, working across end of Shawl, [shell in next sc, shell in next ch-3 lp, shell in next sc] across short edge, rep from * around, join in beg sc, fasten off.

Fringe

Note: *Fringe is worked across each short end of Shawl.* For each Fringe, cut 2 strands of A and 1 strand of MC each 16 inches long.

Holding the 3 strands tog, fold strands in half, insert size K hook from WS to RS into ch-3 lp of short edge, draw strands through at fold to form lp on hook, draw cut ends through lp on hook, pull strands to tighten. Rep in each ch-3 lp on each short end of Shawl. ●

7. Yo and draw through both lps.
Rep steps 5–7 for required length.

SHAWL

Hairpin Lace Strip
Make 7.
With size M hook and MC, work Hairpin Lace Technique until each Strip has 126 lps on each side.

Edging Strip 1
With size K hook and A, *[**shell** *(see Special Stitch)* in each group of 3 lps held tog] across, working across

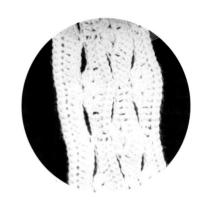

Edelweiss Scarf

DESIGN BY RAYNELDA CALDERON

EASY

Finished Size

4½ x 69 inches

Materials

- Caron Simply Soft medium (worsted) weight yarn (6 oz/330 yds/170g per skein): 1 skein #9702 off-white
- Size H/8/5mm crochet hook or size needed to obtain gauge
- Tapestry needle

4 MEDIUM

Gauge

11 dc = 3 inches

Pattern Notes

Weave in loose ends as work progresses.

Scarf is crocheted lengthwise.

Join rounds with a slip stitch unless otherwise stated.

Pattern Stitches

3-double crochet cluster (3-dc cl): [Yo, insert hook in st, yo, draw up a lp, yo, draw through 2 lps on hook] 3 times in same st, yo, draw through all 4 lps on hook.

2-double crochet cluster (2-dc cl): [Yo, insert hook in next st, yo, draw up a lp, yo, draw through 2 lps on hook] twice in same st, yo, draw through all 3 lps on hook.

SCARF

Row 1: Ch 280, dc in 4th ch from hook, dc in each of next 276 chs, turn. *(278 dc)*

CONTINUED ON PAGE 30

Fabulous Felted Tote

DESIGN BY JEWDY LAMBERT

INTERMEDIATE

Finished Size
Felted: 13 inches tall x 19
  inches long x 5¼ inches
  deep

Materials

4 MEDIUM

- 100 percent
  wool medium
  (worsted) weight yarn (3½
  oz/175 yds/99g per skein):
    6 skeins gray and pink
    tones
- Size I/9/5.5mm crochet
  hook or size needed to
  obtain gauge
- Tapestry needle
- Sewing needle
- Sewing thread
- Stitch markers

Gauge
4 dc sts = 1½ inches; 4 dc rows = 2¾ inches

Pattern Notes
Weave in loose ends as work progresses.
Do not join rounds unless otherwise stated.

TOTE

Bottom & Ends
Row 1: Beg at center bottom, ch 32, dc in 4th ch
from hook *(sk 3 chs count as first dc)*, dc in each rem ch
across, turn. *(30 dc)*
Row 2: Ch 3 *(counts as first dc)*, dc in each dc across, turn.

Rows 3–104: Rep row 2. At end of row 104,
fasten off.

First Side
Note: *For Tote corners, place first st marker in side edge
of row 36 of Bottom and Ends section and 2nd
st marker in side edge of row 69 of Bottom and Ends
section.*
Row 1: Attach yarn in first corner, ch 3, 2 dc in same
st, 3 dc in side edge of each row, ending with last 3
in side edge of 2nd corner *(34 sts across bottom)*, turn.
(102 dc)
Row 2: Ch 3, dc in each dc across, turn.
Rows 3–35: Rep row 2. At the end of row 35,
fasten off.

2nd Side
Rows 1–35: Rep rows 1–35 on opposite edge of Tote.

Pocket
Row 1: Ch 62, dc in 4th ch from hook, dc in each rem
ch across, turn. *(60 dc)*
Rows 2–20: Ch 3, dc in each dc across, turn. At the
end of row 20, fasten off.

Handle
Rnd 1: Ch 3, join with sl st to form a ring, 7 dc in ring,
use st marker to mark rnds. *(7 dc)*

CONTINUED ON PAGE 31

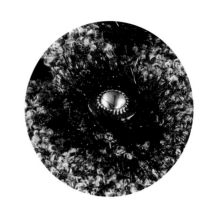

Posh Purse

DESIGN BY ALEXANDRA LOCKHART

EASY

Finished Size

7 inches tall, excluding
  Handles, 10 inches wide
  at base

Materials

- Plymouth Alpaca
  Boucle bulky
  (chunky) weight yarn (1¾
  oz/65 yds/50g per ball):
    2 balls #15 black and
      white variegated *(MC)*
- Erdal Glowlash bulky
  (chunky) weight yarn (1¾
  oz/104 yds/100g per ball):
    1 ball #04 black *(CC)*
- Size K/10½/6.5mm crochet
  hook or size needed to
  obtain gauge
- Tapestry needle
- Stitch markers
- 28mm decorative shank
  button

Gauge

4 sc = 1⅜ inch; 4 rows = 1½ inches

Pattern Notes

Weave in loose ends as work progresses.
Join rounds with a slip stitch unless otherwise stated.

PURSE

Body

Rnd 1 (RS): Starting at bottom of Purse, with MC, ch 25, sc in 2nd ch from hook, sc in each rem ch across, ending with 3 sc in last ch, working on opposite side of foundation ch, sc in each ch across, ending with 2 sc in same ch as beg sc. *(50 sc)*

Note: *Place a stitch marker in the first sc of each 3-sc group of each corner.*

Rnd 2: 2 sc in first sc, sc in each of next 22 sc, [2 sc in next sc] 3 times, sc in each of next 22 sc, [2 sc in next sc] twice. *(56 sc)*

Rnd 3: Sc in each sc around.

Rnds 4–22: Rep rnd 3.

Rnd 23: Rep rnd 3, turn.

Rnd 24 (WS): Draw up a strand of CC, holding 1 strand of both MC and CC tog, sc in each sc around.

Rnd 25: Sc in each sc around, sl st in next sc, fasten off both strands.

Button

Find center front of Purse, measure 3½ inches down from top edge, sew button to Purse.

Flap Closure

Row 1: Mark off center 4 sts at top back of Purse, attach MC in first st, ch 1, sc in same st as beg ch, sc in each of next 3 sc, turn. *(4 sc)*

Row 2: Ch 1, sc in each sc across, turn.

Rows 3–10: Rep row 2.

Row 11: Draw up a strand of CC, holding 1 strand of both MC and CC tog, ch 1, sc in each sc across, turn.

Row 12: Ch 1, sc in first sc, ch 2, sk next 2 sc *(buttonhole)*, sc in last sc, turn.

Row 13: Ch 1, sc in first sc, sc in each of next 2 chs, sc in last sc, turn. *(4 sc)*

CONTINUED ON PAGE 31

Classic in Copper Hat & Scarf

DESIGNS BY SHELIA LESLIE

EASY

Finished Size

Adult

Finished Garment Measurements

Hat: 18-inch circumference

Scarf: 3 x 33 inches, excluding
 Tassels

Gauge

With 2 strands yarn held tog: 5 sc = 1½ inches;
5 sc rows = 1½ inches

Pattern Notes

Weave in loose ends as work progresses.
Do not join rounds unless otherwise stated.
Mark first stitch of each round.

HAT

Crown

Rnd 1: Starting at top, with 2 strands held tog,
ch 2, 6 sc in 2nd ch from hook, **do not join**, **place st**

Materials

![4 MEDIUM]

* Red Heart
 Symphony
 medium (worsted) weight
 yarn (3½ oz/310 yds/100g
 per ball):
   2 balls #4906
    persimmon
* Size K/10½/6.5mm crochet
 hook or size needed to
 obtain gauge
* Yarn needle
* Stitch marker
* Pencil

marker (see Pattern Notes). (6 sc)

Rnd 2: 2 sc in each sc around. (12 sc)

Rnd 3: [Sc in next sc, 2 sc in next sc] around. (18 sc)

Rnd 4: [Sc in each of next 2 sc, 2 sc in next sc]
around. (24 sc)

Rnd 5: [2 sc in next sc, sc in each of next 3 sc]
around. (30 sc)

Rnd 6: [Sc in each of next 4 sc, 2 sc in next sc]
around. (36 sc)

Rnd 7: [Sc in each of next 5 sc, 2 sc in next sc]
around. (42 sc)

Rnd 8: [2 sc in next st, sc in each of next 6 sc] around.
(48 sc)

Rnd 9: [Sc in each of next 7 sc, 2 sc in next sc]
around. (54 sc)

Rnds 10–20: Sc in each sc around.

Rnd 21: Sl st in next st, ch 1, sc in same st, ch 2, sk
next 2 sts, [sc in next sc, ch 2, sk next 2 sc] around,
sl st to join in beg sc. (18 ch-2 sps)

Rnd 22: Ch 1, sc in same sc as beg ch-1, 2 sc in next
ch-2 sp, [sc in next sc, 2 sc in next ch-2 sp] around,
sl st to join in beg sc. (54 sc)

Rnd 23: Ch 1, sc in each sc around, sl st to join in
beg sc.

Row 24: Ch 1, sc in each of next 53 sc, 2 sc in next sc,
sl st to join in beg sc. (55 sc)

Rnd 25: Ch 2 (counts as first hdc), hdc in same st, 2
hdc in each of next 3 sc, hdc in next sc, [2 hdc in each
of next 4 sc, hdc in next sc] around, sl st to join in

2nd ch of beg ch-2. *(99 hdc)*

Rnds 26 & 27: Ch 2, hdc in each hdc around, sl st to join in 2nd ch of beg ch-2.

Rnd 28: Ch 1, **reverse sc** *(see illustration)* in each st around, sl st to join in beg sc, fasten off.

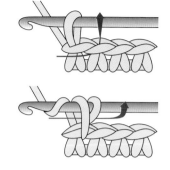

Reverse Single Crochet

Tie

With 2 strands of yarn held tog, ch 110, fasten off. Weave through ch-2 sps of rnd 21 of Hat. Tie ends in a bow.

SCARF

Row 1: With 2 strands of yarn held tog, ch 3, sc in 2nd ch from hook, sc in next ch, turn. *(2 sc)*

Row 2: Ch 1, 2 sc in each sc across, turn. *(4 sc)*

Row 3: Ch 1, sc in each sc across, turn.

Row 4: Ch 1, 2 sc in first sc, sc in each sc across to last sc, 2 sc in last sc, turn. *(6 sc)*

Row 5: Rep row 3.

Row 6: Rep row 4. *(8 sc)*

Rows 7–17: Rep row 3.

First Half Keyhole

Row 18: Ch 1, sc in each of next 4 sc, turn.

Rows 19–27: Rep row 3. At the end of row 27, fasten off.

2nd Half Keyhole

Row 18: Attach 2 strands of yarn in next unworked st

of row 18, ch 1, sc in same st as beg ch-1, sc in each of next 3 sts, turn. *(4 sc)*

Rows 19–27: Rep rows 19–27 of First Half Keyhole.

Row 28: With WS facing, attach 2 strands yarn in first sc, ch 1, sc in same sc as beg ch-1, sc in each of next 3 sc and next 4 sc of opposite edge of Keyhole, turn. *(8 sc)*

Rows 29–97: Rep row 3.

Row 98: Ch 1, **sc dec** *(see Stitch Guide)* in next 2 sc, sc in each of next 4 sc, sc dec in next 2 sc, turn. *(6 sc)*

Row 99: Rep row 3.

Row 100: Ch 1, sc dec in next 2 sc, sc in each of next 2 sc, sc dec in next 2 sc, turn. *(4 sc)*

Row 101: Rep row 3.

Row 102: Ch 1, [sc dec in next 2 sc] twice, fasten off.

Edging

Rnd 1: Working in ends of rows, attach 2 strands of yarn in end of row 102, ch 1, sc in same row as beg ch-1, sc in side edge of each row, at row 1, ch 2, sk opposite side of foundation ch, sc in side edge of row 1 on opposite edge, sc in end of each of next 101 rows, ch 2, sl st to join in first sc, fasten off.

Tassel

Make 2.

Cut 2 strands of yarn each 12 inches long and set aside. Holding 2 strands yarn tog, wrap around 3 spread fingers 16 times. Insert a 12-inch length around center of bundle and tie in a tight knot at top. Cut through lps at bottom edge. At fold, insert pencil between strands of yarn just below knotted section, smooth strands and tie 2nd 12-inch length directly below pencil, remove pencil. Trim ends even. Sew Tassel to the ch-2 sp at end of Scarf. ●

Cozy Evening Slippers

DESIGN BY KATHERINE ENG

BEGINNER

Finished Sizes

Instructions given fit ladies

sizes 6–7 *(small)*, 8–10

(medium) and 10–11 *(large)*

Finished Garment
Measurements

Sole length: 7 inches *(small)*,

8 inches *(medium)* and 9

inches *(large)*

Materials

- Lion Brand Jiffy
  bulky (chunky)
  weight yarn (2½ oz/115
  yds/70g per ball):
    2 balls in color of choice
- Sizes H/8/5mm *(small)*,
  I/9/5.5mm *(medium)* and
  J/10/6mm *(large)* crochet
  hooks or sizes needed to
  obtain gauge
- 12mm blue wooden beads: 2
- Tapestry needle
- Stitch marker

Gauge

Size H hook: 5 sc = 2 inches; 5 sc rows = 2 inches
Size I hook: 6 sc = 2 inches; 6 sc rows = 2 inches
Size J hook: 7 sc = 2 inches; 7 sc rows = 2 inches

Pattern Notes

Weave in loose ends as work progresses.
Join rounds with a slip stitch unless otherwise stated.

CONTINUED ON PAGE 32

Oro Valley Scarf

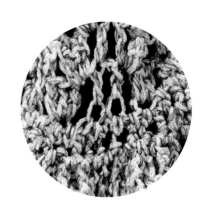

DESIGN BY JOYCE NORDSTROM

EASY

Finished Size

4½ x 45 inches, excluding Trim

Gauge

Dc, ch 1, dc = ¾ inch; 3 dc rows = 3 inches

Pattern Note

Weave in loose ends as work progresses.

SCARF

Row 1: With 1 strand of each held tog, ch 20, dc in 6th ch from hook *(5 sk chs count as first dc, ch-1, sk 1 ch)*, sk next 2 chs, 3 dc in next ch, [sk next ch, ch 1, dc in next ch] twice, ch 1, sk next ch, 3 dc in next ch, sk next 2 chs, dc in next ch, ch 1, dc in last ch, turn. *(12 dc, 5 ch-1 sps)*

Materials

- Bernat Matrix light (DK) weight yarn (1¾ oz/140 yds/50g per ball):
    1 ball #02520 copper wire
- Patons Brilliant light (light worsted) weight yarn (1¾ oz/166 yds/50g per skein):
    1 skein #03008 crystal cream
- Size M/13/9mm crochet hook or size needed to obtain gauge
- Tapestry needle

Row 2: Ch 4 *(counts as first dc, ch-1)*, sk next ch-1 sp, dc in next dc, sk next 3 dc, 3 dc in next ch-1 sp, [ch 1, dc in next dc] twice, ch 1, 3 dc in next ch-1 sp, sk next 3 dc, dc in next dc, ch 1, sk next ch, dc in next ch, turn.

Rows 3–47: Rep row 2. At the end of row 47, **do not fasten off**, turn.

Trim

Row 48: Ch 2 *(counts as first hdc)*, hdc in next ch-1 sp, hdc in each of next 4 dc, [hdc in next ch-1 sp, hdc in next dc] 3 times, hdc in next 3 dc, hdc in next ch-1 sp, hdc in next hdc, turn. *(17 hdc)*

Row 49: (Sl st, ch 6, sl st) in first hdc, (sl st, ch 7, sl st) in next hdc, (sl st, ch 8, sl st) in next hdc, (sl st, ch 9, sl st) in next hdc, (sl st, ch 10, sl st) in next hdc, (sl st, ch 11, sl st) in next hdc, (sl st, ch 12, sl st) in next hdc, (sl st, ch 13, sl st) in next hdc, (sl st, ch 14, sl st) in next hdc, (sl st, ch 13, sl st) in next hdc, (sl st, ch 12, sl st) in next hdc, (sl st, ch 11, sl st) in next hdc, (sl st, ch 10, sl st) in next hdc, (sl st, ch 9, sl st) in next hdc, (sl st, ch 8, sl st) in next hdc, (sl st, ch 7, sl st) in next hdc, (sl st, ch 6, sl st) in next hdc, fasten off. *(17 ch lps)*

Row 50: Working on opposite side of foundation ch, with 1 strand each held tog, attach strands in first ch with sl st, ch 2, hdc in same ch as beg ch-2, hdc in each of next 13 chs, 2 hdc in next ch, turn. *(17 hdc)*

Row 51: Rep row 49. ●

Autumn Wrap

DESIGN BY JENNY KING

EASY

Finished Size
One size fits all

Materials
- Light (light worsted) weight yarn: 37 oz/3330 yds/1049g variegated
- Size G/6/4mm crochet hook or size needed to obtain gauge
- Tapestry needle
- Stitch markers

Gauge
3 shells = 3¼ inches; 5 shell rows = 3 inches

Pattern Notes
Weave in loose ends as work progresses.
Join rounds with a slip stitch unless otherwise stated.

Special Stitches
Shell: (2 dc, ch 1, 2 dc) in indicated ch sp.
Beginning shell increase (beg shell inc): (Ch 4, 2 dc, ch 1, 2 dc) in first st.
End shell increase (end shell inc): (2 dc, ch 1, 3 dc) in last st.

WRAP
Row 1: Starting at center bottom back, ch 5, (2 dc, ch 1, 3 dc) in 5th ch from hook *(4 sk chs count as first dc)*, turn. *(1 shell)*
Row 2 (RS): Ch 4 *(counts as first dc)*, **shell** *(see Special Stitches)* in ch sp of next shell, dc in last st, turn.
Row 3: Beg shell inc *(see Special Stitches)* in first st,

shell in ch sp of next shell, **end shell inc** *(see Special Stitches)* in last st, turn. *(3 shells)*
Row 4: Ch 4, shell in ch sp of each shell across to last st, dc in last st, turn.
Row 5: Beg shell inc in first st, shell in ch sp of each shell across to last st, end shell inc in last st, turn. *(5 shells)*
Rows 6–37: [Rep rows 4 and 5] 16 times alternately.
Row 38: Rep row 4. *(1 dc, 37 shells, 1 dc)*
Rows 39–78: Rep row 4.

First Front
Row 79: Ch 4, shell in ch sp of each of next 15 shells, dc in last st of last worked shell, leaving last 22 shells and dc unworked, turn. *(1 dc, 15 shells, 1 dc)*
Rows 80–148: Rep row 4. At the end of row 148, fasten off. *(1 dc, 15 shells, 1 dc)*

2nd Front
Row 79: With RS facing, sk next 7 shells of row 78 for back neck, join with sl st in first dc of 8th shell, ch 4, shell in ch-1 sp of each rem shell across, dc in last st, turn. *(1 dc, 15 shells, 1 dc)*
Rows 80–148: Rep row 4. At the end of row 148, **do not turn**.

Edging
Rnd 1: Working around entire outer edge of Wrap, ch 1, sc in each st and in each ch, 2 sc in end of each dc row around with 3 sc in each corner, join in beg sc.
Rnd 2: Working in **front lps** *(see Stitch Guide)*, ch 1, sc in each st around with 3 sc in center st of each 3-sc corner group, join in beg sc, fasten off. ●

Winter Warmers

DESIGNS BY MICHELE MAKS THOMPSON

EASY

Finished Sizes

Scarf: 6 x 60 inches

Mitts: 7 x 8 inches

Hat: Loosely fits small head
size; changes for loosely
fit medium and loosely fit
large are in [ ].

Legwarmers: Instructions
given fit size small–
medium; changes for size
medium–large are in [ ].

Finished Garment Measurements

Hat: 20¼ inches in
circumference *(small)* [23½
inches in circumference
(medium), 26½ inches in
circumference *(large)*]

Legwarmers: 11 inches wide
(before sewing edges tog)
x 18 inches long *(small–
medium)* [12½ inches wide
(before sewing edges tog) x
22 *(medium–large)*] inches

Gauge

[Sc, V-st] twice = 3 inches; 9 rows = 6 inches

Materials

- Lion Brand Jiffy
bulky (chunky)
weight yarn (3 oz/135
yds/85g per ball):
    8 balls #195 dusty pink
- Size K/10½/6.5mm crochet
hook or size needed to
obtain gauge
- Tapestry needle

5 BULKY

Pattern Notes

Weave in loose ends as work progresses.

Join rounds with a slip stitch unless otherwise stated.

Use 1 skein for Mitts, 2 skeins each Hat and Scarf and 3 skeins for Legwarmers.

Special Stitches

V-stitch (V-st): (Dc, ch 1, dc) in indicated st or sp.

Picot: Ch 2, sk next sc, sl st in each of next 2 sc.

SCARF

Row 1 (RS): Starting at end of Scarf, ch 14, sc in 2nd ch from hook, sc in each rem ch across, turn. *(13 sc)*

Row 2: Ch 1, sc in first sc, [sk 1 sc, **V-st** *(see Special Stitches)* in next sc, sk 1 sc, sc in next sc] 3 times, turn. *(4 sc, 3 V-sts)*

Row 3: Ch 3 *(counts as first dc)*, dc in same st as beg ch-3, sk next dc, sc in next ch-1 sp, sk next dc, [V-st in next sc, sk next dc, sc in next ch-1 sp, sk next dc] twice, 2 dc in last sc, turn. *(2 V-sts, 3 sc, 4 dc)*

Row 4: Ch 1, sc in same dc as beg ch-1, [sk next dc, V-st in next sc, sk next dc, sc in next ch-1 sp] across, ending with sc in last dc, turn. *(4 sc, 3 V-sts)*

Rows 5–100: [Rep rows 3 and 4] 48 times alternately, turn.

Row 101: Ch 3, [hdc in next dc, sc in ch-1 sp, hdc in next dc, dc in next sc] across, fasten off. *(13 sts)*

Edging

Rnd 1 (RS): Attach yarn in top right edge, ch 1, 3 sc in first st, sc in each st across to last st, 3 sc in last st, sc evenly spaced across long edge of Scarf, sl st

across opposite side of foundation ch, sc evenly spaced across long edge, join in beg sc.
Rnd 2: Picot *(see Special Stitches)* around outer edge of Scarf, fasten off.

MITT

Make 2.

Row 1: Ch 22, sc in 2nd ch from hook, sc in each rem ch across, turn. *(21 sc)*

Row 2: Rep row 2 of Scarf. *(6 sc, 5 V-sts)*

Rows 3–12: Rep rows 3 and 4 of Scarf alternately.

Row 13: Rep row 101 of Scarf, **do not fasten off**, turn. *(21 sts)*

Top Edging

Row 1: Ch 1, sc in each of next 21 sts, turn.

Row 2: Ch 1, sl st in first st, **picot** *(see Special Stitches)* across edge, leaving a 12-inch length of yarn, fasten off.

Bottom Edging

Row 1: Attach yarn in opposite side of foundation ch, ch 1, sc same ch as beg ch 1, sc in each of next 20 chs, turn. *(21 sc)*

Row 2: Ch 1, sl st in first sc, picot across edge, fasten off.

Beg at top edge of Mitt, hold rows 1 and 13 of Mitt tog, sew down 1 inch from top for seam, sk next 2½ inches *(thumb opening)*, sew rem 5½ inches of rows 1 and 13 tog.

HAT

Row 1: Beg at bottom edge and working toward top, ch 54 [62, 70] sc in 2nd ch from hook, sc in each rem ch across, turn. *(53 [61, 69] sc)*

Row 2: Rep row 2 of Scarf. *(13 [15, 17] V-sts)*

Rows 3–8 [3–10, 3–12]: Rep rows 3 and 4 of Scarf alternately until Hat measures 5½ [6, 6½] inches from beg, ending with row 4.

Row 9 [11, 13]: Ch 3, [hdc in next dc, sc in next ch-1 sp, hdc in next dc, dc in next sc] across, fasten off. *(53 [61, 69] sts)*

Row 10 [12, 14]: Ch 1, sc in first st, [**sc dec** *(see Stitch Guide)* in next 2 sts] across, turn. *(27 [31, 35] sc)*

Row 11 [13, 15]: Ch 1, sc in first sc, [sc dec in next 2 sc] across, turn. *(14 [16, 18] sc)*

Row 12 [14, 16]: Ch 1, [sc dec in next 2 sc] across, leaving a 24-inch length of yarn, fasten off. *(7 [8, 9] sc)*

Brim

Row 1: Attach yarn in opposite side of foundation ch, ch 1, sc in same ch as beg ch-1, sc in each rem ch across, turn.

Rows 2–5: Ch 1, sc in each sc across, turn.

Row 6: Ch 1, sl st in first st, **picot** *(see Special Stitches)* across row, fasten off.

CONTINUED ON PAGE 33

Glitzy Cell Phone Pouch

DESIGN BY JOYCE BRAGG

EASY

Finished Size

1½ inches wide x 3½ inches
long, excluding Neck Chain

Materials

- Erdal Terry light
  (DK) weight yarn
  (1¾ oz/165 yds/50g
  per ball):
  1 ball #2939
- Size F/5/3.75mm crochet
  hook or size needed to
  obtain gauge
- Size 10/1.15mm steel
  crochet hook
- Tapestry needle
- 11 x 13mm barrel wood
  beads: 5
- ¾-inch red floral button
- Stitch marker

Gauge

Size F hook: [Hdc in next st, sl st in next st] 3 times =
1 inch; 3 rows = 1 inch

Pattern Notes

Weave in loose ends as work progresses.
Do not join rounds unless otherwise stated.

POUCH

Rnd 1: With size F hook, ch 36, hdc in 2nd ch from
hook, [sl st in next ch, hdc in next ch] 17 times, place

CONTINUED ON PAGE 33

Chic & Classy Laptop Bag

DESIGN BY JOYCE BRAGG

EASY

Finished Size
11½ inches tall x 13½ inches wide x 1¼ inches deep, excluding Handles and Flap

Materials
- Ecolution TW6C400 hemp Fine Beading Twine (400 yds/80g per ball):
  1 ball natural
- Ecolution TWD6/200 hemp Fine Dyed Beading Twine (200 yds/40g per ball):
  20 yds red
  10 yds purple
  2 yds yellow
- Size G/6/4mm crochet hook or size needed to obtain gauge
- Tapestry needle

Gauge
15 sc = 4 inches; 3 sc rows and 1 dc row = 1¼ inches

Pattern Notes
Weave in loose ends as work progresses.
Join rounds with a slip stitch unless otherwise stated.

BAG

Front
Row 1 (RS): Starting at bottom of Front with natural, ch 46, sc in 2nd ch from hook, sc in each rem ch across, turn. *(45 sc)*

Row 2: Ch 1, sc in each st across, turn.

Row 3: Ch 1, working in **front lps** *(see Stitch Guide)* for this row only, sc in each st across, turn.

Rows 4 & 5: Rep rows 2 and 3.

Row 6: Rep row 2.

Row 7: Ch 2 *(counts as first dc)*, dc in each st across, turn.

Row 8: Rep row 3.

Rows 9 & 10: Rep rows 2 and 3.

Row 11: Rep row 7.

Rows 12–31: [Rep rows 8–11 consecutively] 5 times.

Rows 32–35: [Rep rows 3 and 4 alternately] twice. At the end of row 35, **do not turn**.

Row 36: Ch 1, work 40 sc evenly spaced down side edge of Front rows, fasten off. *(40 sc)*

Row 37: Attach natural with sl st in opposite side of foundation ch, ch 1, work 40 sc evenly spaced up side edge of Front rows, fasten off. *(40 sc)*

Back
Row 1 (RS): Starting with flap, with natural, ch 46, sc in 2nd ch from hook, sc in each rem ch across, turn. *(45 sc)*

Rows 2–31: Rep rows 2–31 of Front.

Rows 32–37: [Rep rows 3 and 4] alternately 3 times.

Row 38: Rep row 7.

Rows 39–42: Rep rows 8–11.

Rows 43 & 44: Rep rows 3 and 4.

Row 45: Ch 1, sc evenly spaced up side edge of rows 45–1, sl st in each st across opposite side of

facing RS of Bag, position Gusset edge below Flap and working through both thicknesses, sl st evenly spaced down side edge, across bottom edge and up opposite edge, fasten off.

Handle
Make 2.
Row 1: With natural, ch 71, sc in 2nd ch from hook, sc in each rem ch across, turn. *(70 sc)*
Row 2: Ch 1, working in front lps for this row only, sc in each st across, turn.
Row 3: Ch 1, sc in each st across, turn.
Row 4: Rep row 2, leaving a length of natural, fasten off. With tapestry needle, sew each end of first Handle to Front over rows 24–26 with 6 inches free at center between ends of Handle.
With tapestry needle, sew each end of 2nd Handle over rows 21–23 with 6 inches free at center between ends of Handle.

Flower
Make 2 red and 1 purple.
Rnd 1: With yellow, ch 2, 11 sc in 2nd ch from hook, **do not join**, draw up a lp of red *(purple)*, fasten off yellow. *(12 sc)*
Rnd 2: Ch 1, [(hdc, 4 dc, hdc) in next st, sk next st] 6 times, join in first hdc. *(6 petals)*
Rnd 3: Ch 1, sc in each st around, join in beg sc, fasten off.
With tapestry needle, alternating colors, center and sew Flowers on edge of flap. ●

foundation ch, sc evenly spaced down side edge of rows 1–45, fasten off.

Gusset
Row 1: With natural, ch 127, sc in 2nd ch from hook, sc in each rem ch across, turn. *(126 sc)*
Row 2: Ch 1, working in front lps for this row only, sc in each st across, turn.
Row 3: Ch 1, sc in each st across, turn.
Row 4: Rep row 2. At the end of row 4, **do not fasten off**.

Assembly
Row 1: With Front of Bag facing, holding Gusset edge to row 37 of Front and working through both thicknesses, sl st evenly spaced down side edge, across bottom edge and up opposite edge, fasten off.
Row 2: Sl st in each sc of row 1, fasten off.
Row 3: With Back of Bag facing, hold Gusset with RS

Edelweiss Scarf continued from page 11

Row 2: Ch 1, sc in each dc across, turn.
Row 3: Ch 1, sc in next sc, [ch 4, sk next 7 sc, ({**3-dc cl**— *see Special Stitches*, ch 2} twice, 3-dc cl) in next sc, ch 4, sk next 7 sc, sc in next sc] 17 times, ch 4, sk next 4 sc, 3-dc cl in next sc, turn.
Row 4: Ch 3 *(counts as first dc)*, [dc in each of next 3 chs, **dc dec** *(see Stitch Guide)* in next 2 chs, sk sc between these 2 chs, dc in each of next 3 chs, dc in next cl, 2 dc

in ch-2 sp, 3-dc in center dc cl, 2 dc in next ch-2 sp, dc in next cl] across, ending with dc in each of next 3 chs, dc dec in next 2 sts, turn.
Row 5: Ch 1, sc in each st across, turn.
Row 6: Ch 1, sc in next sc, ch 4, sk next 3 sc, [({3-dc cl, ch 2} twice, 3-dc cl) in next sc, ch 4, sk next 7 sc, sc in next sc, ch 4, sk next 7 sc] 17 times, (3-dc cl, ch 2, **2-dc cl**—*see Special Stitches*) in last sc, turn.

Row 7: Ch 3, dc in same st as beg ch-3, 2 dc in next ch-2 sp, dc in next cl, [dc in each of next 3 chs, dc dec in next 2 chs, sk sc between these 2 chs, dc in each of next 3 chs, dc in next cl, 2 dc in next ch-2 sp, 3 dc in next cl, 2 dc in next ch-2 sp, dc in next cl] 17 times, dc in each of next 4 chs, dc in last sc, turn.

Row 8: Ch 1, sc in each dc across, turn.

Row 9: Rep row 3.

Row 10: Rep row 4.

Rnd 11: Ch 1, sc in each st across row 10, ch 1, sc in same st as last st, working in ends of rows, work 17 sc evenly spaced across ends of rows, ch 1, sc in same st as last sc, working across opposite side of foundation ch, sc in each st across, ch 1, sc in same st as last sc, work 17 sc evenly spaced across ends of rows, ch 1, join in beg sc, fasten off. ●

Fabulous Felted Tote continued from page 12

Rnd 2: Dc in each of next 7 dc.

Rep rnd 2 until Handle measures 80 inches from beg, sl st in next dc, fasten off.

Assembly

Holding First Side and End tog, working through both thicknesses, sl st in each st across edge. Rep sl st on opposite First Side and End.

Holding 2nd Side and End tog, rep sl st across each edge.

With sewing needle and doubled sewing thread, sew Pocket centered on inside edge 7 rows below top edge of First Side.

Handle is woven through 4th row of dc down from top edge. Beg at joined edge of Side and End, *weave from outside in and under 2 sts and back to outside, [weave over 10 dc, weave under 10 dc] twice, with Handle at inside, tie an overhand knot in Handle at the point of Handle on inside edge; leaving approximately 18 inches, tie another overhand knot, sk approximately 23 sts, pass Handle to outside, [weave over 10 dc, weave under 10 dc] twice, pass under 2 dc sts at corner, sk over sts of End, rep from * around. Sew beg and end of tie tog. After felting, the overhand knots will be adjustable.

If, after felting, handle is too long, adjust and tie each section in a knot at each End.

Felting

Place crocheted piece in washer with hot water and a small amount of detergent, wash in a normal cycle. Sometimes two wash cycles are necessary to make a dense fabric. While wet, shape over large shoebox or anything that will maintain Tote shape until dry. ●

Posh Purse continued from page 15

Row 14: Ch 1, sc in each of next 4 sc, fasten off.

Handles

Measure and mark 2 inches on either side of Flap Closure.

With MC, ch 80, sl st in 2nd ch from hook, sl st in each rem ch across, leaving an 8-inch length at end, fasten off.

Beg at back of Purse, holding 1 end of Handle on inside of Purse, weave other end of Handle from WS to RS through one 2-inch mark, weave same end from RS to WS through next 2-inch mark on same side of Purse, then from WS to RS through adjacent 2-inch mark on front of Purse and from RS to WS through 2-inch mark on same side of Purse. With tapestry needle, sew ends of Handle tog. Pull Handles at center front and back to shape sides of Purse, folding the 3-inch section at each center end inward. ●

Cozy Evening Slippers continued from page 19

SLIPPER
Make 2.

Sole
Row 1 (RS): Beg at heel, ch 6, sc in 2nd ch from hook, sc in each rem ch across, turn. *(5 sc)*
Row 2: Ch 1, sc in each sc across, turn.
Rows 3–14: Rep row 2.
Row 15: Ch 1, 2 sc in first sc, sc in each of next 3 sc, 2 sc in next sc, turn. *(7 sc)*
Rows 16–23: Rep row 2.
Row 24: Ch 1, sc in each of next 2 sc, hdc in next sc, 2 dc in next sc, hdc in next sc, sc in each of next 2 sc, turn. *(8 sts)*
Rnd 25: Now working in rnds, ch 1, sc in first st, 2 sc in next st, sc in each of next 4 sts, 2 sc in next st, sc in last st, working in side edge of rows, sc in end of each of next 3 rows, 2 sc in side edge of each of next 3 rows, sc in each of next 17 rows, working across heel in opposite side of foundation ch, sc in first ch, 2 sc in each of next 3 chs, sc in last ch, working in side edges of rows, sc in each of next 17 rows, 2 sc in end of each of next 3 rows, sc in side edge of each of next 3 rows, join in beg sc, fasten off. *(70 sc)*

Top
Rnd 1 (RS): Place st marker in center 2 sc of heel, draw up a lp of yarn in center left sc, ch 1, sc in same sc as beg ch-1, sc in each of next 69 sc, join in beg sc. *(70 sc)*
Rnd 2: Ch 1, sc in same sc as beg ch-1, ch 1, sk 1 sc, [sc in next sc, ch 1, sk 1 sc] around, join in beg sc. *(35 sc, 35 ch-1 sps)*
Rnd 3: Ch 1, sc in same sc as beg ch-1, ch 1, sk next ch-1 sp, [sc in next sc, ch 1, sk next ch-1 sp] around, join in beg sc.
Rnd 4: Ch 1, sc in same sc as beg ch-1, [ch 1, sk next ch-1 sp, sc in next sc] 9 times, [ch 1, sk next ch-1 sp, hdc in next sc] 5 times, [ch 1, sk next ch-1 sp, dc in next sc] 6 times, [ch 1, sk next ch-1 sp, hdc in next sc] 5 times, [ch 1, sk next ch-1 sp, sc in next sc] 9 times, ch 1, sk next ch-1 sp, join in beg sc. *(35 sts, 35 ch-1 sps)*

Rnd 5: Ch 1, sc in same sc as beg ch-1, [ch 1, sk next ch-1 sp, sc in next sc] 9 times, [ch 1, sk next ch-1 sp, hdc in next hdc] 5 times, [ch 1, sk each of next ch-1 sp, next dc and next ch-1 sp *(3 sts)*, dc in next dc] 3 times, [ch 1, sk next ch-1 sp, hdc in next hdc] 5 times, [ch 1, sk next ch-1 sp, sc in next sc] 9 times, ch 1, sk next ch-1 sp, join in beg sc. *(32 sts, 32 ch-1 sps)*
Rnd 6: Ch 4 *(counts as first dc, ch-1)*, sk next ch-1 sp, dc in next st, [ch 1, sk next ch-1 sp, dc in next st] 13 times, [ch 1, sk each of next 3 sts, dc in next st] twice, [ch 1, sk next ch-1 sp, dc in next st] 13 times, join in 3rd ch of beg ch-4. *(30 dc, 30 ch-1 sps)*
Rnd 7: Ch 1, sc in same st as beg ch-1 *(3rd ch of ch-4 of previous rnd)*, sk next ch-1 sp, [(sc, ch 3, sc) in next dc, sk next ch-1 sp] around, join in beg sc, fasten off.

Flower
Make 2.
Rnd 1: Ch 5, join in first ch to form a ring, ch 1, (sc, ch 3) 8 times in ring, join in beg sc. *(8 sc, 8 ch-3 sps)*
Rnd 2: Working behind and between ch-3 sps of rnd 1 of same ring, ch 1, sc in sp between sc, ch 6, [sc in next sp between sc, ch 6] 7 times, join in beg sc, leaving a 12-inch length, fasten off.
Sew Flower to center front over rnd 5. Sew a bead to center of Flower.

Tie
Make 2.
With a 2 strands of yarn held tog, leaving 5-inch length at beg, ch 85, leaving 5-inch length at end, fasten off.

Finishing
Starting under first dc to left of center front dc of rnd 6, weave tie under and over dc around.
Cut two 10-inch lengths of yarn for each end of Tie. Pass strands through end of Tie. With strands folded in half, tie all 6 strands, including 5-inch length, in an overhand knot, trim ends to 1½ inches. Rep on other end of Tie. With toe of Slipper facing, using both ends of Tie, make a bow. ●

Winter Warmers continued from page 26

Weave 24-inch length of yarn through sc of last row of Hat, draw yarn tightly to close opening, knot to secure, matching rows, sew seam with remainder of 24-inch length, fasten off.

LEGWARMER
Make 2.
Row 1: Beg at lower edge, ch 30 [34], sc in 2nd ch from hook, sc in each rem ch across, turn. *(29 [33] sc)*
Row 2: Rep row 2 of Scarf. *(7 [8] V-sts)*
Rows 3–18 [3–20]: Rep rows 3 and 4 until Legwarmer measures 18½ [19½] inches, ending with row 4.
Row 19 [20]: Ch 3, [hdc in next dc, sc in next ch-1 sp, hdc in next dc, dc in next sc] across, turn.

Top Edging
Row 20 [21]: Ch 1, sc in each st across, turn.
Row 21 [22]: Ch 1, sl st in first st, **picot** *(see Special Stitches)* across edge, fasten off.

Bottom Edging
Row 1: Attach yarn in opposite side of foundation ch, ch 1, sc in each ch across, turn.
Row 2: Ch 1, sl st in first st, picot across, leaving a 30-inch length, fasten off.
Holding rows 1 and 19 [20] of Legwarmer tog, sew seam closed. ●

Glitzy Cell Phone Pouch continued from page 27

st marker and move to each rnd as work progresses. *(17 sl sts, 18 hdc)*
Rnd 2: [Sl st in hdc, hdc in sl st] around.
Rep rnd 2 until Pouch measures 3½ inches, ending with sl st, fasten off.
With size F hook, working in opposite side of foundation ch through both thicknesses, attach yarn with a sl st, ch 1, work 17 sc across edge, fasten off.

Bead Preparation
Make 5.
Thread tapestry needle with a double strand of yarn, work yarn in and out of bead hole until bead is covered with yarn, secure and fasten off.

Neck Chain
Row 1: With size F hook, attach yarn with a sl st in side edge of last rnd of Pouch, ch 25, draw up a small lp, remove hook, *insert size 10 steel crochet hook in the bead hole and out opposite edge, pick up dropped lp of ch-25 and draw through bead, draw up a lp, remove hook, pick up size F hook, pick up dropped lp, ch 25, rep from * 4 times, sl st in opposite side edge of Pouch, fasten off.

Finishing
Sew red floral button to center front, centered at top edge. ●

Fashions
in a Flash

In this chapter you'll find great-looking, year-round fashions in a wide range of sizes. They are easy to make using simple construction.

Blue Hawaii Jacket

DESIGN BY RENEE' BARNES

Finished Sizes

Instructions given fit 36–38-
inch bust *(medium)*;
changes for 40–42-inch
bust *(large)*, 44–46-inch
bust *(X-large)*, 48–50-inch
bust *(2X-large)* and 52–54-
inch bust *(3X-large)* are
in [ ].

Finished Garment Measurements

Bust: 35 inches *(medium)*, [38
inches *(large)*, 40 inches *(X-
large)*, 44 inches *(2X-large)*,
47 inches *(3X-large)*]

*Note: V-st and scalloped edge
trim is not included in the
bust measurements, adding
approximately 6 inches.*

Length: 43 inches *(medium)*,
[43 inches *(large)*, 45 inches
(X-large), 45 inches *(2X-
large)*, 45 inches *(3X-large)*]

Gauge

4 dc = 1 inch; 2 dc rows = 1 inch

Materials

- RYC Cashsoft
  Aran medium
  (worsted) weight yarn (1¾
  oz/95 yds/50g per ball):
  13 [14, 16, 17, 18] balls
  #008 tornado
- Size G/6/4mm crochet
  hook or size needed to
  obtain gauge
- Yarn needle
- 18mm decorative buttons:
  2
- Large hook and eye
- Stitch markers

Pattern Notes

Weave in loose ends as work progresses.

Join rounds with a slip stitch unless otherwise stated.

Special Stitches

V-stitch (V-st): (Dc, ch 1, dc) in indicated st.

Corner V-stitch (corner V-st): (V-st, ch 3, V-st) in
indicated st.

Shell: (2 dc, ch 2, 2 dc) in indicated st.

JACKET

Left Front

Row 1: Starting at bottom edge, ch 32 [35, 38, 41, 44],
dc in 4th ch from hook *(first 3 sk chs count as first dc)*,
dc in each rem ch across, turn. *(30 [33, 36, 39, 42] dc)*

Rows 2–40 [40, 42, 42, 42]: Ch 3 *(counts as first dc)*,
dc in each dc across, turn.

Row 41 [41, 43, 43, 43]: Ch 3, dc in each dc across,
do not turn, working down side edge of rows, work
2 sc in side edge of each dc row, fasten off. *(82 [82,
86, 86, 86] sc)*

Row 42 [42, 44, 44, 44]: Attach yarn in top of beg
ch-3 of previous row, ch 3, dc in each of next 12 [16,
15, 18, 21] dc, [sk next 2 dc, **V-st** *(see Special Stitches)*
in next dc] 5 [5, 6, 6, 6] times, **corner V-st** *(see Special
Stitches)* in corner st, [sk next 2 sc, V-st in next sc] 26
[26, 28, 28, 28] times, dc in last st, turn.

Row 43 [43, 45, 45, 45]: Ch 3, V-st in ch sp of each

V-st up front edge to ch-3 corner sp, corner V-st in corner ch-3 sp, V-st in ch sp of each of next 6 [6, 7, 7, 7] V-sts, dc in each of next 13 [17, 16, 19, 22] dc, turn.

Row 44 [44, 46, 46, 46]: Ch 3, dc in each of next 12 [16, 15, 18, 21] dc, V-st in ch sp of each V-st to corner ch-3 sp, corner V-st in corner ch-3 sp, V-st in ch sp of each V-st down front edge, turn.

Row 45 [45, 47, 47, 47]: Ch 1, sc in each dc and in each ch-1 sp to corner ch-3 sp, 3 sc in corner ch-3 sp, sc in each dc and in each ch-1 sp across top edge, fasten off.

Right Front

Rows 1–40 [40, 42, 42, 42]: Rep rows 1–40 [40, 42, 42, 42] of Left Front.

Row 41 [41, 43, 43, 43]: Ch 3, dc in each dc across, draw up a lp, remove hook. Attach another ball of yarn in side edge of row 1, ch 1, work 82 [82, 86, 86, 86] sc evenly spaced up side edge of rows, fasten off. *(82 [82, 86, 86, 86] sc)*

Row 42 [42, 44, 44, 44]: Pick up dropped lp of previous row, ch 3, turn, dc in each of next 11 [15, 14, 17, 20] dc, [sk next 2 dc, V-st in next dc] 5 [5, 6, 6, 6] times, corner V-st in corner st, [sk next 2 sc, V-st in next sc] 26 [26, 28, 28, 28] times, dc in last st, turn.

Rows 43–45 [43–45, 45–47, 45–47, 45–47]: Rep rows 43–45 [43–45, 45–47, 45–47, 45–47] of Left Front.

Back

Row 1: Ch 82 [88, 94, 100, 106], dc in 4th ch from hook *(first 3 sk chs count as first dc)*, dc in each rem ch across, turn. *(80 [86, 92, 98, 104] dc)*

Rows 2–43 [2–43, 2–45, 2–45, 2–45]: Ch 3, dc in each dc across, turn. At the end of last row, fasten off.

Assembly

Holding RS of Left Front facing RS of Back, working through both thicknesses, attach yarn with sl st at bottom edge, sl st evenly spaced in ends of rows 1–24 [24, 26, 24, 24], fasten off.

Work sl st across shoulder seam at top edge, starting at outer edge and working through both thicknesses, sl st in each of next 21 [26, 29, 32, 35] sc, fasten off.

Holding RS of Right Front facing RS of Back, working through both thicknesses, attach yarn with sl st at bottom edge, sl st evenly spaced in ends of rows 1–24 [24, 26, 24, 24], fasten off.

Work sl st across shoulder seam at top edge, starting at outer edge and working through both thicknesses, sl st in each of next 21 [26, 29, 32, 35] sc, fasten off.

Sleeve

Make 2.

Rnd 1: Attach yarn with sl st at underarm, ch 3 *(counts as first dc)*, work 77 [77, 77, 85, 85] dc evenly spaced around armhole opening in end of rows, join in 3rd ch of beg ch-3, **do not turn.** *(78 [78, 78, 86, 86] dc)*

Rnd 2: Ch 3, dc in each dc around, join in 3rd ch of beg ch-3.

Rnd 3: Ch 3, **dc dec** *(see Stitch Guide)* in next 2 dc, dc in each of next 73 [73, 73, 81, 81] dc, dc dec in next 2 dc, join in 3rd ch of beg ch-3. *(76 [76, 76, 84, 84] dc)*

Rnds 4–20: Ch 3, dc dec in next 2 dc, dc in each dc across to last 2 dc, dc dec in last 2 dc, join in 3rd ch of beg ch-3. (42 [42, 42, 50, 50] dc)

Right Sleeve Trim

Note: Take care to follow Sleeve Trim instructions, working in rows and rnds as indicated.

Row 1: Sl st in each of next 11 dc, ch 3, sl st in 3rd st to the right of ch-3 just made, *ch 2, dc in last sl st, rep from * 5 times, sk next 2 sts, sl st in 3rd st on last rnd of Sleeve, ch 3, sk next 2 sts, sl st in 3rd st of last rnd of Sleeve, turn.

Row 2: Ch 2, *(dc, ch 1, dc) in next ch-2 sp, rep from * 5 times, ch 2, sk next 2 sts, sl st in 3rd st on last rnd of Sleeve, ch 3, sk next 2 sts, sl st in 3rd st of last rnd of Sleeve, turn.

Row 3: (Dc, ch 1, dc) in next ch-2 sp, [(dc, ch 1, dc) in next ch-1 sp] 3 times, ch 4, [(dc, ch 1, dc) in next ch-1 sp] 3 times, (dc, ch 1, dc) in next ch-2 sp, sk next 2 sts, sl st in 3rd st on last rnd of Sleeve, ch 3, sk next 2 sts, sl st in next st on last rnd of Sleeve, turn.

Row 4: [Ch 3, dc in next ch-1 sp] 4 times, 10 dc in next ch-4 sp, dc in next ch-1 sp, [ch 3, dc in next ch-1 sp] 3 times, ch 3, sk next 2 sts, sl st in next st on last rnd of Sleeve, ch 3, sk next 2 sts, sl st in next st on last rnd of Sleeve, turn.

Row 5: Sk first ch-3 sp, 10 tr in next ch-3 sp, sk next ch-3 sp, (2 dc, ch 1, 2 dc) in next ch-3 sp, sk next dc, dc in first dc of 10-dc group, [ch 1, dc in next dc] 9 times, sk next dc, (2 dc, ch 1, 2 dc) in next ch-3 sp, sk next ch-3 sp, 10 tr in next ch-3 sp, sl st across to top of ch-3 that is joined to last rnd of Sleeve, ch 4, sk next 3 sts, sl st in next st on last rnd of Sleeve, turn.

Row 6: Dc in first tr of 10-tr group, [ch 1, dc in next tr] 9 times, **shell** (see Special Stitches) in next ch-1 sp, ch 2, sc in next ch-1 sp, [ch 4, sc in next ch-1 sp] 8 times, ch 2, shell in next ch-1 sp, dc in first tr of 10-tr group, [ch 1, dc in next tr] 9 times, ch 3, sk next 3 sts, sl st in 4th st of last rnd of Sleeve, turn.

Row 7: Ch 6, sc in first ch-1 sp, [ch 4, sc in next ch-1 sp] 8 times, ch 4, shell in ch-2 sp of next shell, ch 4, sc in first ch-4 sp, [ch 4, sc in next ch-4 sp] 7 times, ch 4, shell in ch-2 sp of next shell, ch 4, sc in next ch-1 sp, [ch 4, sc in next ch-1 sp] 8 times, ch 6, sl st in next st on last rnd of Sleeve, turn.

Row 8: Ch 8, sc in first ch-4 sp, [ch 4, sc in next ch-4 sp] 7 times, ch 5, sk next ch-4 sp, shell in ch-2 sp of next shell, ch 5, sk next ch-4 sp, sc in next ch-4 sp, [ch 4, sc in next ch-4 sp] 6 times, ch 5, shell in ch-2 sp of next shell, ch 5, sk next ch-4 sp, sc in next ch-4 sp, [ch 4, sc in next ch-4 sp] 7 times, ch 8, sl st in next st on last rnd of Sleeve, sc in each of next 7 [7, 7, 15, 15] sts of last rnd of Sleeve, **do not turn.**

Rnd 9: Now working in rnds, ch 10, sc in next ch-4 sp, [ch 4, sc in next ch-4 sp] 6 times, ch 7, shell in ch-2 sp of next shell, ch 7, sc in next ch-4 sp, [ch 4, sc in next ch-4 sp] 5 times, ch 7, shell in ch-2 sp of next shell, ch 7, sc in next ch-4 sp, [ch 4, sc in next ch-4 sp] 6 times, ch 10, sc in each of next 7 [7, 7, 15, 15] sc, **do not turn.**

Rnd 10: Ch 12, sc in next ch-4 sp, [ch 4, sc in next ch-4 sp] 5 times, ch 8, shell in ch-2 sp of next shell, ch 8, sc in next ch-4 sp, [ch 4, sc in next ch-4 sp] 4 times, ch 8, shell in ch-2 sp of next shell, ch 8, sc in next ch-4 sp, [ch 4, sc in next ch-4 sp] 5 times, ch 12, sc in each of next 6 [6, 6, 14, 14] sc, **do not turn.**

Rnd 11: Ch 15, sc in next ch-4 sp, [ch 4, sc in next ch-4 sp] 4 times, ch 9, shell in ch-2 sp of next shell, ch 9, sc in next ch-4 sp, [ch 4, sc in next ch-4 sp] 3 times, ch 9, shell in ch-2 sp of next shell, ch 9, sc in next ch-4 sp, [ch 4, sc in next ch-4 sp] 4 times, ch 15, sc in each of next 5 [5, 5, 13, 13] sc, **do not turn.**

Rnd 12: Ch 18, sc in next ch-4 sp, [ch 4, sc in next ch-4 sp] 3 times, ch 12, shell in ch-2 sp of next shell, ch 12, sc in next ch-4 sp, [ch 4, sc in next ch-4 sp] twice, ch 12, shell in ch-2 sp of next shell, ch 12, sc in next ch-4 sp, [ch 4, sc in next ch-4 sp] 3 times, ch 18, sc in next 3 [3, 3, 11, 11] sc, **do not turn.**

Rnd 13: Ch 21, sc in next ch-4 sp, [ch 4, sc in next ch-4 sp] twice, ch 16, shell in ch-2 sp of next shell, ch 16, sc in next ch-4 sp, ch 4, sc in next ch-4 sp, ch 16, shell in ch-2 sp of next shell, ch 16, sc in next ch-4 sp, [ch 4, sc in next ch-4 sp] twice, ch 21, sc in each of next 2 [2, 2, 10, 10] sc, **do not turn.**

Rnd 14: Work 21 sc in next ch-21 sp, sc in next ch-4 sp, ch 4, sc in next ch-4 sp, 16 sc in next ch-16 sp, sc in each of next 2 dc, 3 sc in next ch-2 sp, sc in each of

CONTINUED ON PAGE 71

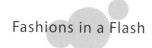

Floral Cluster Skirt

DESIGN BY SVETLANA AVRAKH

INTERMEDIATE

Finished Sizes

Instructions given fit women's X-small/small; changes for medium, large and X-large are in [ ].

Finished Garment Measurements

Hips: 36 inches *(X-small/small)* [39 inches *(medium)*, 42 inches *(large)*, 47 inches *(X-large)*]

Gauge

20 sc = 4 inches

Pattern Notes

Weave in loose ends as work progresses.
Join rounds with a slip stitch unless otherwise stated.

Special Stitches

Half cluster (half cl): [Yo, insert hook in indicated st, yo, draw up a lp, yo, draw through 2 lps on hook] 3 times in indicated st.

Cluster (cl): [Yo, insert hook in indicated st, yo, draw up a lp, yo, draw through 2 lps on hook] 3 times in indicated st, yo, draw through all 4 lps on hook.

Materials

- Bernat Cool Crochet light (light worsted) weight yarn (1¾ oz/200 yds/50g per ball):
    4 [4, 5, 6] balls #74008 summer cream
- Size F/5/3.75mm crochet hook or size needed to obtain gauge
- Tapestry needle

3 LIGHT

SKIRT

Front & Back

Make 2.

Row 1 (RS): Starting below waistline, ch 121 [129, 137, 153] sc in 2nd ch from hook, *ch 5, **half cl** *(see Special Stitches)* in 3rd ch from hook, sk next ch of foundation ch, half cl in next ch, sk next 3 chs of foundation ch, half cl in next ch, yo and draw through all 10 lps on hook—*half flower made,* ch 3, **cl** *(see Special Stitches)* in top of half flower just made, ch 3, sk next ch of foundation ch, sc in next ch, rep from * across, turn. *(15 [16, 17, 19] half flowers)*

Row 2: Ch 4 *(counts as first dc, ch-1),* dc in next ch-3 sp, *ch 1, (cl, ch 3, cl) in top of next half flower, ch 1, **dc dec** *(see Stitch Guide)* in next 2 ch-3 sps, rep from * to last half flower, ch 1, (cl, ch 3, cl) in top of last half flower, ch 1, yo, draw up a lp in sp formed by 3 sk chs of ch-5 sp, yo, draw through 2 lps on hook, yo, insert hook in last st, yo, draw up a lp, yo, draw through 2 lps on hook, yo, draw through 3 lps on hook.

Row 3: Ch 3 *(counts as first dc),* yo, draw up a lp in first st, yo, draw through 2 lps on hook, half cl in top of next cl, yo, draw through all 5 lps on hook, ch 3, cl in top of st just made, ch 3, sc in next ch-3 sp, *ch 5, half cl in 3rd ch from hook, half cl in each of next 2 cls, yo, draw through all 10 lps on hook—*half flower made,* ch 3, cl in top of half flower just made, ch 3, sc in next ch-3 sp, rep from * across, ch 5, half cl in 3rd ch from hook, half cl in next cl, yo, draw up a lp in next dc, yo, draw through 2 lps on hook, yo, draw through all 8 lps on hook, turn.

Row 4: Ch 4, cl in first st, *ch 1, dc dec in each of next 2 ch-3 sps, ch 1, (cl, ch 3, cl) in top of next half flower, rep from * across to sp formed by 3 sk chs of beg ch-5, ch 1, dc dec in sp formed by sk chs and next ch-3 sp, ch 1, (cl, ch 1, cl) in last st, turn.

Row 5: Ch 1, sc in first dc, *half flower over next 2 chs, ch 3, sc in next ch-3 sp, rep from * to last 2 cls, half flower over last 2 cls, ch 3, sc in 3rd ch of beg ch-4 of previous row, turn.

Rep rows 2–5 consecutively until piece measures 24 inches or desired length from beg, ending with a WS row 2 or 4 so that bottom edge has a completed flower, fasten off.

Assembly
Sew side seams.

Waistband
Rnd 1 (RS): Beg at top edge, join yarn with a sl st in first ch sp of opposite side of foundation ch, ch 1, 2 sc in same ch sp, *3 sc in next ch-3 sp, sc in each of next 2 ch-1 sps, rep from * around, join in beg sc.

Rnd 2: Ch 1, sc in same sc as beg ch-1, sc in each rem sc around, join in beg sc.

Rnds 3–5: Rep rnd 2. At the end of rnd 5, fasten off.

Drawstring
With 2 strands held tog, make a ch 58 inches long, fasten off.
Beg at center Front, weave Drawstring through Waistband. Tie in a bow at center front. ●

Hot Spots Top

DESIGN BY DARLA SIMS

EASY

Finished Size

Instructions given fit 32–34-inch bust *(small)*; changes for 36–38-inch bust *(medium)*, 40–42-inch bust *(large)* and 44–46-inch bust *(X-large)* are in [ ].

Finished Garment Measurements

Bust: 36 inches *(small)* [40 inches *(medium)*, 44 inches *(large)*, 48 inches *(X-large)*]

Materials

3 LIGHT

- Fine (sport) weight yarn:
  7½ [10, 10, 12½] oz/675–750 [900–1000, 900–1000, 1125–1250] yds/213 [284, 284, 354] g turquoise
  2½ [2½, 2½, 2½] oz/225–250 [225–250, 225–250, 225–250] yds/71 [71, 71, 71] g each white, fuchsia, lavender and purple
- Sizes G/6/4mm and H/8/5mm crochet hooks or sizes needed to obtain gauge
- Tapestry needle

Gauge

Size H hook: 4 V-sts = 1 inch

Pattern Notes

Weave in loose ends as work progresses.
Join rounds with a slip stitch unless otherwise stated.
All rows are worked with right side facing.

Special Stitch

V-stitch (V-st): 2 dc in indicated st.

TOP

Back

Row 1: Starting at bottom with size H hook and turquoise, ch 73 [81, 89, 97], 2 dc in 5th ch *(beg 4 sk chs count as dc, ch-1)*, [sk next ch, **V-st** *(see Special Stitch)* in next ch] across to last 2 chs, sk next ch, dc in last ch, fasten off. *(34 [38, 42, 46] V-sts)*

Row 2: With purple, make slip knot on hook and join with a sc in sp between beg 4 sk chs and next V-st, [ch 1, sc between V-sts] across to last V-st, sc in sp between last V-st and last dc, fasten off.

Row 3: Attach turquoise in 3rd ch of beg 4 chs of row 1, ch 3 *(counts as first dc)*, V-st in each ch-1 sp on previous row, dc in last dc of row 1, fasten off.

Row 4: With fuchsia, make slip knot on hook and join with a sc in sp between beg ch-3 and next V-st, [ch 1, sc between V-sts] across to last V-st, sc in sp between last V-st and last dc, fasten off.

Row 5: Join turquoise in 3rd ch of beg ch-3 on 2nd row below, ch 3, V-st in each ch-1 sp on previous row, dc in last dc on 2nd row below, fasten off.

Row 6: With lavender, make slip knot on hook and join with a sc in sp between beg ch-3 and next V-st, [ch 1, sc between V-sts] across to last V-st, sc in sp between last V-st and last dc, fasten off.

Row 7: Rep row 5.

Row 8: With white, make slip knot on hook and attach with sc in sp between beg ch-3 and next V-st, [ch 1, sc between V-sts] across to last V-st, sc in sp between last V-st and last dc, fasten off.

Row 9: Rep row 5.

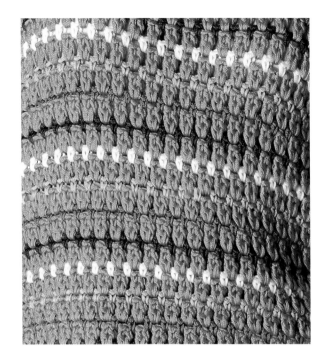

Row 10: With purple, make slip knot on hook and join with a sc in sp between beg ch-3 and next V-st, [ch 1, sc between V-sts] across to last V-st, sc in sp between last V-st and last dc, fasten off.

Row 11: Rep row 5.

Rep rows 4–11 consecutively until piece measures 10 inches, ending with an even-numbered row.

Sleeves

Notes: Hold piece with RS facing, attach turquoise in 3rd ch of ch-3 of previous RS row, ch 4 for Sleeve, fasten off.

Attach turquoise in last dc of same row for 2nd, ch 4 for 2nd Sleeve, fasten off.

Row 1: Attach turquoise in first ch of first ch-4, ch 3, sk next ch, V-st in next ch, sk next ch, V-st in 3rd ch of beg ch-3 on 2nd row below, V-st in each ch-1 sp on previous row, sk next ch, V-st in next ch, sk next ch, dc in next ch, turn.

Working in same color sequence, work as established until armhole measures 6½ [7, 7½, 8] inches, ending with an even-numbered row.

Right Neck & Shoulder Shaping

Row 1: With next color in sequence, make slip knot

and place on hook, sc in sp between beg ch-3 and next V-st, *ch 1, sc between V-sts, rep from * 11 [13, 15, 17] times, leaving rem sts unworked, fasten off.

Row 2: Attach turquoise in 3rd ch of beg ch-3 on 2nd row below, ch 3, V-st in each ch-1 sp, dc between dc of next V-st on 2nd row below, fasten off. *(12 [14, 16, 18] V-sts)*

Continuing in same color sequence, work as established until armhole measures 8½ [9, 9½, 10] inches, ending with an odd-numbered row, fasten off.

Left Neck & Shoulder Shaping

Row 1: With RS facing, sk next 13 V-sts from Right Shoulder, with next color in sequence, make slip knot on hook and attach with sc in sp between beg 13th unused V-st and next V-st, *ch 1, sc between V-sts, rep from * 11 [13, 15, 17] times, fasten off.

Row 2: Attach turquoise between dc of 13th unused V-st from Right Shoulder, ch 3, V-st in each ch-1 sp, dc in next dc on 2nd row below, fasten off. *(12 [14, 16, 18] V-sts)*

Continuing in same color sequence, work as established until armhole measures 8½ [9, 9½, 10] inches, ending with an odd-numbered row, fasten off.

Front

Rows 1–11: Rep rows 1–11 of Back.

Rep rows 4–11 consecutively until piece measures 10 inches, ending with an even-numbered row.

Sleeves

Row 1: Rep row 1 of Sleeves.

Working in same color sequence as Back Sleeve, work 4 rows as established.

Left Neck & Shoulder Shaping

Row 1: With next color in sequence make slip knot on hook and attach with sc in sp between beg ch-3 and next V-st, *ch 1, sc between V-sts, rep from * 11 [13, 15, 17] times, leaving rem sts unworked, fasten off.

Row 2: Attach turquoise in 3rd ch of beg ch-3 on 2nd row below, ch 3, V-st in each ch-1 sp, dc between dc of next V-st on 2nd row below, fasten off. *(12 [14, 16, 18] V-sts)*

Continuing in same color sequence, work as established until armhole measures 8½ [9, 9½, 10] inches, ending with an odd-numbered row, fasten off.

Right Neck & Shoulder Shaping

Row 1: With RS facing, sk next 13 V-sts from Left Shoulder, with next color in sequence make a slip knot on hook and attach with sc in sp between 13th unused V-st and next V-st, *ch 1 sc between V-sts, rep from * 11 [13, 15, 17] times, fasten off.

Row 2: Attach turquoise between dc of 13th V-st from Right Shoulder, ch 3, V-st in each ch-1 sp, dc in next dc on 2nd row below, fasten off. *(12 [14, 16, 18] V-sts)*

Continuing in same color sequence, work as established until armhole measures 8½ [9, 9½, 10] inches, ending with an odd-numbered row, fasten off.

Assembly

With tapestry needle and turquoise, sew Shoulder seams. Sew side and Sleeve seam in one continuous seam.

Lower Edging

Rnd 1: With RS facing, working in opposite side of foundation ch, with size G hook, attach turquoise in side seam, ch 1, sc in same sp as beg ch-1, working in chs and unused lps of chs of beg foundation ch, sc in each st around, join in beg sc, draw up a lp of white, fasten off turquoise.

Rnd 2: Ch 1, sc in same sc as beg ch-1, sc in each sc around, join in beg sc.

Rnd 3: *Ch 6, sl st in 2nd ch from hook, sc in next ch, hdc in next ch, dc in next ch, tr in next ch *(sawtooth point made)*, sk next 3 sc, sl st in next sc, rep from * around, join on beg sl st, fasten off.

Arm Edging

Rnd 1: With RS of Sleeve facing and size G hook, attach turquoise at seam, ch 1, working in sps formed by edge of dc of armhole, 2 sc in each sp, join in beg sc, draw up a lp of white, fasten off turquoise.

Rnds 2 & 3: Rep rnds 2 and 3 of Lower Edging.

Neck Edging

Rnd 1: With RS facing, with size G hook, attach turquoise in Left Shoulder seam, ch 1, sc in same sp, working along Left Front Neck Edge in sps formed by edge, 2 sc in each sp, working across sk V-sts of Front, sc in each dc, working across Right Front Neck Edge in sps formed by edge dc, 2 sc in each sp, sc in next seam, working across Right Back Neck Edge, 2 sc in each sp, working across sk V-sts of Back, sc in each dc, working across Left and Back Neck Edges, 2 sc in each sp, join in beg sc, draw up a lp of white, fasten off turquoise.

Rnd 2: Ch 1, sc in same sc and in each rem sc, join in beg sc, fasten off. ●

Denim Vest

DESIGN BY ROSALIE JOHNSTON

INTERMEDIATE

Finished Sizes

Instructions given fit 32–34-inch bust *(small)*; changes for 36–38-inch bust *(medium)*, 40–42-inch bust *(large)*, 44–46-inch bust *(X-large)*, 48–50-inch bust *(2X-large)* and 52–54-inch bust *(3X-large)* are in [ ].

Finished Garment Measurements

Bust: 41 inches (small), [45 inches (medium), 49 inches (large), 52½ inches (X-large), 56 inches (2X-large), 60 inches (3X-large)]

Gauge

6 hdc = 2 inches; 4 hdc rows = 2 inches

Pattern Notes

Weave in loose ends as work progresses.
Join rounds with a slip stitch unless otherwise stated.
Place a stitch marker to mark right side of each panel as work progresses.

Materials

4 MEDIUM

- TLC Amore medium (worsted) weight yarn (6 oz/278 yds/170g per skein):
    2 [2, 3, 3, 4, 4] skeins #3823 lake blue
- Size I/9/5.5mm crochet hook or size needed to obtain gauge
- Tapestry needle
- ⅝-inch gold shank buttons: 2
- Stitch markers

VEST

Basic Panel

Row 1 (RS): Ch 42 [42, 43, 43, 44, 44], hdc in 2nd ch from hook, hdc in each rem ch across, turn. *(41 [41, 42, 42, 43, 43] hdc)*
Row 2: Ch 2 *(does not count as hdc)*, working in **front lps** *(see Stitch Guide)* only, hdc in each hdc across, turn.
Row 3: Ch 2, working in **back lps** *(see Stitch Guide)* only, hdc in each hdc across, turn.
Rows 4–7 [4–9, 4–9, 4–11, 4–11, 4–13]: [Rep rows 2 and 3] alternately 2 [3, 3, 4, 4, 5] times.

For Sizes Medium, X-large & 3X-large Only
At the end of row [9, 11, 13], fasten off.

For Sizes Small, Large & 2X-large Only
Row 8 [10, 12]: Rep row 2, fasten off.

Right Lower Front

Make 2 Basic Panels and place side-by-side *(with first row of one panel next to last row of other panel)* and RS facing. Whipstitch long sides of the Basic Panels tog using 1 lp from each panel.

Right Upper Front

Row 1 (WS): Join yarn to top right corner of piece with sl st, ch 2 *(counts as first hdc)*, hdc across top, work 14 [15, 17, 18, 20, 21] hdc per Basic Panel, turn. *(28 [30, 34, 36, 40, 42] hdc)*
Row 2: Working in **front lps** *(see Stitch Guide)* only,

hdc and in each hdc across, turn.

Row 8: Ch 2, working in front lps only, hdc in first hdc, and in each hdc across, turn.

Rows 9–12: [Rep rows 7 and 8] alternately twice.

Row 13: Working in back lps only, sl st in each of first 3 hdc, sc in next hdc, hdc in each hdc across, turn.

Row 14: Ch 2, working in front lps only, hdc in first hdc and in each hdc across to last hdc, leaving sc and sl sts unworked, turn. *(17 [19, 23, 25, 29, 31] hdc)*

Row 15: Ch 1, working in back lps only, sk first hdc, hdc in each hdc across, turn. *(16 [18, 22, 24, 27, 29] hdc)*

Row 16: Ch 2, working in front lps only, hdc in first hdc, hdc in each hdc across to last hdc, sc in last hdc, turn.

Row 17: Ch 1, working in back lps only, sk first sc, hdc in each hdc across, turn. *(15 [17, 21, 23, 26, 28] hdc)*

Row 18: Ch 2, working in front lps only, hdc in first st, hdc in each st across, turn.

For Sizes Small & Medium Only
At the end of row 18, fasten off.

For Sizes Large, X-large, 2X-large & 3X-large Only
Row 19: Ch 2, working in back lps only, hdc in first hdc, hdc in each rem hdc across, turn.

For Size Large Only
At the end of row 19, fasten off.

For Sizes X-large, 2X-large & 3X-large Only
Row 20: Ch 2, working in front lps only, hdc in first hdc, hdc in each rem hdc across, turn.

For Size X-large Only
At the end of row 20, fasten off.

For Sizes 2X-large & 3X-large Only
Row 21: Rep row 19, fasten off.

Left Lower Front
Rep Right Lower Front.

sl st in 2nd hdc, ch 1, hdc in next hdc, **hdc dec** *(see Stitch Guide)* in next 2 hdc, hdc in each rem hdc across, turn. *(26 [28, 32, 34, 38, 40] hdc)*

Row 3: Ch 2 *(does not count as hdc)*, working in back lps only, hdc in first hdc and in each hdc across to last 2 hdc, hdc dec in next 2 hdc, leaving sl st un-worked, turn. *(24 [26, 30, 32, 36, 38] hdc)*

Row 4: Ch 2, working in front lps only, hdc in 2nd hdc, hdc in each rem hdc across, turn. *(23 [25, 29, 31, 35, 37] hdc)*

Row 5: Ch 2, working in back lps only, hdc in first hdc and in each hdc across to last 2 hdc, hdc dec in next 2 hdc, turn. *(22 [24, 28, 30, 34, 36] hdc)*

Row 6: Rep row 4. *(21 [23, 27, 29, 33, 35] hdc)*

Row 7: Ch 2, working in back lps only, hdc in first

Left Upper Front

Row 1: With RS facing, rep row 1 of Right Upper Front. *(28 [30, 34, 36, 40, 42] hdc)*

Row 2: Ch 2, working in front lps only, hdc in first hdc, hdc across to last 2 hdc, hdc dec in next 2 hdc, leaving last st unworked, turn. *(26 [28, 32, 34, 38, 40] hdc)*

Row 3: Working in back lps only, sl st in 2nd hdc, ch 1, hdc in next hdc, hdc in each rem hdc across, turn. *(25 [27, 31, 33, 37, 39] hdc)*

Row 4: Ch 2, working in front lps only, hdc in first hdc, hdc across to last 2 hdc, hdc dec in next 2 hdc, leaving sl st unworked, turn. *(23 [25, 29, 31, 35, 37] hdc)*

Row 5: Ch 1, working in back lps only, hdc in 2nd hdc, hdc in each hdc across, turn. *(22 [24, 28, 30, 34, 36] hdc)*

Row 6: Ch 2, working in front lps only, hdc in first hdc, hdc in each hdc across to last 2 hdc, hdc dec in next 2 hdc, turn. *(21 [23, 27, 29, 33, 35] hdc)*

Row 7: Ch 2, working in back lps only, hdc in first hdc, hdc in each hdc across, turn.

Row 8: Ch 2, working in front lps only, hdc in first hdc, hdc in each rem hdc across, turn.

Rows 9–12: [Rep rows 7 and 8] alternately twice.

Row 13: Rep row 7.

Row 14: Working in front lps only, sl st in each of next 3 hdc, sc in next hdc, hdc in each rem hdc across, turn.

Row 15: Ch 2, working in back lps only, hdc in first hdc, hdc in each rem hdc across, leaving sc and sl sts unworked, turn. *(17 [19, 23, 25, 29, 31] hdc)*

Row 16: Ch 1, working in front lps only, sk first hdc, hdc in 2nd hdc, hdc in each hdc across, turn. *(16 [18, 22, 24, 28, 30] hdc)*

Row 17: Ch 2, working in back lps only, hdc in first hdc, hdc across to last hdc, sc in last hdc, turn.

Row 18: Ch 1, working in front lps only, sk next sc, hdc in first hdc, hdc in each rem hdc across, turn. *(15 [17, 21, 23, 27, 29] hdc)*

For Sizes Small & Medium Only
At the end of row 18, fasten off.

For Sizes Large, X-large, 2X-large & 3X-large Only
Row 19: Ch 2, working in back lps only, hdc in first hdc, hdc in each rem hdc across, turn.

For Size Large Only
At the end of row 19, fasten off.

For Sizes X-large, 2X-large & 3X-large Only
Row 20: Ch 2, working in front lps only, hdc in first hdc, hdc in each hdc across, turn.

For Size X-large Only
At the end of row 20, fasten off.

For Sizes 2X-large & 3X-large Only
Row 21: Rep row 19, fasten off.

Lower Back

Make 3 Basic Panels and whipstitch long sides tog.

Upper Back

Row 1 (RS): Join yarn at upper right corner of Back, ch 2 *(counts as first hdc)*, hdc across, working 14 [15, 17, 18, 20, 21] hdc across each panel, turn. *(42 [45, 51, 54, 60, 63] hdc)*

Rows 2–17 [2–17, 2–18, 2–19, 2–20, 2–20]: Rep rows 2 and 3 of Basic Panel. At end of last rep, fasten off.

Joining Front & Back

Starting at outer edge *(armhole opening)*, whipstitch Front to Back at shoulders, using 1 lp from each piece for whipstitch.

Side Panels

Make 2.

Row 1 (RS): Ch 42 [42, 43, 43, 44, 44], hdc in 2nd ch from hook, hdc in each rem ch across, turn. *(41 [41, 42, 42, 43, 43] hdc)*

Row 2: Working in front lps only, hdc in 2nd hdc, hdc dec in next 2 hdc, hdc in each rem hdc across, turn. *(39 [39, 40, 40, 41, 41] hdc)*

CONTINUED ON PAGE 71

Square Deal Shrug

DESIGN BY JOYCE NORDSTROM

EASY

Finished Sizes

Instructions given fit 32–38-inch bust *(small/medium)*; changes for 40–46-inch bust *(large/X-large)* are in [ ].

Finished Garment Measurements

Bust: 40 inches *(small/medium)* [43 inches *(large/X-large)*]

Gauge

Size I hook: Rnds 1–5 = 6¾ inches
Size J hook: Rnds 1–5 = 7¼ inches

Pattern Notes

Weave in loose ends as work progresses.
Join rounds with a slip stitch unless otherwise stated.

Materials

MEDIUM 4

- Red Heart Super Saver medium (worsted) weight yarn (7 oz/364 yds/198g per skein):
  1 skein each #380 Windsor blue *(A)*, #313 Aran *(B)*, #657 dusty teal *(C)*, #330 linen *(D)* and #305 aspen print *(E)*
- Sizes I/9/5.5mm *(small/medium)* and J/10/6mm *(large/X-large)* crochet hook or sizes needed to obtain gauge
- Tapestry needle
- Matching ⅞-inch buttons: 2
- Sewing needle and matching thread

Use size I hook throughout for size small/medium and size J hook throughout for size large/X-large.

Special Stitches

Beginning cluster (beg cl): Ch 2, [yo, insert hook in same st as beg ch-2, yo, draw up a lp, yo, draw through 2 lps on hook] twice, yo, draw through all 3 lps on hook.

Cluster (cl): [Yo, insert hook in indicated st, yo, draw up a lp, yo, draw through 2 lps on hook] 3 times, yo, draw through all 4 lps on hook.

Beginning double crochet corner (beg dc corner): Sl st in corner ch-3 sp, ch 3, (2 dc, ch 3, 3 dc) in same corner ch-3 sp as beg ch-3.

Double crochet corner (dc corner): (3 dc, ch 3, 3 dc) in corner ch-3 sp.

SHRUG

Back

Large Motif

Rnd 1 (RS): Beg at center with A, ch 5, join in 5th ch from hook to form a ring, ch 4 *(counts as first dc, ch-1)*, (dc in ring, ch 1) 11 times in ring, join in 3rd ch of beg ch-4. *(12 dc)*

Rnd 2: Sl st in ch-1 sp, **beg cl** *(see Special Stitches)* in same sp, ch 3, [**cl** *(see Special Stitches)* in next ch-1 sp, ch 3] 11 times, join in top of beg cl, fasten off. *(12 cls)*

Rnd 3: Attach B with sl st in any ch-3 sp, ch 1, sc in

same sp, ch 5, [sc in next ch-3 sp, ch 5] 11 times, join in beg sc, fasten off.

Rnd 4: Attach C with sl st in any ch-5 sp, ch 4 *(counts as first tr)*, (3 tr, ch 3, 4 tr) in same sp as beg ch-4 *(beg corner)*, sc in next ch-5 sp, ch 5, sc in next ch-5 sp, *(4 tr, ch 3, 4 tr) in next ch-5 sp *(corner)*, sc in next ch-5 sp, ch 5, sc in next ch-5 sp, rep from * twice, join in 4th ch of beg ch-4, fasten off.

Rnd 5: Attach B with sl st in any corner ch-3 sp, **beg dc corner** *(see Special Stitches)* in corner ch-3 sp, *ch 1, sk next 2 tr, 3 dc in next tr, ch 1, sk next tr, 3 dc in next ch-5 sp, ch 1, sk next sc, sk next tr, 3 dc in next tr, sk next 2 tr, **dc corner** *(see Special Stitches)*, in next corner ch-3 sp, rep from * twice, ch 1, sk next 2 tr, 3 dc in next tr, ch 1, sk next tr, 3 dc in next ch-5 sp, ch 1, sk next sc, sk next tr, 3 dc in next tr, sk next 2 tr, join in 3rd ch of beg ch-3.

Rnd 6: Sl st in next corner ch-3 sp, beg dc corner in same ch-3 sp, *[ch 1, 3 dc in next ch-1 sp] 4 times, ch 1, dc corner in next corner ch-3 sp, rep from * twice, [ch 1, 3 dc in next ch-1 sp] 4 times, ch 1, join in 3rd ch of beg ch-3, fasten off.

Rnd 7: Attach D with sl st in any corner ch-3 sp, beg dc corner in same ch-3 sp, *[ch 1, 3 dc in next ch-1 sp] 5 times, ch 1, dc corner in next corner ch-3 sp, rep from *

twice, [ch 1, 3 dc in next ch-1 sp] 5 times, ch 1, join in 3rd ch of beg ch-3.

Rnd 8: Sl st in next corner ch-3 sp, beg dc corner in same ch-3 sp, *[ch 1, 3 dc in next ch-1 sp] 6 times, ch 1, dc corner in next ch-3 sp, rep from * twice, [ch 1, 3 dc in next ch-1 sp] 6 times, ch 1, join in 3rd ch of beg ch-3, fasten off.

Rnd 9: Attach A with sl st in any corner ch-3 sp, beg dc corner in same ch-3 sp, *[ch 1, 3 dc in next ch-1 sp] 7 times, ch 1, dc corner in next corner ch-3 sp, rep from * twice, [ch 1, 3 dc in next ch-1 sp] 7 times, ch 1, join in 3rd ch of beg ch-3.

Rnd 10: Sl st in corner ch-3 sp, beg dc corner in same ch-3 sp, *[ch 1, 3 dc in next ch-1 sp] 8 times, ch 1, dc corner in next ch-3 sp, rep from * twice, [ch 1, 3 dc in next ch-1 sp] 8 times, ch 1, join in 3rd ch of beg ch-3, fasten off.

Row 11: Now working in rows, attach E with sl st in any corner ch-3 sp, ch 3, 2 dc in same corner ch-3 sp, *ch 1, [3 dc in next ch-1 sp, ch 1] 9 times, dc corner in next corner ch-3 sp, rep from * once, ch 1, [3 dc in next ch-1 sp, ch 1] 9 times, 3 dc in next corner ch-3 sp, turn, leaving rem side unworked.

Row 12: Ch 3, *[3 dc in next ch-1 sp, ch 1] 10 times, dc corner in next corner ch-3 sp, ch 1, rep from * once, ch 1, [3 dc in next ch-1 sp, ch 1] 10 times, dc in 3rd ch of beg ch-3, fasten off.

Small Motif
Make 2.

Rnds 1–5: Rep rnds 1–5 of Back Large Motif. At the end of rnd 5, fasten off.

Left Front
Upper Section

Row 1 (RS): Hold 1 Small Motif with RS facing, attach B with sl st in any corner ch-3 sp, ch 3, 2 dc in same ch-3 sp, [ch 1, 3 dc in next ch-1 sp] 4 times, ch 1, 3 dc in next corner ch-3 sp, leaving rem sides unworked, fasten off.

Row 2: Hold piece with RS facing, attach D with sl st in sp formed by beg ch-3 of row 1, ch 4 *(counts as first dc, ch-1)*, [3 dc in next ch-1 sp, ch 1] 5 times, sk next 2 dc, dc in next dc, turn.

Row 3: Ch 4, [3 dc in next ch-1 sp, ch 1] 5 times, 3 dc in ch-1 sp formed by beg ch-4, fasten off.

Row 4: Hold piece with RS facing, attach A with sl st in first dc, ch 4, [3 dc in next ch-1 sp, ch 1] 5 times, sk next 2 dc, dc in last dc, turn.

Row 5: Ch 3, 2 dc in next ch-1 sp, [ch 1, 3 dc in next ch-1 sp] 4 times, ch 1, 3 dc in ch-1 sp formed by beg ch-4, fasten off.

Neck Shaping

Row 6: Hold piece with RS facing, attach E with sl st in first dc, ch 4, [3 dc in next ch-1 sp, ch 1] 3 times, dc in next ch-1 sp, leaving rem sps unworked, turn.

Row 7: Ch 3, [3 dc in next ch-1 sp, ch 1] twice, 3 dc in ch-1 sp formed by beg ch-4, fasten off.

Lower Section

Row 1: Hold Motif with RS facing and unworked side opposite worked side at top, attach B with sl st in corner ch-3 sp, ch 3, 2 dc in same sp, [ch 1, 3 dc in next ch-1 sp] 4 times, ch 1, 3 dc in next corner ch-3 sp, leaving rem sides unworked, fasten off.

Rows 2–5: Rep rows 2–5 of Upper Section.

Right Front

Upper Section

Rows 1–5: Rep rows 1–5 of Left Front Upper Section.

Neck Shaping

Row 6: Hold piece with RS facing, attach E with sl st in 2nd ch-1 sp on row 5, ch 4, [3 dc in next ch-1 sp, ch 1] 3 times, dc in last dc, turn.

Row 7: Sl st in next ch-1 sp, ch 3, 2 dc in same sp, ch 1, [3 dc in next ch-1 sp, ch 1] twice, dc in ch-1 sp formed by beg ch-4, fasten off.

Lower Section

Rows 1–5: Rep rows 1–5 of Left Front Lower Section.

Sleeve

Make 2.

Rnds 1–5: Rep rnds 1–5 of Large Motif. At the end of rnd 5, fasten off.

First Section

Row 6: Now working in rows, hold piece with RS facing, attach B with sl st in any corner ch-3 sp, ch 3, 2 dc in same sp, [ch 1, 3 dc in next ch-1 sp] 5 times, fasten off.

Row 7: Hold piece with RS facing, attach E with sl st in 3rd ch of beg ch-3, ch 4, [3 dc in next ch-1 sp, ch 1] 4 times, sk next 2 dc, dc in last dc, turn.

Row 8: Ch 3, 2 dc in next ch-1 sp, [ch 1, 3 dc in next ch-1 sp] 4 times, ch 1, 3 dc in sp formed by beg ch-4, fasten off.

Row 9: Hold piece with RS facing, attach A with sl st in first dc, ch 4, [3 dc in next ch-1 sp, ch 1] 5 times, sk next 2 dc, dc in 3rd ch of beg ch-3, turn.

Row 10: Ch 3, 3 dc in next ch-1 sp, [ch 1, 3 dc in next ch-1 sp] 4 times, ch 1, 3 dc in sp formed by ch-1 sp of beg ch-4, fasten off.

Row 11: Hold piece with RS facing, attach E with sl st in first dc, ch 4, [3 dc in next ch-1 sp, ch 1] 5 times, sk next 3 dc, dc in 3rd ch of ch-3, turn.

Row 12: Ch 3, 2 dc in next ch-1 sp, [ch 1, 3 dc in next ch-1 sp] 4 times, ch 1, 3 dc in sp formed by beg ch-4, turn.

Row 13: Ch 4, [3 dc in next ch-1 sp, ch 1] 5 times, sk next 2 dc, dc in 3rd ch of ch-3, turn.

Row 14: Ch 3, 2 dc in next ch-1 sp, [ch 1, 3 dc in next ch-1 sp] 4 times, ch 1, 3 dc in sp formed by beg ch-4, turn.

Row 15: Ch 4, [3 dc in next ch-1 sp, ch 1] 5 times, sk next 2 dc, dc in 3rd ch of beg ch-3, fasten off.

2nd Section

Row 6: Hold piece with RS facing and unworked side opposite worked side at top, attach B with sl st in corner ch-3 sp, ch 3, 2 dc in same sp, [ch 1, 3 dc in next ch-1 sp] 5 times, fasten off.

Rows 7–15: Rep rows 7–15 of First Section.

Side Edging

Hold 1 Sleeve with RS facing and row 15 of First Section to right, attach E with sl st in sp formed by ch-4 of row 15, ch 3, 2 dc in same sp, [ch 1, 3 dc in

CONTINUED ON PAGE 72

Kimono Jacket

DESIGN BY JOYCE BRAGG

INTERMEDIATE

Finished Sizes

Instructions given fit 32–34-
inch bust *(small)*; changes
for 36–38-inch bust
(medium), 40–42-inch bust
(large), 44–46-inch bust
(X-large), 48–50-inch bust
(2X-large) and 52–54-inch
bust *(3X-large)* are in [ ].

Finished Garment
Measurements

Bust: 36 inches *(small)* [40
inches *(medium)*, 44 inches
(large), 48 inches *(X-large)*,
56 inches *(2X-large)*, 64
inches *(3X-large)*]

Gauge

Size I hook: 12 dc = 4 inches
Size J hook: 13 dc = 4 inches
Size K hook: 14 dc = 4 inches

Pattern Notes

Weave in loose ends as work progresses.
Join rounds with a slip stitch unless otherwise stated.

Materials

- Moda Dea
  Spellbound bulky
  (chunky) weight yarn (1¾
  oz/93 yds/50g per ball):
    10 [13, 13, 15] balls
    #2732 wizard
- Sizes C/2/2.75mm,
  G/6/4mm, I/9/5.5mm, J/10/
  6mm and K/10½/6.5mm
  crochet hooks or sizes
  needed to obtain gauge
- Tapestry needle
- Stitch markers

5 BULKY

JACKET

Body

Row 1: Starting at bottom edge with size J [I, I, K, K,
K] hook, ch 94 [126, 139, 162, 202, 225] dc in 4th ch
from hook *(first 3 chs count as first dc)*, dc in each rem
ch across, turn. *(91 [123, 136, 159, 202, 222] dc)*
Row 2: Ch 3 *(counts as first dc)*, dc in each st across, turn.
Row 3: Ch 3, dc in next st, [ch 1, sk next st, dc in next
st] across, turn.
Row 4: Ch 3, [dc in next ch-1 sp, dc in next dc]
across, turn.
Rows 5–22: [Rep rows 2–4] consecutively 6 times.
Rows 23 & 24: Rep rows 2 and 3.

Left Front

Row 1: Ch 3, dc in each of next 20 [30, 40, 50, 60, 70]
sts, turn.
Row 2: Ch 3, dc in next st, [ch 1, sk 1 st, dc in next st]
across, turn.

For Sizes Small & Medium Only
Row 3: Ch 3, [dc in next ch sp, dc in next dc]
across, turn.

For Sizes Large, X-large, 2X-large & 3X-large Only
Row 3: Sl st in next sp, ch 3, dc in next dc, [dc in next
sp, dc in next dc] across, turn. *([39, 49, 59, 69] sts)*

For All Sizes
Row 4: Ch 3, dc in each st to last st at neckline edge,
leaving last st unworked, turn. *(19 [29, 38, 48, 58, 68] sts)*

Row 17: Rep row 5.
Row 18: Rep row 6. *([19, 28, 38, 48, 58] sts)*

For Size Medium Only
Row 19: Sl st in each of next 2 sts, dc in each of next 15 sts, sl st in each of next 2 sts, fasten off. *([15] sts)*

For Sizes Large, X-large, 2X-large & 3X-large Only
Row 19: Rep row 7. *([27, 37, 47, 57] sts)*
Row 20: Rep row 5.
Row 21: Rep row 6. *([26, 36, 46, 56] sts)*
Row 22: Rep row 7. *([25, 35, 45, 55] sts)*
Row 23: Rep row 5.
Row 24: Rep row 3. *([24, 34, 44, 54] sts)*

For Size Large Only
Row 25: Sl st in each of next 2 sts, dc in each of next 20 sts, sl st in each of last 2 sts, fasten off. *([20] sts)*

For Sizes X-large, 2X-large & 3X-large Only
Row 25: Rep row 7. *([33, 43, 53] sts)*
Row 26: Rep row 5.
Row 27: Rep row 3. *([32, 42, 52] sts)*
Row 28: Rep row 7. *([31, 41, 51] sts)*

For Size X-large Only
Row 29: Sl st in each of next 2 sts, dc in each of next 27 sts, sl st in each of last 2 sts, fasten off. *([27] sts)*

For Size 2X-large Only
Row 29: Rep row 7. *([40] sts)*
Row 30: Rep row 5.
Row 31: Rep row 3. *([39] sts)*
Row 32: Rep row 7. *([38] sts)*
Row 33: Sl st in each of next 2 sts, dc in each of next 34 sts, sl st in each of last 2 sts, fasten off. *([34] sts)*

For Size 3X-large Only
Row 29: Rep row 7. *([50] sts)*
Row 30: Rep row 5.
Row 31: Rep row 3. *([49] sts)*
Row 32: Rep row 7. *([48] sts)*
Rows 33–36: Rep rows 29–32. *([45] sts)*

Row 5: Ch 3, dc in next st, [ch 1, sk 1 st, dc in next st] across, turn.
Row 6: Ch 3, dc in each st to last st at neckline edge, leaving last st unworked, turn. *(18 [28, 37, 47, 57, 67] sts)*
Row 7: Sl st in next st, ch 3, dc in each st across, turn. *(17 [27, 36, 46, 56, 66] sts)*
Row 8: Rep row 5.
Row 9: Rep row 6. *(16 [26, 35, 45, 55, 65] sts)*
Row 10: Rep row 7. *(15 [25, 34, 44, 54, 64] sts)*
Row 11: Sl st in next st, ch 3, dc in next st, [sk next st, ch 1, dc in next st] across, turn. *(14 [24, 33, 43, 53, 63] sts)*
Row 12: Rep row 6. *(13 [23, 32, 42, 52, 62] sts)*

For Size Small Only
Row 13: Sl st in each of next 2 sts, dc in each of next 9 sts, sl st in each of next 2 sts, fasten off.

For Sizes Medium, Large, X-large, 2X-large & 3X-large Only
Row 13: Rep row 7. *([22, 31, 41, 51, 61] sts)*
Row 14: Rep row 5.
Row 15: Rep row 6. *([21, 30, 40, 50, 60] sts)*
Row 16: Rep row 7. *([20, 29, 39, 49, 59] sts)*

Rows 37–39: Rep rows 29–31. *([43] sts)*

Row 40: Sl st in each of next 2 sts, dc in each of next 39 dc, sl st in each of last 2 sts, fasten off. *([39] sts)*

Right Front

Attach yarn in first st at outer edge of row 24 of Body with a sl st, work as for Left Front *(design is reversible)*.

Back

Row 1: Sk next 5 [7, 7, 8, 8, 8] sts for underarm, attach yarn in next st with sl st, rep row 4 of Body. *(44 [52, 45, 46, 66, 69] sts)*

Rows 2–13 [2–19, 2–25, 2–29, 2–33, 2–40]: [Rep rows 2–4 of Body] consecutively 4 [6, 8, 9, 10, 11] times, then rep row 0 [0, 0, 2, 3, 0] ending last rep with row 4 [4, 4, 2, 3, 4], fasten off.

With size C hook, matching top edge of Left Front to Back, attach yarn with sl st in first st, ch 1, working through both thicknesses, sc in each st across for shoulder, fasten off.

Rep with Right Front and Back.

Sleeve

Make 2.

For All Sizes

Foundation ch: With size J [I, I, K, K, K] hook, ch 40 [55, 65, 70, 75, 75], using care not to twist ch, join in first ch to form a ring. *(40 [55, 65, 70, 75, 75] sts)*

Rnd 1: Ch 3, dc in each st around, join in 3rd ch of ch-3, turn.

Rnd 2: Ch 3, dc in each st around, join in 3rd ch of ch-3, turn.

Rnd 3: Ch 4, sk next st, [dc in next st, ch 1, sk next st] around, join in 3rd ch of beg ch-4.

For Size Small Only

Rnds 4–12: Rep rnds 1–3.

Rnd 13: Ch 3, *2 dc in next sp, [dc in next dc, dc in next sp] 4 times, dc in next dc, rep from * around, join in 3rd ch of beg ch-3, turn. *(44 sts)*

Rnds 14 & 15: Rep rnds 2 and 3.

Rnd 16: Rep rnd 13, inc 4 dc evenly spaced around in ch-1 sps. *(48 sts)*

Rnds 17 & 18: Rep rnds 2 and 3.

Rnd 19: Rep rnd 13, inc 6 dc evenly spaced around in ch-1 sps. *(54 sts)*

Rnds 20 & 21: Rep rnds 2 and 3.

Rnd 22: Rep rnd 13, inc 4 dc evenly spaced around in ch-1 sps. *(58 sts)*

Rnds 23 & 24: Rep rnds 2 and 3.

For Size Medium Only

Rnds 4–6: Rep rnds 4–6 of small Sleeve.

For Size Large Only

Rnd 4: Ch 3, dc in each st around, inc 3 dc, join in 3rd ch of beg ch-3, turn. *([68] sts)*

Rnd 5: Rep rnd 2.

Rnd 6: Rep rnd 3.

For Sizes Medium & Large Only

Rnd 7: Ch 3, dc in each st around, inc 4 dc around, join in 3rd ch of beg ch-3, turn. *([58, 72] sts)*

Rnds 8 & 9: Rep rnds 2 and 3 of Sleeve.

Rnd 10: Rep rnd 7, inc [4, 2] sts. *([62, 74] sts)*

Rnd 11: Ch 3, dc in each st around, join in 3rd ch of ch-3. *([62, 74] sts)*

Rnd 12: Rep rnd 3.

Rnds 13–15: Rep rnds 1–3.

Rnd 16: Rep rnd 7, inc [4, 5] sts. *([66, 79] sts)*

Rnds 17 & 18: Rep rnds 2 and 3.

Rnds 19–21: Rep rnds 1–3 of Sleeve.

For Size Medium Only

Rnd 22: Rep rnd 7, inc 7 sts. *([73] sts)*

Rnd 23: Rep rnd 2, fasten off.

For Size Large Only

Rnd 22: Rep rnd 7, inc [5] sts. *([84] sts)*

Rnds 23 & 24: Rep rnds 2 and 3.

Rnds 25 & 26: Rep rnds 1 and 2. At the end of rnd 26, fasten off.

CONTINUED ON PAGE 74

Easy Summer Vest or Top

DESIGN BY DARLA SIMS

EASY

Finished Sizes

Instructions given fit 32–34-inch bust *(small)*; changes for 36–38-inch bust *(medium)*, 40–42-inch bust *(large)*, 44–46-inch bust *(X-large)*, 48–50-inch bust *(2X-large)*, 52–54-inch bust *(3X-large)*, 56–58-inch bust *(4X-large)* and 60–62-inch bust *(5X-large)* are in [ ].

Finished Garment Measurements

Bust: 36 inches *(small)* [40 inches *(medium)*, 44 inches *(large)*, 48 inches *(X-large)*, 52 inches *(2X-large)*, 56 inches *(3X-large)*, 60 inches *(4X-large)*, 64 inches *(5X-large)*]]

Gauge

Size H hook: 3 dc = 1 inch

Pattern Notes

Weave in loose ends as work progresses.

Materials

- Aunt Lydia's Quick Crochet medium (worsted) weight thread (400 yds per ball): 2 [2, 3, 3, 4, 5, 5, 6] balls #1007 cranberry
- Sizes F/5/3.75mm, G/6/4mm and H/8/5mm crochet hooks or sizes needed to obtain gauge
- Tapestry needle
- Stitch markers

4 MEDIUM

Join rounds with a slip stitch unless otherwise stated. Top is made of 2 pieces worked vertically. Each piece is folded in half horizontally *(short ends together)* to create 1 half of garment, going up and over shoulders from lower edge of front to lower edge of back. Pieces are joined at center front and back to create V-neck openings.

Front & Back

Make 2.

Row 1: With size H hook, ch 122 [126, 126, 126, 128, 128, 132, 132], dc in 4th ch from hook *(beg 3 chs count as first dc)*, dc in each rem ch across, turn. *(120 [124, 124, 126, 126, 130, 130] dc)*

Row 2: Ch 3 *(counts as first dc)*, dc in each dc across, turn.

Rep row 2 until piece measures 9 [10, 11, 12, 13, 14, 15, 16] inches wide, fasten off.

Assembly

Fold each piece in half *(see Pattern Notes)* and place st marker at both ends of fold to mark shoulder line *(fold line)*. For all sizes, measure 8 inches down from shoulder line on both pieces for front neck opening. Place pieces side by side. Beg at lower front and working through **back lps** *(see Stitch Guide)* only, sew pieces tog to st markers. For all sizes, place markers 6 inches down from shoulder line

CONTINUED ON PAGE 74

Ravishing in Red Top

DESIGN BY ANN PARNELL

INTERMEDIATE

Finished Sizes

Instructions given fit 32–34-
inch bust *(small)*; changes
for 36–38-inch bust
(medium) and 40–42-inch
bust *(large)* are in [ ].

Finished Garment
Measurements

Bust: 36 inches *(small)* [38
inches *(medium)*, 40 inches
(large)]

Gauge

3 V-sts = 1 inch; 15 V-st rows = 4 inches

Pattern Notes

Weave in loose ends as work progresses.
Join rounds with a slip stitch unless otherwise stated.

Special Stitches

V-stitch (V-st): 2 dc in next ch or in sp between sts of
next V-st.
Shell: 4 dc in next ch or sp between 2nd and 3rd sts
of next shell.
Cluster (cl): [Yo, insert hook in indicated st or sp, yo,
draw up a lp, yo, draw through 2 lps on hook] twice

Materials

• DMC Cebelia crochet
cotton size 10 (282 yds/50g
per ball):
   1,526 [1,744, 1,744] yds
   #666 bright red
• Size E/4/3.5mm crochet
hook or size needed to
obtain gauge
• Tapestry needle
• Stitch markers

in same st or sp, yo, draw through all 3 lps on hook.

TOP

Back

Row 1 (WS): Starting at bottom edge, ch 127 [135,
143], **V-st** *(see Special Stitches)* in 5th ch from hook,
[sk next ch, V-st in next ch] 20 [22, 24] times, sk next
ch, dc in next ch, [sk next 2 chs, **shell** *(see Special
Stitches)* in next ch, sk next 2 chs, dc in next ch] 6
times, [sk next ch, V-st in next ch] 21 [23, 25] times, sk
next ch, dc in last ch, turn. *(9 dc, 6 shells, 42 V-sts, [9 dc,
6 shells, 46 V-sts and 9 dc, 6 shells, 50 V-sts])*
Row 2: Ch 3 *(counts as first dc)*, V-st in each V-st to next
shell, sk last dc of V-st, **fpdc** *(see Stitch Guide)* around
next dc, [fpdc around 2nd dc of next shell, V-st in center of same shell, fpdc around 3rd dc of same shell,
sk last dc of same shell, fpdc around next dc] 6 times,
V-st in each V-st across to last st, dc in last st, turn.
Row 3: Ch 3, V-st in each V-st across to next fpdc, sk
last dc of V-st, **bpdc** *(see Stitch Guide)* around next
fpdc, [sk next dc, sk next fpdc, bpdc around next dc
of V-st at center of shell, V-st in center sp of same V-st,
bpdc around 2nd dc of same V-st, sk next fpdc, sk next
dc, bpdc around next fpdc between shells] 6 times,
V-st in each V-st across to last st, dc in last st, turn.
Row 4: Ch 3, V-st in each V-st across to post sts, sk
last dc of V-st, fpdc around next bpdc, [sk next dc, sk
next bpdc, fpdc around next dc of V-st, V-st in center

sp of same V-st, fpdc around 2nd dc of same V-st, sk next bpdc, sk next dc, fpdc around next bpdc between shells] 6 times, V-st in each V-st across to last st, dc in last st, turn.

Rows 5–54 [5–56, 5–58]: [Rep rows 3 and 4] alternately 25 [26, 27] times.

Row 55 [57, 59]: Rep row 3.

First Shoulder

Row 56 [58, 60]: Ch 1, sl st in each of first 5 sts, 2 sc in next V-st, 2 hdc in next V-st, V-st in each V-st across to last 2 V-sts before next shell, **cl** (see Special Stitches) in each of next 2 V-sts, sk last dc of V-st, dc in next st, leaving rem sts unworked, turn. (15 [17, 19] V-sts)

Row 57 [59, 61]: Ch 3, dc in each of next 2 cls (counts as V-st), V-st in each V-st across to next hdc, sl st in next hdc, leaving rem sts unworked, turn. (14 [16, 18] V-sts)

Row 58 [60, 62]: Ch 1, sl st in each of next 4 dc, 2 sc in next V-st, 2 hdc in next V-st, V-st in each V-st across to last 2 V-sts, cl in each of next 2 V-sts, dc in last st, turn. (10 [12, 14] V-sts)

Rows 59 & 60 [61 & 62, 63 & 64]: Rep rows 57 and

58 [59 and 60, 61 and 62].

Row 61 [63, 65]: Rep row 57 [59, 61], fasten off.

2nd Shoulder

Row 56 [58, 60]: Sk center shell section of row 55 [57, 59], attach cotton with sl st in next fpdc, ch 3, cl in each of next 2 V-sts, V-st in each V-st across to last 4 V-sts, 2 hdc in next V-st, 2 sc in next V-st, leaving rem sts unworked, turn. (15 [17, 19] V-sts)

Row 57 [59, 61]: Ch 1, sl st in each of first 4 sts, V-st in each V-st across to next 2 cls, dc in each of next 2 cls (counts as a V-st), dc in last st, turn.

Row 58 [60, 62]: Ch 3, cl in each of next 2 V-sts, V-st in each V-st across to last 4 sts (4 sts before sl sts), 2 hdc in next V-st, 2 sc in next V-st, leaving rem sts unworked, turn.

Rows 59 & 60 [61 & 62, 63 & 64]: Rep rows 57 and 58 [59 and 60, 61 and 62].

Row 61 [63, 65]: Rep row 57 [59, 61], fasten off.

Front

Rows 1–45 [1–47, 1–49]: Rep rows 1–45 [1–47, 1–49] of Back.

First Shoulder

Row 46 [48, 50]: Ch 3, V-st in each st across to last 2 V-sts before next shell, cl in each of next 2 V-sts, dc in next post st, leaving rem sts unworked, turn.

Row 47 [49, 51]: Ch 3, dc in each of next 2 cls (counts as V-st), V-st in each V-st across to last st, dc in last st, turn.

Row 48 [50, 52]: Ch 3, V-st in each V-st across to last 2 V-sts, cl in each of next 2 V-sts, dc in last st, turn.

Rows 49 & 50 [51 & 52, 53 & 54]: Rep rows 47 and 48 [49 and 50, 51 and 52].

Row 51 [53, 55]: Rep row 47 [49, 51].

Rows 52–55 [54–57, 56–59]: Ch 3, V-st in each V-st across, ending with dc in last st, turn.

Row 56 [58, 60]: Ch 1, sl st in each of first 5 sts, 2 sc in next V-st, 2 hdc in next V-st, V-st in each V-st across, ending with dc in last st, turn. (14 [16, 18] V-sts)

Row 57 [59, 61]: Ch 3, V-st in each V-st across to next hdc, sl st in next hdc, leaving rem sts unworked, turn.

Row 58 [60, 62]: Sl st in each of next 4 dc, 2 sc in next V-st, 2 hdc in next V-st, V-st in each V-st across, ending with dc in last st, turn.

Rows 59 & 60 [61 & 62, 63 & 64]: Rep rows 57 and 58 [59 and 60, 61 and 62].

Row 61 [63, 65]: Rep row 57 [59, 61], fasten off.

2nd Shoulder

Row 46 [48, 50]: Sk center shell section of row 45 [47, 49], attach cotton with sl st in next post st, ch 3, cl in each of next 2 V-sts, V-st in each V-st across, ending with dc in last st, turn.

Row 47 [49, 51]: Ch 3, V-st in each V-st across to next 2 cls, dc in each of next 2 cls (counts as V-st), dc in last st, turn.

Row 48 [50, 52]: Ch 3, cl in each of next 2 V-sts, V-st in each V-st across, dc in last st, turn.

Rows 49–51 [51–53, 53–55]: Rep rows 47 and 48 [49 and 50, 51 and 52] alternately once, ending last rep with row 47 [49, 51].

Rows 52–55 [54–57, 56–59]: Ch 3, V-st in each V-st across, dc in last st, turn.

Row 56 [58, 60]: Ch 3, V-st in each V-st across to last 4 V-sts, 2 hdc in next V-st, 2 sc in next V-st, leaving rem sts unworked, turn.

Row 57 [59, 61]: Ch 1, sl st in each of first 4 sts, V-st in each st across, with dc in last st, turn.

Rows 58–61 [60–63, 62–65]: Rep rows 56 and 57 [58 and 59, 60 and 61]. At the end of last row, fasten off. Sew shoulder seams. For side seams, sew ends of rows 1–28 tog on each side leaving rem rows for armhole opening.

Neckline Trim

Rnd 1: Working in ends of rows and in sts around neckline opening, attach cotton with sc in any st, sc in each st around, evenly spacing sts in multiples of 4, join in beg sc.

Rnd 2: Sk next st, shell in next st, sk next st, [sl st in next st, sk next st, shell in next st, sk next st] around, join with sl st in first st, fasten off.

Bottom Band

Rnd 1: Working around bottom in sps between V-sts on opposite side of foundation ch of Row 1, attach cotton with sl st in either side seam, ch 3, *shell in sp between first 2 V-sts, [dc in next sp, shell in next sp] across to last dc before next shell, fpdc around next dc, [shell in center of next shell, fpdc around next dc] 6 times, shell in sp between last dc and next V-st, [dc in next sp, shell in next sp], rep from * to next side seam, dc in next side seam, rep from * to *, join with sl st in top of ch-3, **turn**.

Rnd 2: Ch 3, [bpdc around 2nd dc of next shell, V-st in center of same shell, bpdc around 3rd dc of same shell, sk last dc of same shell, bpdc around next st] around, join, turn.

Rnd 3: Ch 3, [fpdc around first dc of next V-st, V-st in center of same V-st, fpdc around 2nd dc of same V-st, sk next st, fpdc around next bpdc] around, join, turn.

Rnd 4: Ch 3, [bpdc around first dc of next V-st, V-st in center of same V-st, bpdc around 2nd dc of same V-st, sk next st, bpdc around next fpdc] around to last V-st, join, turn.

Rnds 5–8: [Rep rnds 3 and 4] alternately twice.

Rnd 9: Ch 1, sc in first st, [**fpsc** (see Stitch Guide) around first dc of next V-st, V-st in center of same V-st, fpsc around 2nd dc of same V-st, sk next bpdc, sc in next bpdc] around to last V-st, join in first sc, fasten off.

Sleeve Trim

Rnd 1: Working in ends of rows around armhole, attach cotton with sl st at underarm seam, ch 3, sk next row, shell in next row, [dc in sp between next 2 rows, sk next row, shell in next row] around, sk last 1 or 2 rows if necessary, join in 3rd ch of beg ch-3, turn.

Rnds 2–9: Rep rnds 2–9 of Bottom Band. ●

Jazzy Diamonds

DESIGN BY MARY ANN FRITS

INTERMEDIATE

Finished Sizes

Instructions given fit 32–34-
inch bust *(small)*; changes
for 36–38-inch bust
(medium) and 40–42-inch
bust *(large)* are in [ ].

Finished Garment Measurements

Bust: 36 inches *(small)* [40
inches *(medium)*, 44 inches
(large)]

Gauge

Size D hook: Motif = 3 inches
Size E hook: Motif = 3½ inches
Size F hook: Motif = 4 inches

Pattern Notes

Weave in loose ends as work progresses.
Join rounds with a slip stitch unless otherwise stated.
Refer to individual diagrams for placement of Motifs
and number of Motifs required for each section of
garment.

JACKET

Back

Motif A
Row 1 (RS): Ch 14, dc in 6th ch from hook *(beg 5 sk*

Materials

2 FINE

- Red Heart
  LusterSheen fine (sport)
  weight yarn (4 oz/335
  yds/113g per skein):
    3 [3, 4] skeins #0007
      vanilla
- Sizes D/3/3.25mm,
  E/4/3.5mm and
  F/5/3.75mm crochet hooks
  or sizes needed to obtain
  gauge
- Tapestry needle

chs count as ch-1 sp, dc and ch-1 sp), [ch 1, sk next ch,
dc in next ch] 4 times, turn. *(6 dc, 5 ch-1 sps)*
Row 2: Ch 4 *(counts as first dc, ch-1),* [dc in next dc, ch
1] 4 times, sk next ch, dc in next ch, turn.
Row 3: Ch 4, [dc in next dc, ch 1] 4 times, sk next ch,
dc in next ch, turn.
Row 4: Rep row 3.
Row 5: Ch 4, [dc in next dc, ch 1] 4 times, sk next ch,
dc in next ch, **do not turn**.
Rnd 6: Now working in rnds, ch 1, working around
edge of piece, 2 sc in each of next 4 sps, [5 sc in next
sp *(corner)*, 2 sc in each of next 3 sts] 3 times, 3 sc in
same sp as beg 2 sc *(corner)*, join in beg sc.
Rnd 7: Ch 1, sl st in each of next 3 sc, [ch 6, sk next 2
sc, sl st in each of next 4 sc, ch 1, sc in next sc, ch 1,
sl st in each of next 4 sc] 3 times, ch 6, sk next 2 sc, sl
st in each of next 4 sc, ch 1, sc in next sc, ch 1, sl st in
next sc, join in beg sl st.
Rnd 8: Sl st in each of next 2 sts, sl st in each of next 2
chs of next ch-6 sp, ch 7, [sk next 2 chs, sc in next ch,
ch 6, sk next ch, sk next 4 sl sts, sk next ch, sc in next
sc, ch 6, sk next ch, sk next 4 sl sts, sk first ch of next
ch-6 sp, sc in next ch, ch 6] 3 times, sk next 2 chs, sc
in next ch, ch 6, sk next ch, sk next 4 sl sts, sk next ch,
sc in next sc, ch 6, join with sl st in first ch of beg ch-7.
Rnd 9: Sl st in next sp, ch 1, (3 sc, ch 3, 3 sc) in same
sp as beg ch-1 *(corner)*, [7 sc in each of next 2 ch-6
sps, (3 sc, ch 3, 3 sc) in next ch-6 sp *(corner)*] 3 times, 7
sc in each of next 2 ch-6 sps, join in first sc, fasten off.

Motif B
Rows 1–5: Rep rows 1–5 of Motif A.

holding WS of completed Motif facing WS of working Motif and matching sts, sl st in 2nd ch of corresponding corner ch-3 sp on completed Motif, ch 1, 3 sc in same ch-6 sp on working Motif as previous 3 sc *(joined corner)*, [4 sc in next ch-6 sp, sc around post of 4th sc of corresponding ch-6 sp on completed Motif, on working Motif, 3 sc in same sp as previous 4 sc] twice, 3 sc in next ch-6 sp, ch 1, sc in center of joining sc of corresponding ch-3 sps on completed Motifs, ch 1, on working Motif, 3 sc in same sp as previous 3 sc, 7 sc in each of next 2 ch-6 sps, join in first sc, fasten off.

Motifs D & E

Referring to Back diagram for number and placement, work same as Motif C of Back, joining sides in same manner.

Right Front

Motifs A–C

Referring to Right Front diagram for number and placement, work same as Motifs A, B and C of Back, joining sides in same manner.

Motif E

Referring to Right Front diagram for number and placement, work same as Motif C of Back, joining sides in same manner.

Half Motif A

Row 1 (RS): Rep row 1 of Motif A of Back. *(6 dc, 5 ch-1 sps)*

Row 2: Ch 3 *(counts as first dc)*, [dc in next dc, ch 1] 3 times, dc in next dc, sk next ch, dc in next ch, turn. *(6 dc, 3 ch-1 sps)*

Row 3: Sl st in next dc, ch 3, dc in next dc, ch 1, dc in next dc, sk next dc, dc in next ch, turn. *(4 dc, 1 ch-1 sp)*

Row 4: Sl st in next dc, ch 3, dc in next dc, turn, leaving ch-3 unworked. *(2 dc)*

Rnd 5: Now working in rnds, ch 1, working around edge of piece, [2 sc in each of next 3 sps, 5 sc in next sp *(corner)*] twice, 2 sc in each of next 2 sps, 3 sc in same sp as beg 2 sc *(corner)*, join in first sc. *(29 sc)*

Rnds 6–8: Rep rnds 6–8 of Motif A.

Rnd 9: Sl st in next sp, ch 1, (3 sc, ch 3, 3 sc) in same sp as beg ch-1 *(corner)*, 7 sc in each of next 2 ch-6 sps, 3 sc in next ch-6 sp, ch 1, holding WS of last completed Motif facing WS of working Motif and matching sts, sl st in 2nd ch of corresponding corner ch-3 sp on completed Motif, ch 1, 3 sc in same corner ch sp on working Motif as previous 3 sc *(joined corner)*, [4 sc in next ch-6 sp, sc around **post** *(see Stitch Guide)* of 4th sc of corresponding ch-6 sp on completed Motif, 3 sc in same ch-6 sp as previous 4 sc] twice, 3 sc in next ch-6 sp, ch 1, sl st in 2nd ch of corresponding corner ch-3 sp on completed Motif, ch 1, 3 sc in same ch-6 sp as previous 3 sc on working Motif *(joined corner)*, 7 sc in each of next 2 ch-6 sps, (3 sc, ch 3, 3 sc) in next ch-6 sp *(corner)*, 7 sc in each of next 2 ch-6 sps, join in first sc, fasten off.

Motif C

Rows 1–5: Rep rows 1–5 of Motif A.

Rnds 6–8: Rep rnds 6–8 of Motif A.

Rnd 9: Sl st in next sp, ch 1, (3 sc, ch 3, 3 sc) in same sp as beg ch-1 *(corner)*, 7 sc in each of next 2 ch-6 sps, (3 sc, ch 3, 3 sc) in next ch-6 sp *(corner)*, 7 sc in each of next 2 ch-6 sps, 3 sc in next ch-6 sp, ch 1,

Rnd 6: Sl st in each of next 3 sc, ch 6, sk next 2 sc, sl st in each of next 2 sc, ch 1, sc in next sc (sc corner), ch 1, sl st in each of next 10 sc, ch 1, sc in next sc (sc corner), ch 1, sl st in each of next 2 sc, ch 6, sk next 2 sc, sl st in each of next 4 sc, ch 1, sc in next sc (sc corner), ch 1, sl st in next sc, join in first sl st, fasten off.

Row 7: Now working in rows, hold piece with WS facing and straight edge at bottom, attach yarn with sl st in corner sc of right-hand bottom corner, ch 7, sc in 2nd ch of next ch-6 sp, ch 6, sk next 2 chs, sc in next ch, ch 6, sc in next corner sc, ch 2, sc in 2nd ch of next ch-6 sp, ch 6, sk next 2 chs, sc in next ch, ch 6, sc in next sc corner, turn.

Row 8 (joining): 7 sc in next ch-6 sp, 3 sc in next ch-6 sp, ch 1, holding WS of completed Motif facing WS of working Motif and matching sts, sc in 2nd ch of corresponding corner ch-3 sp on completed Motif, ch 1, on working Motif, 3 sc in same ch-6 sp as previous 3 sc, [4 sc in next ch-6 sp, sc around post of 4th sc on corresponding ch-6 sp on completed Motif, on working Motif, 3 sc in same ch sp as previous 4 sc] twice, 3 sc in next ch-6 sp, ch 1, sc in center of joining sc of corresponding ch-3 sps on completed Motifs, ch 1, on working

Motif, 3 sc in same ch-6 sp as previous 3 sc, 7 sc in next ch-6 sp, fasten off.

Half Motif B

Rows 1–4: Rep rows 1–4 of Half Motif A.

Rnds 5 & 6: Rep rnds 5 and 6 of Half Motif A.

Row 7: Rep row 7 of Half Motif A.

Row 8 (joining): 4 sc in next ch-6 sp, holding WS of Half Motif A facing WS of working Motif and matching sts, sc around post of 4th sc of corresponding ch-6 sp on Half Motif A, on working Motif, 3 sc in same sp as previous 4 sc, 3 sc in next ch-6 sp, ch 1, sc in center of joining sc of corresponding ch-3 sps on completed Motifs, ch 1, on working Motif, 3 sc in same sp as previous sc, [4 sc in next ch-6 sp, sc around post of 4th sc on corresponding ch-6 sp on completed Motif; on working Motif, 3 sc in same sp as previous 4 sc] twice, 3 sc in next ch-6 sp, ch 1, sc in center of joining sc of corresponding ch-3 sps on completed Motifs, ch 1, on working Motif, 3 sc in same sp as previous sc, 7 sc in next ch-6 sp, fasten off.

Left Front

Referring to Left Front diagram for number and placement, work Motifs in same manner as Right Front.

Sleeve

Make 2.

Referring to Sleeve diagram for number and placement, work Motifs A–D of Back and Half Motifs A and B of Right and Left Fronts.

Motif F

Rows 1–5: Rep rows 1–5 of Motif A of Back. (6 dc, 5 ch-1 sps)

Rnd 6: Rep Rnd 6 of Motif A of Back.

Row 7: Now working in rows, ch 1, sc in same sc as beg ch-1, sl st in each of next 3 sc, [ch 6, sk next 2 sc, sl st in each of next 4 sc, ch 1, sc in next sc (sc corner), ch 1, sl st in each of next 4 sc] twice, ch 6, sk next 2 sc, sl st in each of next 4 sc, ch 1, sc in next sc (sc cor-

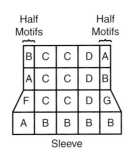

Jazzy Diamonds Assembly Diagram

CONTINUED ON PAGE 75

Wear Anywhere Skirt

DESIGN BY KATHERINE ENG

INTERMEDIATE

Finished Sizes

Instructions given fit women's sizes 4–6 small; changes for sizes 8–10 medium and sizes 12–14 large are in [ ].

Finished Garment Measurements

Hip unstretched: 30½ inches (small) [37½ inches (medium), 44½ inches (large)]

Materials

- TLC Amore medium (worsted) weight yarn (6 oz/278 yds/170g per skein): 2 skeins #3628 dark thyme
- Red Heart Plush medium (worsted) weight yarn (6 oz/278 yds/170g per skein): 1 skein #9324 chocolate
- Size I/9/5.5mm crochet hook or size needed to obtain gauge
- Tapestry needle
- Stitch markers
- ⅞-inch brown La Bouton buttons: 5

MEDIUM 4

Gauge

[Sc, shell] twice = 3½ inches; 5 shell rows = 5 inches

Pattern Notes

Weave in loose ends as work progresses.
Join rounds with a slip stitch unless otherwise stated.

Special Stitch

Shell: 5 dc in st indicated.

SKIRT

Row 1 (RS): Starting below waistline with dark thyme, ch 114 [136, 158], 2 dc in 4th ch from hook (first 3 chs count as first dc), sk next 2 chs, sc in next ch, sk next 2 chs, **shell** (see Special Stitch) in next ch, sk next 2 chs, sc in next ch, *ch 3, sk next 3 chs, sc in next ch**, [sk next 2 chs, shell in next ch, sk next 2 chs, sc in next ch] 3 times, rep from * across, ending last rep at **, sk next 2 chs, shell in next ch, sk next 2 chs, sc in next ch, 3 dc in last ch, turn.

Row 2: Ch 1, sc in same dc as beg ch-1, ch 2, dc in next sc, ch 2, sc in center dc of next shell, ch 2, dc in next sc, *ch 1, sc in next ch-3 sp, ch 1, dc in next sc **, [ch 2, sc in center dc of next shell, ch 2, dc in next sc] rep from * across, ending last rep at **, ch 2, sc in center dc of next shell, ch 2, dc in next sc, ch 2, sc in last dc, turn.

Row 3: Ch 3 (counts as first dc), 2 dc in same sc as beg ch-3, sc in next dc, shell in next sc, sc in next dc, *ch 3, sc in next dc **, [shell in next sc, sc in next dc] 3 times, rep from * across, ending last rep at **, shell in next sc, sc in next dc, 3 dc in last sc, turn.

Rows 4–15: [Rep rows 2 and 3] 6 times.

Row 16: Rep row 2.

Row 17: Ch 3, 2 dc in first sc, sc in next dc, shell in next sc, sc in next dc, *ch 5, sc in next dc **, [shell in next sc, sc in next dc] 3 times, rep from * across, ending last rep at **, shell in next sc, sc in next dc, 3 dc in last sc, turn.

Row 18: Ch 1, sc in first dc, ch 2, dc in next sc, ch 2, sc in center dc of next shell, ch 2, dc in next sc, *ch 2, sc in next ch-5 sp, ch 2, 1 dc in next sc **, [ch 2, sc in center dc of next shell, ch 2, dc in next sc] 3 times, rep from * across, ending last rep at **, ch 2, sc in center dc of next shell, ch 2, dc in next sc, ch 2, sc in last dc, turn.

Rows 19–32: [Rep rows 17 and 18] alternately 7 times.

Row 33: Ch 3, 2 dc in first sc, sc in next dc, [shell in each sc, sc in each dc] across, ending with 3 dc in last sc, turn.

Border

Note: *Work Border in top of and around post of dc at end of rows and in sc at end of rows.*

Rnd 1 (RS): Working up right front opening to top, with dark thyme, ch 1, (sc, ch 2, sc) in top of last dc, sc in post of same dc, sc in end of each sc row, sc in top of and in post at end of each dc row to top, ending with (sc, ch 2, sc) in top corner ch; working across opposite side of foundation ch, 2 sc in each ch-2 sp, sc in each ch *(under sc of row 1)*, sc in each ch *(under shell of row 1)* and 3 sc in each ch-3 sp across, ending with (sc, ch 2, sc) in last corner ch, rep sts worked up right-front opening in reverse down left-front opening; working in post of dc and then in top of dc and ending with (sc, ch 2, sc) in bottom corner dc; working across bottom, sc in each rem st across; working (sc, ch 2, sc) in center dc of each shell, join in beg sc, fasten off.

Rnd 2 (RS): Draw up a lp of chocolate in top left-hand corner ch-2 sp of previous rnd, ch 1, (sc, ch 2, sc) in same ch-2 sp, sc in each sc to bottom, working (sc, ch 2, sc) in corner ch-2 sp, working across

bottom, sc in each of next 3 sc, *sk next sc **, sc in each of next 3 sc, (sc, ch 2, sc) in next ch-2 sp, sc in each of next 3 sc *, rep between * across, ending last rep at **, sc in each of next 3 sc, (sc, ch 2, sc) in next corner ch-2 sp, working up right-front opening, sc in each of next 9 sc, ch 2, sk next 2 sc *(buttonhole)*, work [sc in each of next 8 sc, ch 2, sk next 2 sc *(buttonhole)*] up right-front opening, (sc, ch 2, sc) in next corner ch-2 sp, sc in each sc across waistline, join in beg sc, fasten off.

Rnd 3 (RS): Draw up a lp of dark thyme in top right-front corner ch-2 sp, ch 1, (sc, ch 3, sc) in same ch-2 sp as beg ch-1, working across top, ch 3, sk next 2 sc, [sc in next sc, ch 3, sk next 2 sc] across, (sc, ch 2, sc) in corner ch-2 sp, ch 3, sk next 2 sc, [sc in next sc, ch 3, sk next 2 sc] down left front, working across bottom edge, ch 3, sk next 3 sc, **sc dec** *(see Stitch Guide)*, *ch 3, sk next 3 sc, (sc, ch 3, sc) in next ch-2 sp, ch 3, sk next 3 sc, sc dec in next 2 sc, rep from * across bottom edge, ending with ch-3, sk next 3 sc, (sc, ch 3, sc) in next corner ch-2 sp, working up right-front opening, ch 2, sk 1 sc, sc in next sc, [{ch 3, sk next 2 sc, sc in next sc} twice, ch 3, sk next 2 sc, 2 sc in next ch-2 sp] across, ending with ch-2, sk last sc, join in beg sc, fasten off.

Finishing

Sew buttons to left-front opening opposite buttonholes.

Tie

Leaving 6-inch length at beg, with 2 strands of dark thyme held tog, ch 200 [220, 240] leaving 6-inch length, fasten off.

Weave Tie through ch-3 sps of rnd 3 of Border. Attach 4 lengths of dark thyme to each end of Tie. Fold lengths in half and tie in an overhand knot tying in tails. Trim tails to 3 inches. Tie ends in a bow. ●

Blue Hawaii Jacket continued from page 39

next 2 dc, 16 sc in next ch-16 sp, sc in next ch-4 sp, 16 sc in next ch-16 sp, sc in each of next 2 dc, 3 sc in next ch-2 sp, sc in each of next 2 dc, 16 sc in next ch-16 sp, sc in next ch-4 sp, ch 4, sc in next ch-4 sp, 21 sc in next ch-21 sp, sl st in next sc, **do not turn.**

Rnd 15: Sk next st, 5 hdc in next st, sk next st, [sl st in next st, sk next st, 5 hdc in next st, sk next st] around, fasten off.

Left Sleeve Trim

Row 1: Sl st in each of next 35 dc, ch 3, sl st in 3rd st to the right of the ch-3 just made, *ch 2, dc in last sl st, rep from * 5 times, sl st in 3rd st on last rnd of Sleeve, ch 3, sl st in 3rd st of last rnd of Sleeve, turn.

Rows 2–8: Rep rows 2–8 of Right Sleeve Trim.

Rnds 9–15: Rep rnds 9–15 of Right Sleeve Trim.

Scalloped Trim

Rnd 1: Join yarn at center back neckline, ch 3, dc in each dc to shoulder seam, *ch 1, sk next st, dc in next st*, rep between * 8 [9, 10, 11, 12] times to corner, ch 3, dc in same st as last dc (neckline corner completed), rep between * 46 [46, 48, 48, 48] times to bottom corner, ch 3, dc in same st as last dc (bottom corner completed), rep between * 79 [85, 91, 97, 103] times across bottom of Jacket to corner, ch 3, dc in same st as last dc (bottom corner completed), rep between * 46 [46, 48, 48, 48] times to corner, ch 3, dc in same st as last dc (neckline corner completed), rep between * 8 [9, 10, 11, 12] times to shoulder seam, dc in each rem dc across back neckline, join in 3rd ch of beg ch-3, fasten off.

Rnd 2: Join yarn to Left Front in 3rd dc from shoulder seam, sk next dc, *tr in next dc, [ch 1, tr in next dc] 4 times in same dc as previous tr, sk next dc, sl st in next dc, sk next dc, rep from * around, ending with sl st in 3rd dc from opposite shoulder, fasten off.

Finishing

Attach a button to each front in center of 5th Scallop down from neckline. Sew large hook and eye to underside of each side of same scallop to which buttons are attached. ●

Denim Vest continued from page 49

Row 3: Ch 2 (does not count as hdc), working in back lps only, hdc in first hdc, hdc in each hdc across to last 4 hdc, [hdc dec in next 2 hdc] twice, turn. (37 [37, 38, 38, 39, 39] hdc)

Row 4: Ch 2, working in front lps only, hdc in each hdc across, turn.

Row 5: Ch 2, working in back lps only, hdc in each hdc across, turn.

Rows 6 & 7 [6–9, 6–9, 6–11, 6–11, 6–13]: [Rep rows 4 and 5] alternately 1 [2, 2, 3, 3, 4] times.

Row 8 [10, 10, 12, 12, 14]: Ch 2, working in front lps only, 2 hdc in each of next 2 hdc, hdc in each rem hdc across, turn. (39 [39, 40, 40, 41, 41] hdc)

Row 9 [11, 11, 13, 13, 15]: Ch 2, working in back lps only, hdc in first hdc, hdc in each rem hdc across to last 2 hdc, 2 hdc in each of next 2 hdc, fasten off. (41 [41, 42, 42, 43, 43] hdc)

Inserting Side Panels

Starting at bottom of Vest, whipstitch right Side Panel to Right Front piece and then sew to Back. Whipstitch left Side Panel to Left Front and then sew to Back.

Bottom Border

Row 1 (RS): Join yarn in bottom edge, ch 2 (counts as first hdc), working in both lps across bottom edge, hdc across, working 13 [14, 16, 17, 19, 20] hdc across each Basic Panel and 15 [16, 16, 18, 18, 20] hdc across each Side Panel, turn. (121 [130, 144, 155, 169, 180] hdc)

Row 2: Ch 2, working in front lps only, hdc in first hdc, hdc in each rem hdc across, turn.

Row 3: Ch 2, working in back lps only, hdc in first st,

hdc in each rem hdc across, turn.

Row 4: Rep row 2.

For Sizes Small, Medium & Large Only

At the end of row 4, fasten off.

For Sizes X-large, 2X-large & 3X-large Only

Rows 5 & 6: Rep rows 3 and 4. At the end of Row 6, fasten off.

Armhole Edgings

Rnd 1 (RS): Join yarn at underarm with sl st, ch 1, sc evenly spaced around armhole opening, join in beg sc, fasten off.

Front Opening & Neckline Edging

Row 1 (RS): Join yarn at bottom Right Front edge, ch 1, sc evenly spaced up Right Front edge, working 3 sc in top corner, sc in each sc across Neckline edge, ending with 3 sc in top corner of opposite edge, sc evenly spaced down Left Front edge, fasten off.

Collar

Row 1 (RS): Join yarn in both lps of center sc of 3-sc corner group, sl st in each of next 2 sc *(3 sl sts)*, sc in each of next 3 sc, hdc in next sc, hdc in each sc across to last 6 sc, sc in each of next 3 sc, sl st in each of next 3 sc, ending with last sl st in center sc of 3-sc corner group, fasten off, turn.

Row 2 (RS): Sk sl sts, join yarn with sl st in first sc, ch

1, working in back lps only, sc in next st, hdc in each st across to last 3 sts, sc in each of next 2 sts, sl st through both lps of next sc, turn.

Row 3: Ch 1, working in front lps only, sc in first sl st, hdc in each st across, ending with sc in sl st, turn.

Row 4: Ch 1, working in back lps only, sc in first sc, hdc in each st across to last sc, sc through both lps of next sc, turn.

Row 5: Ch 1, working in front lps only, sc in sc, hdc in each hdc across, ending with sc through both lps of sc, fasten off.

Front Decorative Flap

Make 2.

Row 1: Ch 13 [15, 15, 17, 17, 17], dc in 4th ch from hook, dc in each rem ch across, turn. *(11 [13, 13, 15, 15, 15] dc)*

Row 2: Ch 2, working in front lps only, dc in 2nd dc *(beg dc dec)*, dc in each dc across to last 2 dc, **dc dec** *(see Stitch Guide)* in last 2 dc, turn. *(9 [11, 11, 13, 13, 13] dc)*

Row 3: Working in back lps only, sl st in 2nd dc, sc in next dc, hdc in each of next 1 [2, 2, 2, 2, 2] dc, dc in each of next 2 [2, 2, 4, 4, 4] dc, hdc in each of next 1 [2, 2, 2, 2, 2] dc, sc in next dc, sl st in next dc, fasten off.

With row 3 pointing downward, sew opposite side of foundation ch of Flap centered on Right Front at junction of Right Lower and Right Upper Front. Sew a button centered between rows 2 and 3 of Flap. Tack lower edge of Flap to Front. Attach rem Flap in same manner on Left Front. ●

Square Deal Shrug continued from page 53

continued from page 53

next ch-1 sp] 16 times, fasten off.

Hold rem Sleeve with RS facing and row 15 to left, attach E with sl st in sp formed by ch-4 of row 15, ch 3, 2 dc in same sp, [ch 1, 3 dc in next ch-1 sp] 16 times, fasten off.

Sew shoulder seams.

Left Side & Underarm Sections

Row 1: Hold piece with RS of Left Front facing and

shoulder seam to left, attach E with sl st in sp formed by turning ch of last row to right, ch 4, [3 dc in next sp, ch 1] 22 times, 3 dc in next corner ch-3 sp, turn.

Row 2: Ch 4, [3 dc in next ch-1 sp, ch 1] 22 times, 3 dc in sp formed by beg ch-4, turn.

Row 3: Ch 4, [3 dc in next ch-1 sp, ch 1] 3 times, dc in next ch-1 sp, turn.

Row 4: Ch 3, [3 dc in next ch-1 sp, ch 1] 3 times, 3 dc in next ch-1 sp, turn.

Row 5: Ch 4, [3 dc in next ch-1 sp, ch 1] 3 times, sk next 3 dc, dc in 3rd ch of ch-3, fasten off.

Underarm Section

Row 1: Hold piece with RS of Back facing and shoulder seam to right, sk first three 3 dc groups from left edge, attach E with sl st in first ch-1 sp of last row to left, ch 3, 2 dc in same sp, ch 1, [3 dc in next sp, ch 1] twice, 3 dc in sp formed by turning ch-4, turn.
Row 2: Ch 4, [3 dc in next ch-1 sp, ch 1] 3 times, sk next 2 dc, dc in 3rd ch of beg ch-3, turn.
Row 3: Ch 3, 2 dc in next ch-1 sp, ch 1, [3 dc in next ch-1 sp, ch 1] twice, 3 dc in sp formed by turning ch-4, fasten off.

Right Side & Underarm Sections

Row 1: Hold piece with RS of Back facing and shoulder seam to left, attach E with sl st in first ch-1 sp of last row to right, ch 3, 2 dc in same sp, ch 1, [3 dc in next sp , ch 1] 22 times, dc in last dc of last row of Right Front, turn.
Row 2: Ch 3, 2 dc in next ch-1 sp, ch 1, [3 dc in next ch-1 sp, ch 1] 23 times, ch 1, dc in 3rd ch of beg ch-3, turn.
Row 3: Sl st in next ch-1 sp, ch 3, 2 dc in same sp, ch 1, [3 dc in next ch-1 sp, ch 1] twice, 3 dc in next ch-1 sp, turn.
Row 4: Ch 4, [3 dc in next ch-1 sp, ch 1] 3 times, dc in 3rd ch of beg ch-3, turn.
Row 5: Ch 3, 2 dc in next ch-1 sp, ch 1, [3 dc in next ch-1 sp, ch 1] twice, 3 dc in sp formed by ch-4, fasten off.

Underarm Section

Row 1: Hold piece with RS of Right Front facing and shoulder seam to right, sk first three 3-dc groups from left edge, attach E with sl st in next ch-1 sp to left, ch 3, 2 dc in same sp, ch 1, [3 dc in next ch-1 sp, ch 1] twice, 3 dc in sp formed by ch-4, turn.
Row 2: Ch 4, [3 dc in next ch-1 sp, ch 1] 3 times, sk next 2 dc, dc in 3rd ch of beg ch-3, turn.
Row 3: Ch 3, 2 dc in next ch-1 sp, ch 1, [3 dc in next ch-1 sp, ch 1] twice, 3 dc in sp formed by ch-4, fasten off.

Assembly

With tapestry needle and E, sew side seams. Matching center of Sleeves to shoulder seams, sew Sleeves in place, forming square armholes.

Body Border

Rnd 1: Hold piece with RS facing and lower edge at top, attach E with sl st in first sp to left of Right Underarm seam, ch 3, 2 dc in same sp, ch 1, *3 dc in next sp, ch 1, rep from * to next corner sp, (3 dc, ch 1, 3 dc) in corner sp *(corner)*, ch 1, working up Right Front edge, (3 dc, ch 1) in each sp to next corner, (3 dc, ch 1, 3 dc) in corner sp *(corner)*, ch 1, working around neck edge to next corner, work (3 dc, ch 1) across to next corner, (3 dc, ch 1, 3 dc) in corner sp *(corner)*, ch 1, working down Left Front edge work (3 dc, ch 1) in each sp to next corner, (3 dc, ch 1, 3 dc) in corner sp *(corner)*, ch 1, working across lower edge, (3 dc, ch 1) in each sp to beg ch-3, join in 3rd ch of beg ch-3.
Rnd 2: Sl st in each of next 2 dc, sl st in next ch-1 sp, ch 3, 2 dc in same sp, ch 1, (3 dc, ch 1) in each ch-1 sp and (3 dc, ch 1) twice in each corner sp, join with sl st in 3rd ch of beg ch-3, draw up a lp of C, fasten off E.
Rnd 3: With C, working in **front lps** *(see Stitch Guide)* only, sl st in each dc and in each ch, ending with sl st in same st as first sl st, fasten off.

Sleeve Border

Make 2.
Rnd 1: Hold 1 Sleeve with RS facing, attach E with sl st in first sp to right of underarm seam, ch 3, 2 dc in same sp, ch 1, (3 dc, ch 1) in each rem sp, join in 3rd ch of beg ch-3, draw up a lp of C, fasten off E.
Rnd 2: With C, working in front lps only, sl st in each dc and in each ch, join in beg sl st, fasten off.

Finishing

With sewing needle and matching thread and referring to photo for placement, sew buttons to Left Front. ●

Kimono Jacket continued from page 57

continued from page 57

For Sizes X-large, 2X-large & 3X-large Only
Rnds 4–24: Rep rnds 4–24 of large. *([89, 94, 94] sts)*

For Size X-large Only
Rnds 25 & 26: Rep rnds 1 and 2, fasten off.

For Sizes 2X-large Only
Rnds 25–27: Rep rows 1–3
Rows 28 & 29: Rep rnds 1 and 2, fasten off.

For Size 3X-large Only
Rnds 26–31: [Rep rnds 1–3] consecutively twice.
Rnd 32: Rep rnd 1, fasten off.
Matching sts, place Sleeve inside armhole opening, working through both thicknesses, with size C hook, sc Sleeve to armhole.

Jacket Edging
Rnd 1 (RS): With size G hook, attach yarn at left shoulder, ch 1, sc evenly spaced around entire outer edge of Jacket, working 3 sc in each outer bottom corner, **do not join**, place st marker.
Rnds 2–4: Sc in each sc around, working sc as necessary in outer edge corners to keep work flat. At the end of rnd 4, sl st in next st, fasten off.

Sleeve Edging
Rnd 1: With size G hook, attach yarn in opposite side of foundation ch with sl st, ch 1, sc in each ch around, **do not join**, place st marker.
Rnds 2–4: Sc in each sc around. At the end of rnd 4, sl st in next st, fasten off.

Sash
Row 1: With G hook, attach yarn in bottom front corner of Jacket Edging, ch 1, sc in same st as beg ch-1, sc in each of next 4 sc, turn. *(5 sc)*
Rows 2–26: Ch 3, dc in each of next 4 sts, turn. *(5 dc)*
At the end of row 26, fasten off.
Rep on opposite bottom front corner. ●

Easy Summer Vest or Top continued from page 59

continued from page 59

on both pieces for back neck opening. Beg at lower edge, sew pieces tog to st markers in same manner as for front neck opening.
For armholes, measure and place st markers 8 [8½, 8½, 8½, 9, 9, 9½, 10] inches down from shoulder line on front and back outer edge of each piece. Working through back lps only, sew side seams from lower edge to st markers.

Neck Edging
Rnd 1 (RS): With size G hook, attach yarn with sc in 1 shoulder st marker, ch 1, working in sts down neck edge, work 25 sc evenly spaced from shoulder to 1 st before bottom of V-neck, **sc dec** *(see Stitch Guide)* in next st and in next st on opposite neck edge, work 25 sc evenly spaced up to next shoulder st marker, working on back neck edge, work 18 sc evenly spaced down to 1 st before bottom of V-neck, sc dec in next st and in next st on opposite neck edge, work 18 sc evenly spaced up to first sc, join in beg sc, fasten off. *(88 sc)*

Armhole Edging
Make 2.
Rnd 1 (RS): With size F hook, attach yarn in bottom of armhole opening, ch 1, working in ends of rows around armhole opening, work 25 [27, 27, 27, 29, 29, 31, 33] sc evenly spaced up to shoulder and work 25 [27, 27, 27, 29, 29, 31, 33] sc evenly spaced from shoulder down to underarm on opposite edge, join in beg sc. *(50 [54, 54, 54, 58, 62, 66] sc)*
Rnd 2: Ch 1, sc in same sc as beg ch-1, sc in each rem sc around, join in beg sc.
Rnd 3: Rep rnd 2, fasten off.

Lower Edging

Rnd 1 (RS): With size F hook, attach yarn in right-hand side seam, working in end sts of dc rows, ch 1, work 30 [32, 34, 36, 38, 40, 42, 44] sc evenly spaced to center front and another 30 [32, 34, 36, 38, 40, 42, 44] sc evenly spaced to left-hand side seam, work 30 [32, 34, 36, 38, 40, 42, 44] sc evenly spaced to center back and 30 [32, 34, 36, 38, 40, 42, 44] sc evenly spaced to right-hand side seam, join in beg sc. *(120 [128, 136, 144, 152, 160, 168, 176] sc)*

Rnd 2: Ch 1, sc in same sc as beg ch-1, sc in next sc, sc dec in next 2 sc, [sc in each of next 2 sc, sc dec in next 2 sc] around, join in beg sc. *(90 [96, 102, 108, 114, 120, 126, 132] sc)*

Rnd 3: Ch 1, sc in same sc as beg ch-1, sc in each rem sc around, join in beg sc.

Rnds 4 & 5: Rep rnd 3. At the end of rnd 5, fasten off. ●

Jazzy Diamonds continued from page 67

ner), turn.

Row 8: Ch 6, [sc in 2nd ch of next ch-6 sp, ch 6, sk next 2 chs, sc in next ch, ch 6, sc in next corner sc, ch 6] twice, sc in 2nd ch of next ch-6, sk next 2 chs, sc in next ch, ch 6, sc in next corner sc, turn.

Row 9 (joining): Ch 1, 7 sc in next ch-6 sp, 3 sc in next ch-6 sp, ch 1, holding WS of Motif A facing WS of working Motif and matching sts, sl st in 2nd ch of corresponding corner ch-3 sp on Motif A, *ch 1, work 3 sc in same sp as previous 3 sc on working Motif *(joined corner)*, [4 sc in next ch-6 sp, sc around post of 4th sc of corresponding ch-6 sp on Motif A, 3 sc in same sp as previous 4 sc on working Motif] twice, 3 sc in next ch-6 sp, ch 1, sl st in center of joining sc of corresponding ch-3 sps on completed Motifs, rep from * once, 4 sc in next ch-6 sp, sc around post of 4th sc of corresponding ch-6 sp on next Motif, 3 sc in same ch sp as previous 4 sc, fasten off.

Motif G

Rows 1–5: Rep rows 1–5 of Motif A of Back. *(6 dc, 5 ch-1 sps)*

Rnd 6: Rep rnd 6 of Motif A of Back.

Rows 7 & 8: Rep rows 7 and 8 of Motif F.

Row 9 (joining): Ch 1, 4 sc in next ch-6 sp, holding WS of Half Motif B facing WS of working Motif and matching sts, sc around post of 4th sc of corresponding ch-6 sp on Half Motif B, on working Motif, 3 sc in same sp as previous 4 sc, 3 sc in next ch-6 sp, ch 1, 2 sc in 2nd ch of corresponding ch-3 sp on Motif D, ch 1, on working Motif, 3 sc in same sp as previous sc *(joined corner)*, [4 sc in next ch-6 sp, sc around post of 4th sc of corresponding ch-6 sp on Motif D, on working Motif, 3 sc in same sp as previous 4 sc] twice, 3 sc in next ch-6 sp, ch 1, sl st in center of joining sc of corresponding ch-3 sps on completed Motifs, ch 1, on working Motif, 3 sc in same sp as previous sc, [4 sc in next sp, sc around post of 4th sc of corresponding ch-6 sp on Motif B, on working Motif, 3 sc in same sp as 4 sc] twice, 3 sc in next ch-6 sp, ch 1, sc in 2nd ch of corresponding ch-3 sp on Motif B, ch 1, on working Motif, 3 sc in same sp as previous sc, 7 sc in next ch-6 sp, fasten off.

Assembly

Block pieces if necessary. Sew shoulder seams, matching Motif joining and using 2 or 3 sts at each joining. Matching center of Sleeve to shoulder seam, sew in Sleeve. Sew side and Sleeve seams. ●

Great Gifts
in a Dash

Our wonderful collection of great
gift ideas for friends and family
will help you be ready for any
special occasion.

Blushing Rose Sachet

DESIGN BY DIANE STONE

EASY

Finished Size
4¼ inches across

Gauge
Rnds 1 and 2 = 1 inch across

Pattern Notes
Weave in loose ends as work progresses.
Join rounds with a slip stitch unless otherwise stated.

Special Stitches
Beginning 4-double crochet popcorn (beg 4-dc pc): Ch 3, 3 dc in same st or ch sp, drop lp from hook, insert hook in 3rd ch of beg ch-3, pick up dropped lp and draw through st on hook.

Materials
- Size 10 crochet cotton:
    100 yds white
    25 yds pink
    10 yds green
- Size 6/1.80mm steel crochet hook or size needed to obtain gauge
- Sewing needle
- Sewing thread
- 4-inch square white tulle: 2
- 30 inches ¼-inch-wide ribbon
- 5 cotton balls
- Scented oil
- Washable fabric glue

4-double crochet popcorn (4-dc pc): 4 dc in next st or ch sp, drop lp from hook, insert hook in top of first st of dc group, pick up dropped lp and draw through st on hook.

Beginning 3-double crochet popcorn (beg 3-dc pc): Ch 3, 2 dc in same st or ch sp, drop lp from hook, insert hook in 3rd ch of beg ch-3, pick up dropped lp and draw through st on hook.

3-double crochet popcorn (3-dc pc): 3 dc in next st or ch sp, drop lp from hook, insert hook in top of first st of dc group, pick up dropped lp and draw through st on hook.

SACHET

Front
Rnd 1: With white, form a ring with end of cotton, ch 1, 12 sc in ring, pull end of thread tightly to close ring, join in beg sc. *(12 sc)*

Rnd 2: Ch 3 *(counts as first dc)*, 2 dc in next st, [dc in next st, 2 dc in next st] around, join in 3rd ch of beg ch-3. *(18 dc)*

Rnd 3: Ch 1, sc in first st, [ch 2, sc in next st] around, hdc in beg sc to form last ch sp. *(18 ch-2 sps)*

Rnd 4: Sl st in ch sp formed by hdc, **beg 4-dc pc** *(see Special Stitches)* in next ch-2 sp, ch 3, [**4-dc pc** *(see Special Stitches)* in next ch-2 sp, ch 3] around, join in top of beg pc. *(18 pc)*

Rnd 5: Sl st in ch-3 sp, (beg 4-dc pc, ch 2, 4-dc pc) in

same ch sp, [ch 2, (4-dc pc, ch 2, 4-dc pc) in next ch-3 sp] around, ending with hdc in beg 4-dc pc to form last ch sp.

Rnd 6: Sl st in ch sp just formed, ch 1, sc in same ch sp as beg ch-1, ch 3, [sc in next ch-2 sp, ch 3] around, join in beg sc, fasten off.

Back

Rnds 1–6: Rep rnds 1–6 of Front.

Scented Pouch

Use Front of Sachet to measure tulle, cut 2 pieces of tulle slightly larger than Front of Sachet. Place 2 drops of scented oil on each cotton ball. Sew the 2 pieces of tulle tog, placing cotton balls inside before closing.

Sachet Pouch

Rnd 1: Holding Front and Back WS tog with Scented Pouch between, working through both thicknesses, attach white with sl st in any ch-3 sp, ch 1, sc in same ch sp as beg ch-1, ch 3, [sc in next ch sp, ch 3] around, join in beg sc.

Rnd 2: Sl st in next ch-3 sp, (**beg 3-dc pc**—see Special Stitches, ch 3, sl st in 3rd ch from hook, **3-dc pc**—see Special Stitches) in same ch sp, (3-dc pc, ch 3, sl st in 3rd ch from hook, 3-dc pc) in each ch sp around, join in top of beg 3-dc pc, fasten off.

Rose

Rnd 1: With pink, form a ring with end of cotton, ch 3, 9 dc in ring, pull end of thread tightly to close ring, join in 3rd ch of beg ch-3. *(10 dc)*

Rnd 2: Ch 1, sc in same st as beg ch-1, ch 3, sk next st, [sc in next st, ch 3, sk next st] around, join in beg sc. *(5 ch-3 sps)*

Rnd 3: Sl st in first ch-3 sp, ch 1, (sc, 6 dc, sc) in same ch sp and in each rem ch-3 sp around, join in beg sc. *(5 petals)*

Rnd 4: Ch 1, working in same ch-3 sps as previous rnd, sc between 3rd and 4th dc of first petal, ch 5, [sc between 3rd and 4th dc on next petal, ch 5] around, join in beg sc. *(5 ch-5 sps)*

Rnd 5: Sl st into first ch-5 sp, (ch 3, 7 dc, ch 3, sl st) in same ch-5 sp, (sl st, ch 3, 7 dc, ch 3, sl st) in each rem ch-5 sp around, join in beg sl st, fasten off. *(5 petals)*

Leaf

Make 5.

With green, ch 6, sl st in 2nd ch from hook, sc in next ch, dc in each of last 3 chs, fasten off.

Finishing

Weave ribbon through ch sps of rnd 1 of Sachet Pouch, trim and glue ends.

Cut an 8-inch length of ribbon and fold in half to form a hanging lp, glue hanging lp to ends of ribbon weave on rnd 1. Fold rem length of ribbon into a bow and glue to base of hanging lp.

Glue Rose and Leaves to center of Sachet. ●

Linen Straps

DESIGNS BY BELINDA "BENDY" CARTER

EASY

Finished Size

3¼ x 12½ inches

Materials
- DMC Cebelia crochet cotton size 20 (405 yds/50g per ball):
  - 1 ball blanc
- Size 11/1.10mm steel crochet hook or size needed to obtain gauge
- Tapestry needle
- 63 inches 1½-inch-wide ribbon for each Strap

Gauge

9 mesh = 2 inches; 10 rows = 2 inches

Pattern Notes

Weave in loose ends as work progresses.

Join rounds with a slip stitch unless otherwise stated.

Graph-reading knowledge is necessary.

Special Stitches

Beginning mesh (beg mesh): Ch 5 *(first 3 chs count as first dc)*, sk next 2 sts or chs, dc in next st.

Mesh: Ch 2, sk next 2 sts or chs, dc in next st.

Block: Dc in each of next 3 sts or 2 dc in next ch sp,

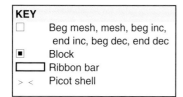

KEY
- ☐ Beg mesh, mesh, beg inc, end inc, beg dec, end dec
- ■ Block
- ▭ Ribbon bar
- > < Picot shell

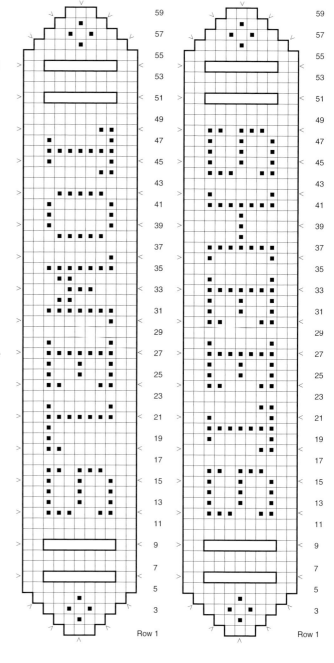

dc in next st.

Ribbon bar: Ch 20, sk next 20 sts and chs, dc in next st.

Beginning increase (beg inc): Ch 7, dc in same st.

End increase (end inc): Ch 2, dtr in same st.

Beginning decrease (beg dec): Sl st in each of first 4 sts.

End decrease (end dec): Leave last 3 sts unworked.

Picot shell: (3 dc, ch 5, sl st in top of last dc made, 3 dc) in indicated sp.

Strap

Row 1: Ch 14, dc in 8th ch from hook *(first mesh)*, [ch 2, sk next 2 chs, dc in next ch] twice, turn. *(3 mesh)*

Rows 2–59: Work according to graph using Special Stitches as needed, at end of last row, turn.

Border

Rnd 1: Working across short edge, ch 1, sc in top of last dc, *[**picot shell** (see Special Stitches) in next corner, sc in next corner] twice, working across 1 long edge, [picot shell in next row, sk next row, sc in top of next st on next row, sk next row] 16 times, picot shell in next row, sc in next corner, [picot shell in next corner, sc in next corner] twice, picot shell in next mesh**, sc in next corner, rep from * around, ending last rep at **, join in beg sc, fasten off.

Weave ribbon WS to RS to WS through each ribbon bar. ●

Spa Set

DESIGNS BY ELAINE BARTLETT

EASY

Finished Sizes

Washcloth: 8½ x 8¼ inches

Scrubbie Washcloth: 7½
 inches square

Back Scrubbie: 3 x 18½,
 excluding Handles

Soap Sachet: 3½ x 6 inches

Materials

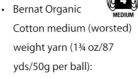

- Bernat Organic
 Cotton medium (worsted)
 weight yarn (1¾ oz/87
 yds/50g per ball):
  3 balls #43244 cactus
- Size H/8/5mm crochet
 hook or size needed to
 obtain gauge
- Tapestry needle
- Large-eyed tapestry needle
- Stitch marker
- Mesh sponge in
 desired color

Gauge

14 sc = 4 inches; 20 sc rows = 4 inches

Pattern Notes

Weave in loose ends as work progresses.

Join rounds with a slip stitch unless otherwise stated.

WASHCLOTH

Row 1 (WS): Ch 29, sc in 2nd ch from hook, sc in each rem ch across, turn. *(28 sc)*

Rows 2–38: Ch 1, sc in each sc across, turn.

Row 39: Ch 1, sc in each sc across, **do not turn**.

Rnd 40: Now working in rnds, ch 1, work 24 sc across side edge of Washcloth, ending with (sc, ch 2, sc) in corner st, sc in each ch across opposite side of foundation ch, work (sc, ch 2, sc) in corner st, work 24 sc across side edge of Washcloth, (sc, ch 2, sc) in corner st, sc in each sc across row 39, (sc, ch 2, sc) in corner st, join in first sc.

Rnd 41: Ch 1, sc in each sc around, working 3 sc in each corner ch-2 sp, join in beg sc, fasten off.

SCRUBBIE WASHCLOTH

Rnd 1 (RS): Starting at center, ch 4, join in first ch to form a ring, ch 2 *(counts as first dc)*, 2 dc in ring, ch 2, [3 dc in ring, ch 2] 3 times, join in 3rd ch of ch-3. *(12 dc, 4 ch-2 sps)*

Rnd 2: Ch 2, dc in each of next 2 dc, *(2 dc, ch 2, 2 dc) in corner ch-2 sp **, dc in each of next 3 dc, rep from * around, ending last rep at **, join in 2nd ch of ch-2. *(28 dc, 4 ch-2 sps)*

Rnd 3: Ch 2, dc in each dc around, working (2 dc, ch 2, 2 dc) in each corner ch-2 sp, join in 2nd ch of ch-2. *(44 dc, 4 ch-2 sps)*

Rnd 4: Ch 2, dc in each dc around, working (dc, ch 2, dc) in each corner ch-2 sp, join in 2nd ch of ch-2. *(52 dc, 4 ch-2 sps)*

Rnd 5: Rep rnd 3. *(68 dc, 4 ch-2 sps)*

Rnd 6: Rep rnd 4. *(76 dc, 4 ch-2 sps)*

Rnd 7: Rep rnd 3. *(92 dc, 4 ch-2 sps)*

Rnd 8: Ch 1, sc in same st as beg ch-1, sc in each dc around, working 3 sc in each corner ch-2 sp, join in beg sc, fasten off. *(104 sc)*

Assembly

Prepare mesh sponge by cutting the tie that holds the sponge tog. Cut the mesh sponge in half. Using a 24-inch length of yarn, gather half of the mesh tog and tie yarn around the middle of the mesh and knot

securely, leaving 2-inch lengths of yarn, fasten off. Thread rem 2-inch lengths onto large-eyed tapestry needle. Pass needle through center of mesh from RS to WS of Washcloth. Remove 1 length from needle, pass needle back through to RS of Washcloth slightly left of center, remove rem length from needle. Thread length on WS of Washcloth onto needle and pass needle back through to RS of Washcloth slightly left of center, knot ends to secure and weave each rem end into Washcloth.

BACK SCRUBBIE

Row 1 (WS): Ch 10, sc in 2nd ch from hook, sc in each rem ch across, turn. *(9 sc)*

Row 2: Ch 1, sc in each sc across, turn.

Rows 3–5: Rep row 2.

Row 6: Ch 1, sc in each of next 2 sc, [tr in next sc, sc in next sc] 3 times, sc in last sc, turn. *(6 sc, 3 tr)*

Row 7: Rep row 2.

Row 8: Ch 1, sc in each of next 3 sc, [tr in next sc, sc in next sc] twice, sc in each of next 2 sc, turn. *(7 sc, 2 tr)*

Row 9: Rep row 2.

Rows 10–69: [Rep rows 6–9 consecutively] 15 times.

Row 70: Rep row 6.

Rows 71–76: Rep row 2.

Rnd 77: Now working in rnds, work 2 more sc in same st as last sc of row 76 *(3 sc in corner)*, working in ends of rows, work 1 sc in each row across, ending with 3 sc in first ch of opposite side of foundation ch, sc in each of next 7 chs, 3 sc in last ch, sc in side edge of each row, ending with 2 sc in same sc as first sc of row 76, join in first sc of row 76.

Rnd 78: Sl st in each st around to middle st of last corner *(before joining)*, ch 20 *(for first Handle)*, using care not to twist ch, sl st in middle st of next corner, turn, sl st in back bump of each ch of ch-20, fasten off. Attach yarn in center st of next corner 3-sc group, ch 20 *(for 2nd Handle)*, taking care not to twist ch, sl st in back bump of each ch of ch-20, fasten off.

SOAP SACHET

Body

Make 2.

Row 1 (RS): Ch 12, sc in 2nd ch from hook, sc in each rem ch across, turn. *(11 sc)*

Rows 2–24: Ch 1, sc in each sc across, turn. At the end of row 24, fasten off.

Assembly

Rnd 1: Holding Body pieces tog matching rows and working through both thicknesses, attach yarn in side edge of row 24, ch 1, sc in same st as beg ch-1 *(RS row)*, [sk next WS row, sc in next row] across, working across opposite side of foundation ch, 3 sc in corner, sc in each ch across to last ch, 3 sc in last ch, working up side edge of rows, sc in side edge of row 1, [sk next WS row, sc in next row] across edge, **do not fasten off**.

Top Edging

Rnd 1: Ch 1, sc evenly spaced around top opening, join in beg sc.

Rnd 2: Ch 3 *(counts as first dc)*, dc in each sc around, join in 3rd ch of beg ch-3.

Rnd 3: Ch 1, sc in same st as beg ch-1, sc in each dc around, join, fasten off.

Tie

Leaving a 6-inch length at beg, ch 50 tightly, leaving a 6-inch length, fasten off.

Starting at center front of Soap Sachet, weave Tie through sps between dc sts of rnd 2 of Top Edging, knot ends tog, trim each end to approximately 1 inch. ●

Medallion Bookmarks

DESIGNS BY MICHELLE CREAN

EASY

Finished Sizes
2½ inches wide

Materials
- Size 10 crochet cotton:
  125 yds each white and yellow
- Size 7/1.65mm steel crochet hook or size needed to obtain gauge
- ⅛-inch-wide satin ribbon:
  1 yd each pink and green
- Fabric spray starch

Gauge
9 dc = 1 inch

Pattern Notes
Weave in loose ends as work progresses.
Join rounds with a slip stitch unless otherwise stated.

Special Stitch
Picot: Ch 3, sc in top of last sc.

SUMMER SUNSHINE
Rnd 1: With yellow, ch 4, 11 dc in 4th ch from hook *(3 sk chs count as first dc)*, join in top of 4th ch. *(12 dc)*
Rnd 2: Ch 3 *(counts as first dc)*, dc in same st as beg ch-3, 2 dc in each rem dc around, join in 3rd ch of ch-3. *(24 dc)*
Rnd 3: Ch 5 *(counts as first dc, ch-2)*, (dc, ch 2, dc) in same dc as beg ch-5, sk next 2 sts, [({dc, ch 2} twice,

dc) in next dc, sk next 2 dc] around, join in 3rd ch of ch-5. *(24 dc, 16 ch-2 sps)*
Rnd 4: Ch 1, sc in first ch sp, *ch 3, sc in next st, **picot** *(see Special Stitch)*, ch 3**, sc in each of next 2 ch sps, rep from * around, ending last rep at **, sc in last ch sp, join in first sc, fasten off.

CONTINUED ON PAGE 94

Teddy Bear Magnet

DESIGN BY SUE PENROD

EASY

Finished Size
5 inches tall

Gauge
8 sc = 1 inch; 8 sc rnds = 1 inch

Pattern Notes
Weave in loose ends as work progresses.
Do not join rounds unless otherwise stated.
Use stitch marker to mark rounds.

MAGNET

Head & Body
Rnd 1: Starting at top of Head, ch 4, sl st in first ch

Materials
- Size 10 crochet cotton:
  50 yds tan
- Size B/1/2.25mm crochet
  hook or size needed to
  obtain gauge
- Tapestry needle
- Embroidery needle
- 12 inches each black,
  pink and white 6-strand
  embroidery floss
- 6 round ¾-inch magnets
- 12 inches ⅛-inch-wide
  pink ribbon
- Fiberfill
- Stitch marker

to form a ring, ch 1, 8 sc in ring, do not join, place st marker (see Pattern Notes). (8 sc)

Rnd 2: 2 sc in each sc around. (16 sc)

Rnd 3: [Sc in next sc, 2 sc in next sc] around. (24 sc)

Rnd 4: Sc in each sc around.

Rnds 5–11: Rep row 4.

Rnd 12: [Sc in next sc, sk next sc, sc in next sc] around. (16 sc)

Rnd 13: [Sk next sc, sc in next sc] around. (8 sc)

Rnd 14: Rep rnd 2. (16 sc)

Rnd 15: [Sc in next sc, 2 sc in next sc] around. (24 sc)

Rnds 16–18: Rep rnd 4.

Rnd 19: [Sc in each of next 2 sc, 2 sc in next sc] around. (32 sc)

Rnds 20–24: Rep rnd 4. Stuff lightly and shape. Continue stuffing as work progresses.

Rnd 25: [Sc in each of next 2 sc, sk next sc, sc in next sc] around. (24 sc)

Rnd 26: Rep rnd 4. Place 2 magnets into back of Body, securing with fiberfill.

Rnd 27: Rep rnd 12. (16 sc)

Rnd 28: Rep rnd 13. (8 sc)

Rnd 29: [Sk next st, sl st in next st] around, join with sl st in beg sl st, fasten off.

Ear
Make 2.
Attach tan with sl st at top right-hand side of Head, (ch 3, 5 dc, ch 3, sl st) in same st, fasten off.

Rep Ear on top left-hand side of Head.

Arm
Make 2.
Rnd 1: Ch 4, sl st in beg ch to form a ring, ch 1, 8 sc in ring. *(8 sc)*
Rnd 2: 2 sc in each sc around. *(16 sc)*
Rnd 3: Sc in each sc around.
Rnds 4–8: Rep rnd 3. At the end of rnd 8, insert 1 magnet.
Rnd 9: [Sk next st, sc in next st] around. *(8 sc)*
Rnds 10–12: Rep rnd 3.
Row 13: Now working in rows, flatten rnd 12 horizontally, working through both thicknesses, ch 1, work 4 sc across, fasten off.
Sew row 13 of each Arm between rnds 15–18 on each side of Body.

Leg
Make 2.
Rnds 1–12: Rep rnds 1–12 of Arm.
Row 13: Rep row 13 of Arm.
Sew row 13 of each Leg to center bottom of Body.

Facial Features
With black floss, using French knots, embroider eyes to rnd 6 of Head ¼ inch apart.
With black floss, using satin stitch, embroider nose centered below eyes.
With white floss, using straight stitch, embroider a highlight st on left-hand side of each eye.
With black floss, using backstitch, embroider mouth.
With pink floss, using French knots, embroider cheeks on each side of nose. ●

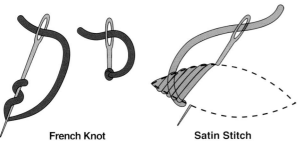 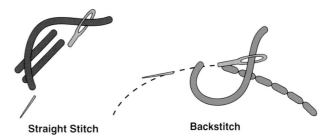

French Knot   **Satin Stitch**   **Straight Stitch**   **Backstitch**

Bride's Bag

DESIGN BY JOYCE BRAGG

EASY

Finished Size

12¼ x 13½ inches

Materials

- Cotton/rayon blend fine (sport) weight yarn (1 oz/100 yds/28.35g per ball):

  3 oz/300 yds/85.5g white
- Size G/6/4mm crochet hook or size needed to obtain gauge
- Tapestry needle
- Bead needle and thread
- 8mm pearl bead

Gauge

7 dc = 1½ inches; 3 dc, ch 1, 3 dc = 1½ inches; 5 dc rows = 2 inches

Pattern Notes

Weave in loose ends as work progresses.
Join rounds with a slip stitch unless otherwise stated.

BAG

Body

Rnd 1: Starting at bottom edge of Bag, ch 120, taking care not to twist ch, join in first ch, ch 1, sc in same ch as beg ch-1, sc in each rem ch around, join in beg sc, **do not turn**. *(120 sc)*

Rnd 2: Ch 3 *(counts as first dc)*, dc in each st around, join in 3rd ch of ch-3. *(120 dc)*

Rnd 3: Ch 3, dc in each of next 2 sts, ch 1, sk next st, [dc in each of next 3 sts, ch 1, sk next st] 29 times, join in 3rd ch of ch-3. *(30 groups of 3 dc, 30 ch-1 sps)*

Rnd 4: Ch 4 *(counts as first dc, ch-1)*, sk next dc, dc in next dc, dc in ch-1 sp, [dc in next dc, ch 1, sk next dc, dc in next dc, dc in next ch-1 sp] around, join in 3rd ch of beg ch-4.

Rnd 5: Ch 3, dc in next ch-1 sp, dc in next dc, ch 1, sk next dc, [dc in next dc, dc in next ch-1 sp, dc in next dc, ch 1, sk 1 dc] around, join in top of ch-3.

Rnds 6–29: [Rep rnds 4 and 5 alternately] 12 times.

Rnd 30: Rep rnd 4.

Top Edging

Rnd 31: Ch 4, sk next st, [dc in next st, ch 1, sk next st] around, join in 3rd ch of beg ch-4.

Rnd 32: Working in ch-1 sps only, ch 1, [sc in next ch-1 sp, (hdc, dc, hdc) in next ch-1 sp] around, join in beg sc.

Rnd 33: Ch 1, [(hdc, dc, hdc) in sc, sk next hdc, sc in next dc, sk next hdc] around, join in beg hdc, fasten off.

Bottom Closure

Row 1: Lay piece flat, working in opposite side of foundation ch through both thicknesses, attach yarn with sl st in first ch, ch 1, sc in each st across, turn. *(60 sc)*

Row 2: Ch 3, sc in next sc, [ch 3, sc in next sc] across, fasten off.

Drawstring

Make 2.

Leaving a 2-inch length, ch 100, leaving a 2-inch length, fasten off.

Starting at side edge of Bag front, weave first Drawstring through dc sts of rnd 31 across front only, tie beg and end tog.

Starting at side edge of Bag back, weave 2nd Drawstring through dc sts of rnd 31 across back only, tie beg and end tog.

Corkscrew

Make 2.

Ch 12, sk next 2 chs, 4 hdc in next ch, 4 hdc in each rem ch across, fasten off.

Attach Corkscrew to joining of each Drawstring.

Rose

Rnd 1: Ch 4, join in first ch to form a ring, ch 3, 9 dc in ring, join in 3rd ch of ch-3. *(10 dc)*

Rnd 2: Ch 1, sc in same st as beg ch-1, (hdc, 3 dc, hdc) in next dc, [sc in next dc, (hdc, 3 dc, hdc) in next dc] 4 times, join in beg sc. *(5 petals)*

Rnd 3: Ch 1, sc in same sc as beg ch-1, ch 3, [sc in next sc, ch 3] 4 times, join in beg sc. *(5 ch-3 sps)*

Rnd 4: Ch 1, sc in same sc as beg ch-1, (hdc, 5 dc, hdc) in next ch-3 sp, [sc in next sc, (hdc, 5 dc, hdc) in next ch-3 sp] around, join in beg sc.

Rnd 5: Ch 1, sc in same sc as beg ch-1, ch 5, [sc in next sc, ch 5] around, join in beg sc.

Rnd 6: Ch 1, (sc, hdc, 7 dc, hdc, sc) in each ch-5 sp around, join in beg sc, fasten off.

Sew 8mm pearl bead to the center of rnd 1. Sew Rose to front bottom left corner of Bag. ●

Wedding Favor Bags

DESIGNS BY FEROSA HAROLD

EASY

Finished Sizes
Bag No. 1: 4½ inches in
   diameter
Bag No. 2: 3½ x 4 inches

Gauge
5 dc rows = 1 inch

Pattern Notes
Weave in loose ends as work progresses.
Join rounds with a slip stitch unless otherwise stated.

Special Stitches
Shell: (2 dc, ch 2, 2 dc) in indicated st.
Large Shell: (2 dc, ch 3, 2 dc) in indicated st.

Materials
- Size 10 crochet cotton:
   350 yds white
- Kreinik Blending Filament
   (55 yds per spool):
   4 spools #001 silver
- Size 6/1.80mm steel
   crochet hook or size
   needed to obtain gauge
- 1 yd white ⅛-inch-wide
   ribbon
- Straight pins
- Plastic wrap-covered
   pinning board
- Starch

BAG NO. 1

First Motif
Rnd 1 (RS): With 1 strand each held tog, ch 8, sl st in first ch to form a ring, ch 3 *(counts as first dc)*, 17 dc in ring, join in 3rd ch of ch-3. *(18 dc)*

Rnd 2: Ch 3, dc in each of next 2 dc, [ch 3, dc in each of next 3 dc] around, ch 1, hdc in 3rd ch of beg ch-3 to position hook in center of last ch sp.

Rnd 3: Ch 1, sc in same sp as joining, [ch 5, sc in center dc of 3-dc group, ch 5, sc in next ch-3 sp] 5 times, ch 5, sc in center dc of 3-dc group, ch 2, dc in beg sc. *(12 ch-5 sps)*

Rnd 4: Ch 1, sc in same ch sp, [ch 5, sc in next ch-5 sp] 11 times, ch 2, dc in beg sc.

Rnd 5: Ch 1, sc in same ch sp, [ch 5, (sc, ch 5) twice in next ch-5 sp, sc in next ch-5 sp] around, ending with ch 2, hdc in beg sc. *(18 ch-5 sps)*

Rnd 6: Ch 1, sc in same ch sp, [ch 5, sc in next ch-5 sp] around, ending with ch 2, hdc in beg sc.

Rnd 7: Ch 1, sc in same ch sp, ch 6, [sc in next ch-5 sp, ch 6] around, join in beg sc.

Rnd 8: Ch 3, dc in same sc as beg ch-3, sc in next ch-6 sp, [**large shell** *(see Special Stitches)* in next sc, sc in next ch-6 sp] around, ending with 2 dc in same sc as beg ch-3, ch 3, join in 3rd ch of beg ch-3, fasten off. *(18 shells)*

2nd Motif

Rnds 1–7: Rep rnds 1–7 of First Motif.

Rnd 8: Ch 3, dc in same sc as beg ch-3, sc in next ch-6 sp, [large shell in next sc, sc in next ch-6 sp] around, ending with 2 dc in same sc as beg ch-3, ch 1, hdc in 3rd ch of beg ch-3, **do not fasten off**. *(18 shells)*

Edging

Row 1: Now working in rows, with WS facing, hold motifs tog, matching sts and working through both thicknesses, ch 1, [sc in ch-3 sp of first large shell, ch 6, sc in next sc between large shells, ch 6] 11 times, sc in ch-3 sp of next large shell, ch 6, sc in next sc between large shells, ch 3, dc in next ch-3 sp, turn, leaving 5 large shells unworked for opening of Bag.

Row 2: Ch 1, sc in same ch sp as beg ch-1, [ch 5, sc in next ch-6 sp] 23 times, **do not turn**.

Rnd 3: Now working in rnds, sl st in next sc, working around opening through 1 thickness only, [ch 5, sc in ch-3 sp of next large shell] 5 times, ch 5, sc in first sc of row 1 of Edging, working on opposite side of opening, [ch 5, sc in ch-3 sp of next large shell] 5

times, ch 5, sc in next sc.

Rnd 4: Sl st into ch-5 sp, ch 8 *(counts as first tr, ch-4 sp)*, sl st in 3rd ch from hook, ch 1, [tr, ch 4, sl st in top of last tr, ch 1] 3 times in same ch-5 sp as beg ch-8, [tr, ch 4, sl st in top of last tr, ch 1] 4 times in each

CONTINUED ON PAGE 94

Glass Slippers

DESIGNS BY JO ANN MAXWELL

INTERMEDIATE

Finished Sizes

Each fits 3-inch diameter x
6-inch tall glass

Gauge

8 sts = 1 inch; 11 hdc rnds = 2 inches

Pattern Notes

Weave in loose ends as work progresses.
Join rounds with a slip stitch unless otherwise stated.

Special Stitch

Picot: Ch 2, sl st in top of last st.

YELLOW SLIPPER

Rnd 1: With yellow, ch 4, sl st in first ch to form a

Materials

- Size 10 crochet cotton:
  130 yds each peach,
  pink, light green
  and yellow
  25 yds each medium
  purple, dark purple,
  white and dark green
- Size 5/1.90mm steel
  crochet hook or size
  needed to obtain gauge
- Sewing needle
- Peach sewing thread
- 3 gold round seed beads
- 10 flat assorted ½-inch
  buttons
- Craft glue
- Hot-glue gun

ring, ch 3 *(counts as first dc)*, 19 dc in ring, join in 3rd ch of ch-3. *(20 dc)*

Rnd 2: Ch 3, dc in same st as beg ch-3, dc in next dc, [2 dc in next dc, dc in next dc] around, join in 3rd ch of ch-3. *(30 dc)*

Rnd 3: Rep rnd 2. *(45 dc)*

Rnd 4: Ch 3, dc in same st as beg ch-3, [dc in next dc, 2 dc in next dc] around, join in 3rd ch of ch-3. *(68 dc)*

Rnd 5: Working this rnd in **back lps** *(see Stitch Guide)*, ch 2, hdc in each st around, join in 2nd ch of ch-2.

Rnds 6–35: Ch 2, hdc in each st around, join in 2nd ch of beg ch-2.

Rnd 36: Ch 1, sc in each st around, join in beg sc, fasten off.

Rnd 37: With side of Slipper facing, working this rnd in back lps only, attach pink with a sc in any st, ch 5, sk next 3 sts, [sc in next st, ch 5, sk next 3 sts] around, join in beg sc. *(17 ch sps)*

Rnd 38: Ch 1, sc in each of next 2 chs, (sc, ch 4, sc) in next ch, sc in each of next 2 chs, [sk next sc, sc in each of next 2 chs, (sc, ch 4, sc) in next ch, sc in next 2 chs] around, join in beg sc, fasten off.

PINK SLIPPER

Rnds 1–36: Rep rnds 1–36 of Yellow Slipper with pink.

Yellow Pansy

Rnd 1: With medium purple, ch 4, sl st in first ch to form a ring, ch 1, (sc in ring, ch 2) 5 times, join in beg sc, fasten off. *(5 sc, 5 ch-5 sps)*

Rnd 2: Attach yellow with sc in any sc, ch 1, *(hdc, ch 1, dc, ch 1) in next ch sp, (tr, ch 1) 5 times in same ch sp, (dc, ch 1, hdc) in same ch sp, rep from * once, ch 1, [sc in next sc, (hdc, 5 dc, hdc) in next ch sp] 3 times, join in beg sc, fasten off. *(5 petals)*

Row 3: Now working in rows, attach white with sl st in first sc, [ch 3, sc in next ch sp] 8 times, [sc in next ch sp, ch 3] 8 times, sl st in next sc, leaving rem sts unworked, fasten off.

Purple Pansy

Rnd 1: Rep rnd 1 of Yellow Pansy with dark purple.
Rnd 2: Rep rnd 1 of Yellow Pansy with medium purple.
Row 3: Rep row 3 of Yellow Pansy.

Leaf

Make 3.
With light green, ch 9, sc in 2nd ch from hook, hdc in

next ch, dc in each of next 5 chs, (dc, ch 1, sl st) in last ch, fasten off.

Glue Pansies and Leaves to Slipper.

LIGHT GREEN SLIPPER

Rnds 1–36: Rep rnds 1–36 of Yellow Slipper with light green.

Flower

Make 1 each pink, yellow and medium purple.

Ch 4, sl st in first ch to form a ring, (ch 3, dc in ring, ch 3, sl st in ring) 5 times, ch 3, dc in ring, ch 3, join with sl st in first sl st, fasten off.

Leaves & Stem

Make 3.

With dark green, ch 11 for Leaf, dc in 3rd ch from hook, **picot** (see Special Stitch), ch 2, sl st in same ch as last dc made, ch 6, sl st in 2nd ch from hook, sl st in each of next 4 chs, for Leaf, ch 2, (dc, picot, ch 2, sl st) in last sl st made, sl st in rem chs across, ch-11, fasten off.

Glue Flowers, Leaves and Stems diagonally over Glass Slipper. Glue 1 bead to center of each Flower.

PEACH SLIPPER

Rnds 1–36: Rep rnds 1–36 of Yellow Slipper with peach.

Sew buttons evenly spaced around rnds 31–33 of Slipper. ●

Medallion Bookmarks continued from page 85

Assembly

Spray Bookmark with starch, being careful not to touch crocheted piece with iron, gently steam crocheted piece.

Cut 12 inches from green ribbon. Weave rem 24 inches through 1 ch sp of rnd 3 and secure. Tie knot at each end. Tie rem 12-inch length into a bow and glue to top of long ribbon over rnd 3.

ICE CRYSTAL

Rnd 1: With white, ch 6 (counts as first dc, ch-2), (dc,

ch 2) 5 times in 6th ch from hook, join in 4th ch of ch-6. (6 dc, 6 ch-2 sps)

Rnd 2: Ch 3, dc in same st as beg ch-3, 2 dc in next ch-2 sp, [2 dc in next dc, 2 dc in next ch-2 sp] around, join in 3rd ch of ch-3. (24 dc)

Rnds 3 & 4: Rep rnds 3 and 4 of Summer Sunshine.

Assembly

Rep assembly of Summer Sunshine, using pink ribbon in place of green ribbon. ●

Wedding Favor Bags continued from page 91

rem ch-5 sp, ending with join in 4th ch of beg ch-8, fasten off.

Finishing

Wash and lightly starch Bag, pin to shape on pinning board and let dry.

Cut 18-inch length of ribbon, starting at center large shell of rnd 8 of Bag opening, weave ribbon through ch sps of large shells around opening, tie ends in a bow at center front.

BAG NO. 2

First Motif

Row 1: Working with 1 strand each, ch 33, dc in 4th ch from hook (beg 3 chs count as first dc), dc in next ch, [ch 2, sk next 2 chs, dc in each of next 2 chs] 7 times, turn. (16 dc, 7 ch-2 sps)

Row 2: Ch 3, **shell** (see Special Stitches) in next ch-2 sp, ch 2, 2 dc in next ch-2 sp, ch 2, sk next ch-2 sp, (tr, ch 5, tr) in next ch-2 sp, ch 2, sk next ch-2 sp, 2 dc in

next ch-2 sp, ch 2, shell in next ch-2 sp, dc in top of last dc, turn.

Row 3: Ch 3, shell in next ch-2 sp of next shell, ch 2, sk next ch-2 sp, dc in each of next 2 dc, ch 2, 9 dc in next ch-5 sp, ch 2, dc in each of next 2 dc, ch 2, shell in next ch-2 sp of next shell, dc in last dc, turn.

Row 4: Ch 3, shell in next ch-2 sp of next shell, ch 2, dc in each of next 2 dc, ch 2, [tr in next dc, ch 1] 8 times, tr in next dc, ch 2, dc in each of next 2 dc, ch 2, shell in ch-2 sp of next shell, dc in last dc, turn.

Row 5: Ch 3, shell in ch-2 sp of next shell, ch 2, dc in each of next 2 dc, [ch 3, sc in next ch-1 sp] 8 times, ch 3, dc in each of next 2 dc, ch 2, shell in ch-2 sp of next shell, dc in last dc, turn.

Row 6: Ch 3, shell in ch-2 sp of next shell, ch 2, dc in each of next 2 dc, sk next ch-3 sp, [ch 3, sc in next ch-3 sp] 7 times, ch 3, dc in each of next 2 dc, ch 2, shell in ch-2 sp of next shell, dc in last dc, turn.

Row 7: Ch 3, shell in ch-2 sp of next shell, ch 2, dc in each of next 2 dc, sk next ch-3 sp, [ch 3, sc in next ch-3 sp] 6 times, ch 3, dc in each of next 2 dc, ch 2, shell in ch-2 sp of next shell, dc in last dc, turn.

Row 8: Ch 3, shell in ch-2 sp of next shell, ch 2, dc in each of next 2 dc, sk next ch-3 sp, [ch 3, sc in next ch-3 sp] 5 times, ch 3, dc in each of next 2 dc, ch 2, shell in ch-2 sp of next shell, dc in last dc, turn.

Row 9: Ch 3, shell in ch-2 sp of next shell, ch 2, dc in each of next 2 dc, sk next ch-3 sp, [ch 3, sc in next ch-3 sp] 4 times, ch 3, dc in each of next 2 dc, ch 2, shell in ch-2 sp of next shell, dc in last dc, turn.

Row 10: Ch 3, shell in ch-2 sp of next shell, ch 2, dc in each of next 2 dc, sk next ch-3 sp, [ch 3, sc in next ch-3 sp] 3 times, ch 3, dc in each of next 2 dc, ch 2, shell in ch-2 sp of next shell, dc in last dc, turn.

Row 11: Ch 3, shell in ch-2 sp of next shell, ch 2, dc in each of next 2 dc, sk next ch-3 sp, [ch 3, sc in next ch-3 sp] twice, ch 3, dc in each of next 2 dc, ch 2, shell in ch-2 sp of next shell, dc in last dc, turn.

Row 12: Ch 3, shell in ch-2 sp of next shell, ch 2, dc in each of next 2 dc, ch 3, sk next ch-3 sp, sc in next ch-3 sp, ch 3, dc in each of next 2 dc, ch 2, shell in ch-2 sp of next shell, dc in last dc, turn.

Row 13: Ch 3, shell in ch-2 sp of next shell, ch 2, [dc in each of next 2 dc, ch 2] twice, shell in ch-2 sp of next shell, dc in last dc, turn.

Row 14: Ch 3, shell in ch-2 sp of next shell, ch 2, [**dc dec** *(see Stitch Guide)* in next 2 dc] twice, ch 2, shell in ch-2 sp of next shell, dc in last dc, turn.

Row 15: Ch 3, shell in ch-2 sp of next shell, ch 2, shell in ch-2 sp of next shell, dc in last dc, turn.

Row 16: Ch 2, [dc in next ch sp of shell] twice, dc in last dc, fasten off.

2nd Motif

Rows 1–16: Rep rows 1–16 of First Motif.

Edging

Row 1: Holding both Motifs WS tog and working through both thicknesses, attach 1 strand each inside edge of row 1 of Motifs, ch 1, (sc, ch 3) twice and sc in each ch-3 sp and each dc around outer edge to opposite side of row 1 of Motif.

Rnd 2: Now working in rnds around Bag opening through 1 thickness only, ch 1, sc in same st as beg ch-1, ch 3, sc in next ch-2 sp, [ch 3, sc in sp between next 2 dc , ch 3, sc in next ch-2 sp] around, ending with ch 1, hdc in beg sc.

Rnd 3: Ch 7 *(counts as first tr, ch-3)*, sc in 4th ch from hook, ch 1, [tr, ch 3, sl st in top of last tr, ch 1] in each ch-3 sp around, join in 4th ch of beg ch-7, fasten off.

Finishing

Wash and lightly starch Bag, pin to shape on pinning board and let dry.

Starting at center front, weave 18-inch length of ribbon through ch-2 sps of row 1, tie ends in a bow at center front. ●

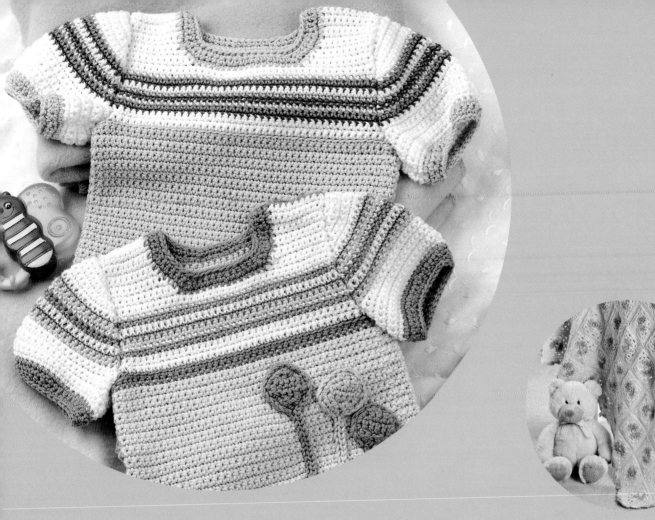

Wee Folk
in a Wink

You'll love making these adorable designs for babies and kids, including a cute variety of blankets, simple wearables, toys, totes and more.

Baby His & Her Onesies

DESIGNS BY NANETTE SEALE

INTERMEDIATE

Finished Sizes

Instructions given fit sizes
0–3 months; changes for
sizes 6, 12, 18, 24 months
are in [ ].

Finished Garment Measurements

Chest: 17 [18, 20, 21, 22]
inches

Materials

- Patons Grace
  light DK weight
  yarn (1¾ oz/136 yds/50g):

  Boy:
  280 [330, 350, 440, 500]
  yds #60603 apricot *(MC)*
  80 [90, 115, 125, 150] yds
  #60005 snow *(A)*
  70 [80, 85, 90, 95] yds
  #60027 ginger *(B)*

Gauge

5 sc = 1 inch; 5 sc rows = 1 inch

16 [19, 20, 21, 22] yds
#60104 azure *(C)*
12 [12, 13, 14, 15] yds
#60604 terracotta *(D)*
Girl:
280 [330, 350, 440, 500]
yds #60416 blush
(MC)
80 [90, 115, 125, 150] yds
#60005 snow *(A)*
105 [113, 130, 135, 145]
yds #60437 rose *(B)*
20 [23, 24, 25, 26] yds
#60130 sky *(C)*
15 [15, 17, 18, 19 yds
#60903 lavender *(D)*
- Size E/4/3.5mm crochet
  hook or size needed to
  obtain gauge
- Tapestry needle
- Sewing needle and
  matching thread
- Snap fasteners: 4
- 12mm white buttons: 4
- Stitch markers

Pattern Notes

Weave in loose ends as work progresses.

Join rounds with a slip stitch unless otherwise stated.

Garment is crocheted from bottom upwards.

When color change is required, do not fasten off;
carry along side edge of work whenever possible.

ONESIES

Front

Row 1 (WS): Starting at bottom with MC, ch 13 [17,
20, 23, 26], sc in 2nd ch from hook, sc in each rem ch
across, turn. *(12 [16, 19, 22, 25] sc)*

Row 2: Ch 1, sc in each st across, turn.

Row 3: Rep row 2.

Row 4: Ch 1, 2 sc in first st, sc in each st across to last
st, 2 sc in last st, turn. *(14 [18, 21, 24, 27] sc)*

Row 5: Rep row 2.

Row 6: Rep row 4. *(16 [20, 23, 26, 29] sc)*

Rows 7–9: Rep row 2.

Row 10: Rep row 4. *(18 [22, 25, 28, 31] sc)*

Rows 11–13: Rep row 2.

Row 14: Rep row 4. *(20 [24, 27, 30, 33] sc)*

Rows 15–17: Rep row 2.

Row 18: Rep row 4. *(22 [26, 29, 32, 35] sc)*

Rows 19 [19–21, 19–22, 19–23, 29–24]: Rep row 2.

Rows 20–24 [22–26, 23–27, 24–28, 25–29]: Ch 4,
sc in 2nd ch from hook, sc in each of next 2 chs, sc in
each rem sc across, turn. At the end of last rep, ch 5,

not come undone, remove hook. With tapestry needle, thread the rem 4-inch length from ch-5 of Front and join to the first st of Back row 24 [26, 27, 28, 29], secure end. Pick up dropped lp from first ch-5 sp.

Body

Rnd 25 [27, 28, 29, 30]. Now working in rnds, ch 1, [sc in each of next 5 chs, sc in each sc across] twice, join in beg sc, turn. *(86 [94, 100, 106, 112] sc)*

Rnd 26 [28, 29, 30, 31]: Ch 1, sc in each sc around, join in beg sc, turn.

Note: *With equal number of sts Front and Back, place st marker at each side. Move st markers as work progresses.*

Rnds 27–60 [29–64, 30–68, 31–72, 32–76]: Ch 1, sc in each sc around, join in beg sc, turn. At the end of last rep, fasten off.

Rnd 61 [65, 69, 73, 77]: Attach B with sl st in first st, ch 1, sc in each sc around, join in beg sc, turn.

Rnd 62 [66, 70, 74, 78]: Ch 1, sc in each sc around, join in beg sc, turn, fasten off.

Upper Back

Row 63 [67, 71, 75, 79]: Now working in rows, working in **front lps** (see Stitch Guide) for this row only, attach MC in first st of back with sc, ch 1, sc in each of next 42 [47, 49, 52, 55] sc, turn. *(43 [48, 50, 53, 56] sc)*

Row 64 [68, 72, 76, 80]: Sl st in each of next 3 sts, ch 1, sc in each sc across to last 3 sc, leaving last 3 sc unworked, turn. *(37 [41, 44, 47, 50] sc)*

Rows 65–80 [69–84, 73–90, 77–96, 81–102]: Ch 1, sc in each sc across, turn.

Left Shoulder

Row 81 [85, 91, 97, 103]: Ch 1, sc in each of next 12

leaving a 4-inch length, fasten off. *(37 [41, 44, 47, 50] sc at end of last row)*

Back

Row 1 (WS): Starting at bottom with MC, ch 15 [19, 22, 25, 28], sc in 2nd ch from hook, sc in each rem ch across, turn. *(14 [18, 21, 24, 27] sc)*

Rows 2–23 [2–25, 2–26, 2–27, 2–28]: Rep rows 2–23 [2–25, 2–26, 2–27, 2–28] of Front. *(36 [40, 43, 46, 49] sc)*

Row 24 [26, 27, 28, 29]: Ch 4, sc in 2nd ch from hook, sc in each of next 2 chs, sc in each rem sc across, ch 5, do not fasten off. *(39 [43, 46, 49, 52] sc)* Take care to make sure the WS of Front and Back are tog and that the ch-5 lengths are not twisted. Join end of ch-5 with sl st to first st of Front row 24 [26, 27, 28, 29], draw up a lp so the joining does

[12, 13, 14, 15] sc, leaving rem sts unworked, turn. *(12 [12, 13, 14, 15] sc)*

Row 82 [86, 92, 98, 104]: Ch 1, **sc dec** *(see Stitch Guide)* in next 2 sc, sc in each rem sc across, turn. *(11 [11, 12, 13, 14] sc)*

Row 83 [87, 93, 99, 105]: Ch 1, sc in each sc across to last 2 sc, sc dec in next 2 sc, turn. *(10 [10, 11, 12, 13] sc)*

Rows 84–87 [88–91, 94–98, 100–104, 106–110]: Ch 1, sc in each sc across, turn. At the end of last rep, fasten off.

Right Shoulder

Row 81 [85, 91, 97, 103]: Sk next 13 [17, 18, 19, 20] sc for back neck opening, attach MC with sc in next st, sc in each of next 11 [11, 12, 13, 14] sc, turn. *(12 [12, 13, 14, 15] sc)*

Row 82 [86, 92, 98, 104]: Ch 1, sc in each sc across to last 2 sc, sc dec in next 2 sc, turn. *(11 [11, 12, 13, 14] sc)*

Row 83 [87, 93, 99, 105]: Ch 1, sc dec in next 2 sc, sc in each rem sc across, turn. *(10 [10, 11, 12, 13] sc)*

Rows 84–87 [88–91, 94–98, 100–104, 106–110]: Ch 1, sc in each sc across, turn. At the end of last rep, fasten off.

Upper Front

Row 63 [67, 71, 75, 79]: Working in front lps only, attach A with sc in first free sc of row 62, [66, 70, 74, 78], sc in each rem sc across, turn. *(43 [47, 50, 53, 56] sc)*

Row 64 [68, 72, 76, 80]: Sl st in each of next 3 sc, sc in each sc across to last 3 sc, leaving rem sc unworked, turn. *(37 [41, 44, 47, 50] sc)*

Row 65 [69, 73 & 74, 77–79, 81–84]: Ch 1, sc in each st across, turn.

Row 66 [70, 75, 80, 85]: With C, ch 1, sc in each st across, turn.

Row 67 [71, 76, 81, 86]: With D, ch 1, sc in each st across, turn.

Row 68 [72, 77, 82, 87]: With A, ch 1, sc in each st across, turn.

Row 69 [73, 78, 83, 88]: With C, ch 1, sc in each st across, turn.

Row 70 [74, 79, 84, 89]: With B, ch 1, sc in each st across, turn.

Row 71 [75, 80, 85, 90]: With A, ch 1, sc in each st across, turn.

Row 72 [76, 81, 86, 91]: With C, ch 1, sc in each st across, turn.

Row 73 [77, 82, 87, 92]: With D, ch 1, sc in each st across, turn.

Rows 74–76 [78–80, 83–86, 88–92, 93–98]: With A, ch 1, sc in each st across, turn.

Right Shoulder

Row 77 [81, 87, 93, 99]: Ch 1, sc in each of next 12 [12, 13, 14, 15] sc, leaving rem sts unworked, turn. *(12 [12, 13, 14, 15] sc)*

Row 78 [82, 88, 94, 100]: Ch 1, sc dec in next 2 sc, sc in each rem sc across, turn. *(11 [11, 12, 13, 14] sc)*

Row 79 [83, 89, 95, 101]: Ch 1, sc in each sc across to last 2 sc, sc dec in next 2 sc, turn. *(10 [10, 11, 12, 13] sc)*

Rows 80–87 [84–91, 90–98, 96–104, 102–110]: Ch 1, sc in each sc across, turn. At the end of last rep, fasten off.

Left Shoulder

Row 77 [81, 87, 93, 99]: Sk center 13 [17, 18, 19, 20] sc for neck opening, attach A in next sc with sc, sc in each of next 11 [11, 12, 13, 14] sc, turn. *(12 [12, 13, 14, 14] sc)*

Row 78 [82, 88, 94, 100]: Ch 1, sc in each sc across to last 2 sc, sc dec in next 2 sc, turn. *(11 [11, 12, 13, 14] sc)*

Row 79 [83, 89, 95, 101]: Ch 1, sc dec in next 2 sc, sc in each rem sc across, turn. *(10 [10, 11, 12, 13] sc)*

Rows 80–87 [84–91, 90–98, 96–104, 102–110]: Ch 1, sc in each st across, turn. At the end of last rep, fasten off.

With tapestry needle and length of A, sew Right Shoulders tog.

Neckband

Note: *The Neckband st count is approximate. If the actual count is a couple of sts different more or less, it is not vital to the design as long as sts rem flat.*

Row 1 (RS): Attach B with sc in outer corner of left front shoulder, sc in each st across shoulder, 3 sc in corner of Front Left Shoulder, sc evenly

Using tapestry needle, position Front Left Shoulder over the Back Left Shoulder and sew tog along armhole edge.

Leg Band

Note: *The Leg Band st count is approximate. If the actual st count is a couple of sts different more or less, it is not vital to the design as long sts rem flat.*

Row 1 (RS): Attach B with a sc in end of first row of leg opening, sc evenly spaced across opening, turn. *(67 [72, 78, 82, 86] sc)*

Row 2: Ch 1, [sc in each of next 5 sc, sc dec in next 2 sc] across, turn. *(58 [62, 67, 71, 74] sc)*

Row 3: Rep row 2. *(50 [54, 58, 61, 64] sc)*

Row 4: Sl st in each st across, fasten off. Rep on rem leg opening

Sleeve

Make 2.

Row 1 (RS): Beg at Band end, with A, ch 42 [44, 45, 47, 49], sc in 2nd ch from hook, sc in each rem ch across, turn. *(41 [43, 44, 46, 48] sc)*

Row 2: Ch 1, sc in each sc across, turn.

Rows 3–5 [3–5, 3–6, 3–6, 3–6]: Rep row 2.

Row 6 [6, 7, 7, 7]: Ch 1, sc dec in next 2 sc, sc in each sc across to last 2 sc, sc dec in next 2 sc, turn. *(39 [41, 42, 44, 46] sc)*

Row(s) 7 [7 & 8, 8 & 9, 8–10, 8–10]: Rep row 2.

Row 8 [9, 10, 11, 11]: With C, sl st in first 4 sts, ch 1, sc in same st as last sl st, sc in next 32 [34, 35, 37, 39] sts, leaving last 3 sts unworked, turn. *(33 [35, 36, 38, 40] sc)*

Row 9 [10, 11, 12, 12]: With D, rep row 6 [6, 7, 7, 7]. *(31 [33, 34, 36, 38] sc)*

Row 10 [11, 12, 13, 13]: With A, rep row 2.

Row 11 [12, 13, 14, 14]: With C, rep row 6 [6, 7, 7, 7]. *(29 [31, 32, 34, 36] sc)*

Row 12 [13, 14, 15, 15]: With B, rep row 2.

spaced around neckline to the inner corner of Back Left Shoulder, do not work across sts of Back Left Shoulder, turn. *(77 [85, 92, 96, 100] sc)*

Row 2: Ch 1, [sc in each of next 5 sts, sc dec in next 2 sc] around neckline, after the last dec sc in each st to the corner st of Left Shoulder, working across sts of Left Shoulder, ch 3, sc in corner st, sc in next st, [ch 3, sk next st, sc in each of next 2 sts] 3 times, sc across, turn. *(4 buttonholes, 65 [73, 79, 83, 87] sc)*

Row 3: Ch 1, working across Left Shoulder, sc in each sc to 2 sc before first ch-3 sp, [sc dec in next 2 sc, 2 sc in next ch-3 sp] 3 times, sc dec in next 2 sc, 3 sc in next ch-3 sp, [sc in each of next 5 sc, sc dec in next 2 sc] around neckline ending with sc across rem sts, turn. *(62 [69, 74, 78, 82] sc)*

Row 4: Sl st in each st across, fasten off.

Row 13 [14, 15, 16, 16]: With A, rep row 6 [6, 7, 7, 7]. *(27 [29, 30, 32, 34] sts)*

Row 14 [15, 16, 17, 17]: With C, rep row 2.

Row 15 [16, 17, 18, 18]: With D, rep row 6 [6, 7, 7, 7]. *(25 [27, 28, 30, 32] sc)*

Row 16 [17, 18, 19, 19]: With A, rep row 2.

Row 17–22 [18–23, 19–25, 20–26, 20–27]: Rep row 6 [6, 7, 7, 7]. At the end of last rep, fasten off. *(13 [15, 14, 16, 16] sc at end of last row)*

Sew ends of rows of Sleeve tog.

Sleeve Band

Rnd 1 (RS): Working in opposite side of foundation ch of Sleeve, attach B with sc in first ch, sc in each ch around, join in beg sc, turn. *(41 [43, 44, 46, 48] sc)*

***Note:** When working dec sts for some sizes after the last sc dec, sc in rem sts to end of rnd.*

Rnd 2: Ch 1, [sc in each of next 5 sc, sc dec in next 2 sc] around, join in beg sc, turn. *(35 [37, 38, 40, 42] sc)*

Rnd 3: Rep rnd 2. *(30 [32, 33, 35, 36] sc)*

Rnd 4: Sl st in each st around, fasten off.

Sew sleeves into armholes matching the colored stripes of upper Body to the stripes on the sleeve as work progresses.

Rep on rem Sleeve.

Finishing

Sew 4 snap fasteners to the bottom over the first couple of rows with front overlapping back. Sew 4 buttons to Left Back Shoulder opposite buttonholes of Left Front Shoulder.

Girl Rump Ruffle

Make 2.

Rnd 1: With B, ch 35 [35, 46, 46, 52], dc in 4th ch from hook *(first 3 sk chs count as first dc)*, ch 1, 2 dc in same ch, [sk next ch, (2 dc, ch 1, 2 dc) in next ch] across, ending with (2 dc, ch 1, 2 dc) in last ch, working on opposite side of foundation ch, [sk next ch, (2 dc, ch 1, 2 dc) in next ch] across, join in top of first ch-3, fasten off.

Sew Rump Ruffles slightly above leg openings, one above the other, to lower back bottom.

Balloon Appliqué

Make 1 each B, C and D.

Row 1: Ch 2, 2 sc in 2nd ch from hook, pull beg length to tighten opening, turn. *(2 sc)*

Row 2: Ch 1, 2 sc in each sc across, turn. *(4 sc)*

Row 3: Ch 1, 2 sc in first sc, sc in each of next 2 sc, 2 sc in next sc, turn. *(6 sc)*

Row 4: Ch 1, sc in each sc across, turn.

Row 5: Ch 1, sc dec in next 2 sc, sc in each of next 2 sc, sc dec in next 2 sc, turn. *(4 sc)*

Row 6: Ch 1, [sc dec in next 2 sc] twice, turn. *(2 sc)*

Row 7: Ch 1, sc dec in next 2 sc, do not turn. *(1 sc)*

Rnd 8: Now working in rnds, ch 15, sl st in 2nd ch from hook, sl st in each ch across, sl st in base of Balloon, sc around outer edge of Balloon with 2 sc in ends of rows and 3 sc in end of row 1, sl st to join in base of Balloon, leaving a 12-inch length of yarn, fasten off.

Using 12-inch length, sew Balloons to left of Front Body of Onesie as shown in photo. ●

Baby His & Her Sailor Suits

DESIGNS BY NANETTE SEALE

INTERMEDIATE

Finished Sizes

Instructions given fit sizes 0–3 months; changes for sizes 6, 12, 18, 24 months are in [ ].

Finished Garment Measurement

Chest: 17 [18, 20, 21, 22] inches

Materials

- Patons Grace light (DK) weight yarn (1¾ oz/136 yds/59g per ball):
  Boy:
  288 [355, 398, 450, 505] yds #60104 azure *(MC)*
  92 [140, 148, 165, 185] yds #60005 snow *(B)*
  7 [7, 7, 7, 7] yds #60130 sky
  Girl:
  418 [504, 578, 655, 735] yds #60705 cardinal *(MC)*
  90 [110, 115, 120, 138] yds #60104 azure *(B)*
  55 [67, 78, 90, 97] yds #60005 snow
- Size E/4/3.5mm crochet hook or size needed to obtain gauge
- Tapestry needle
- Sewing needle and matching thread
- 6 snap fasteners
- White 12mm buttons: 4
- Stitch markers

Gauge

21 hdc = 4 inches; 12 hdc rows = 4 inches

Pattern Notes

Weave in loose ends as work progresses.
Join rounds with a slip stitch unless otherwise stated.
Garment is crocheted from bottom upwards.
Chain-2 at beginning of row does not count as a stitch.
When color change is required, **do not fasten off**, carry along side edge of work whenever possible.

Pattern Stitch

Variation 1: [Hdc in **front lp** *(see Stitch Guide)* of next st, hdc in **back lp** *(see Stitch Guide)* of next st] across, turn.
Variation 2: [Hdc in **back lp** *(see Stitch Guide)* of next st, hdc in **front lp** *(see Stitch Guide)* of next st] across, turn.

SUIT

Front

Row 1: Starting at bottom with MC, ch 14 [16, 20, 22, 24], hdc in 3rd ch from hook, hdc in each rem ch across, turn. *(12 [14, 18, 20, 22] sc)*
Row(s) 2 [2, 2 & 3, 2–4, 2–5]: Ch 2, [hdc in back lp of next st, hdc in front lp of next st] across, turn.
Note: *In the following rows/rnds, if previous row/rnd ends with hdc in front lp, work in variation 2; if previous row/rnd ends with hdc in back lp, work in variation 1.*

Rows 3–14 [3–15, 4–16, 5–17, 6–18]: Ch 2, 2 hdc in first st, work Pattern Stitch across to last st, 2 hdc in last st, turn. At the end of last row, ch 6, leaving a 4-inch length, fasten off. *(36 [40, 44, 46, 48] sts)*

Back

Rows 1–14 [1–15, 1–16, 1–17, 118]: Rep rows 1–14 [1–15, 1–16, 1–17, 1–18] of Front. At the end of last rep, ch 6, sl st to end st of last row of Front, draw up a lp, remove hook. Sl st rem, ch-6 of Front to opposite side of last row of Back, pick up dropped lp, turn. *(36 [40, 44, 46, 48] sts)*

Body

Rnd 15 [16, 17, 18, 19]: Now working in rnds with MC, ch 2, [hdc in each of next 6 chs, work in Pattern Stitch across] twice, join, turn. *(84 [92, 100, 104, 108] sts)*

Rnds 16–25 [17–27, 18–29, 19–32, 20–33]: Work in Pattern Stitch around, join, turn.

Note: With equal number of sts Front and Back, place st marker at each side. Move st markers as work progresses.

Rnd 26 [28, 30, 33, 34]: With B, work in Pattern Stitch in each st around, join, turn.

Rnd 27 [29, 31, 34, 35]: With MC, work in Pattern Stitch in each st around, join, turn.

Rnd 28 [30, 32, 35, 36]: With B, work in Pattern Stitch in each st around, join, turn.

Rnds 29–34 [31–37, 33–40, 36–44, 37–46]: Rep rnds [27 and 28 {29 and 30, 31 and 32, 34 and 35, 35 and 36 alternately}] 3 times.

Upper Front
Note: Continue to alternate MC and B (one row each color) for rem of Upper Front.

Row 35 [38, 41, 45, 47]: Now working in rows, sl st in each of next 3 sts, ch 2, work in Pattern Stitch across 36 [40, 44, 46, 48] sts, leaving rem 3 sts unworked, turn. *(36 [40, 44, 46, 48] sts)*

Rows 36–41 [39–45, 42–49, 46–54, 48–57]: Alternating colors working 1 row each MC and B, ch 2, work in Pattern Stitch across, turn.

Right Shoulder
Row 42 [46, 50, 55, 58]: Ch 2, Pattern Stitch in each of next 12 [12, 13, 14, 15] sts, leaving rem sts unworked, turn. *(12 [12, 13, 14, 15] sts)*

Rows 43–45 [47–50, 51–55, 56–60, 59–65]: Ch 2, Pattern Stitch in each st across, turn. At the end of last rep, fasten off.

Left Shoulder

Row 42 [46, 50, 55, 58]: Sk next 12 [16, 18, 18, 20] sts for neck opening, attach MC with sl st in next st, ch 2, hdc in same st as beg ch-2, Pattern Stitch across rem sts, turn. *(12 [12, 13, 14, 15] sts)*

Rows 43–45 [47–50, 51–55, 56–50, 59–65]: Ch 2, Pattern Stitch across, turn. At the end of last rep, fasten off.

Upper Back

Row 35 [38, 41, 45, 47]: Continue to alternate MC and B, sk next 3 sts from marker, attach yarn with sl st in 4th st, ch 2, hdc in same st, Pattern Stitch across 35 [39, 43, 45, 47] sts, turn. *(36 [40, 44, 46, 48] sts)*

Rows 36–43 [39–47, 42–52, 46–56, 48–61]: Alternating colors working 1 row each MC and B, ch 2, Pattern Stitch across, turn.

Left Shoulder

Row 44 [48, 53, 57, 62]: Ch 2, Pattern Stitch in each of next 12 [12, 13, 14, 14] sts, leaving rem sts unworked, turn. *(12 [12, 13, 14, 14] sts)*

Row(s) 45 [49 & 50, 54 & 55, 58–60, 63–65]: Ch 2, Pattern Stitch in each st across, turn. At the end of last rep, fasten off.

Right Shoulder

Row 44 [48, 53, 57, 62]: Sk center 12 [16, 18, 18, 20] sc for neck opening, attach yarn with sl st in next st, ch 2, hdc in same st as beg ch-2, Pattern Stitch in each rem st across, turn. *(12 [12, 13, 14, 14] sts)*

Row(s) 45 [49 & 50, 54 & 55, 58–60, 63–65]: Ch 2, Pattern Stitch in each st across, turn. At the end of last rep, fasten off.

With tapestry needle and length of A, sew Right Shoulders tog.

Neckband

Note: *The Neckband st count is approximate. If the actual count is a couple of sts different more or less, it is not vital to the design as long as sts rem flat.*

Row 1 (RS): Attach MC with sc in outer corner of Left Front Shoulder, sc in each st across Shoulder, 3 sc in corner of Left Front Shoulder, sc evenly around Neckline to the inner corner of Back Left Shoulder, do not work across Back Left Shoulder sts, turn. *(63 [79, 92, 108, 122] sts)*

Row 2: Ch 1, sc in each st to Left Shoulder, sc in corner st, sc in next st, [ch 3, sk next st, sc in each of next 2 sts] 3 times, ch 3, sk 1 st, sc in last st, turn. *(4 buttonholes)*

Row 3: Ch 1, sc in each st to first ch-3 sp, [2 sc in next ch-3 sp, sc dec in next 2 sc] 3 times, 2 sc in next ch-3 sp, sl st in each rem st, fasten off.

Using tapestry needle, position Front Left Shoulder over Back Left Shoulder, and sew tog along armhole edge.

Leg Band

Note: *The Leg Band st count is approximate. If the actual st counts are a couple of sts different more or less, it is not vital to the design as long as they rem flat.*

Row 1 (RS): Attach MC with a sc in end of first row of leg opening, sc evenly spaced across opening, turn. *(58 [69, 81, 93, 106] sc)*

Row 2: Ch 1, sc in each sc across, turn.

Row 3: Sl st in each st across, fasten off.

Rep on rem leg opening.

Sleeve

Make 2.

Row 1 (RS): Beg at Band end, with MC, ch 43 [45, 47, 49, 51], hdc in 3rd ch from hook, hdc in each rem ch across, turn. *(41 [43, 45, 47, 49] hdc)*

Row 2: Ch 2, Pattern Stitch in each st across, turn.

Row 3: With B *(for Girl)* and sky *(for Boy)*, rep row 2.

Rows 4 [4 & 5, 4 & 5, 4–6, 4–7]: With MC, rep row 2.

Row 5 [6, 6, 7, 8]: Ch 1, sl st in first 3 sts, ch 2, hdc in Pattern Stitch across to last 3 sts, leaving last 3 sts unworked, turn. *(35 [37, 39, 41, 43] sts)*

Rows 6–12 [7–14, 7–14, 8–15, 9–17]: Ch 2, hdc dec in first 2 sts, hdc in Pattern Stitch across to last 2 sts, hdc dec in last 2 sts, turn At the end of last rep, fasten off. *(21 [21, 23, 25, 25] sts)*

Sew ends of Sleeve rows of tog.

31, 35, 37] sc in 2nd ch from hook, sc in each rem ch across, turn. *(24 [28, 30, 34, 36] sc)*
Row 2: Ch 1, sc in each sc across, turn.
Rows 3–12 [3–14, 3–16, 3–17, 3–18]: Rep row 2.

Right Front
Row 13 [15, 17, 18, 19]: Ch 1, sc in each of next 4 [5, 5, 6, 6] sts, turn. *(4 [5, 5, 6, 6] sc)*
Rows 14–36 [16–40, 18–47, 19–50, 20–53]: Rep row 2.
Row 37 [41, 48, 51, 54]: Ch 1, sc dec in next 2 sc, sc in each rem sc across, turn. *(3 [4, 4, 5, 5] sc)*
Row 38 [42, 49, 52, 55]: Rep row 2.
Row 39 [43, 50, 53, 56]: Ch 1, sc dec in next 2 sc, sc in each rem sc across, turn. *(2 [3, 3, 4, 4] sc)*

For Size 0–3 Months Only
Row 40: Ch 1, sc in next 2 sc, fasten off. *(2 sc)*

For Size 6 Months Only
Row 44: Ch 1, sc in first st, sc dec in next 2 sts, turn. *(2 sc)*
Row 45: Ch 1, sc in next 2 sts, fasten off. *(2 sc)*

For Size 12 Months Only
Row 51: Ch 1, sc in first sc, sc dec in next 2 sts, fasten off. *(2 sc)*

For Sizes 18 & 24 Months Only
Row 54, 57: Ch 1, sc in first 2 sc, sc dec in next 2 sc, turn. *([3, 3] sc)*
Rows 55, 58: Ch 1, sc in first sc, sc dec in next 2 sc, turn. *([2, 2] sc)*
Row 56, 59: Ch 1, sc in next 2 sc, fasten off.

Sleeve Band
Rnd 1 (RS): Working in opposite side of foundation ch of Sleeve, attach B *(for Boy)* and snow *(for Girl)* with sc in first ch, sc in each ch around, join in beg sc, turn.
Rnd 2: Sl st in each st around, fasten off.
Sew sleeves into armholes.

Finishing
Sew snap fasteners to the bottom over the first couple of rows with front overlapping back. Sew 4 buttons to Left Back Shoulder opposite buttonholes of Left Front Shoulder.

Collar
Row 1: With B *(for Boy)* and snow *(for Girl)*, ch 25 [29,

Left Front

Row 13 [15, 17, 18, 19]: Sk next 16 [18, 20, 22, 24] sts of row 12 [14, 16, 17, 18], attach B *(for Boy)* and snow *(for Girl)* with sl st in next sc, ch 1, sc in same sc, sc in each rem sc across, turn. *(4 [5, 5, 6, 6] sc)*

Rows 14–36 [16–40, 18–47, 19–50, 20–53]: Rep row 2.

Row 37 [41, 48, 51, 54]: Ch 1, sc in each sc across to last 2 sc, sc dec in next 2 sc, turn. *(3 [4, 4, 5, 5] sc)*

Row 38 [42, 49, 52, 55]: Rep row 2.

Row 39 [43, 50, 53, 56]: Ch 1, sc in each sc across to last 2 sc, sc dec in next 2 sc, turn. *(2 [3, 3, 4, 4] sc)*

For Size 0–3 Months Only

Row 40: Ch 1, sc in next 2 sc, **do not fasten off**. *(2 sc)*

For Size 6 Months Only

Row 44: Ch 1, sc dec in next 2 sc, sc in next sc, turn. *(2 sc)*

Row 45: Ch 1, sc in next 2 sts, **do not fasten off**. *(2 sc)*

For Size 12 Months Only

Row 51: Ch 1, sc dec in next 2 sts, sc in next sc, **do not fasten off**. *(2 sc)*

For Sizes 18 & 24 Months Only

Row 54, 57: Ch 1, sc dec in next 2 sc, sc in each of next 2 sc, turn. *([3, 3] sc)*

Row 55, 58: Ch 1, sc dec in next 2 sc, sc in next sc, turn. *([2, 2] sc)*

Row 56, 59: Ch 1, sc in next 2 sc, **do not fasten off**.

Border

Rnd 41 [46, 52, 57, 60]: Now working in rnds, sc in end of each row and in each st, working 3 sc in each back corner and 2 sc in front inside edge corners, join in beg sc, fasten off.

Row 42 [47, 53, 58, 61]: Now working in rows around the outside edge of Collar only, attach B with a sc, sc in each sc around outer edge only, working 3 sc in each center sc of each back corner, fasten off.

Row 43 [47, 54, 58, 62]: Working in each sc of previous row, attach MC with sc in first sc, sc in each sc working 3 sc in center sc of each back corner, turn.

Row 44 [48, 55, 59, 63]: Sl st in each st of previous row, fasten off.

Sew sk sts of row 12 [14, 16, 17, 18] of Collar to back neck edge.

Tie

Row 1: With MC *(for Girl)* and sky *(for Boy)*, ch 2, 2 sc in 2nd ch from hook, turn. *(2 sc)*

Row 2: Ch 1, 2 sc in first sc, sc in next sc, turn. *(3 sc)*

Rows 3–34: Ch 1, sc in each sc across, turn.

Row 35: Ch 1, sc dec in next 2 sc, sc in next sc, turn. *(2 sc)*

Row 36: Ch 1, sc in each of next 2 sc, fasten off.

Tie piece in a loose knot at center. Attach each side of Tie to Collar with a snap fastener.

Girl's Overskirt

Rnd 1: With MC, ch 3, hdc in first ch of ch-3, [turn, ch 2, hdc in top of last hdc] 45 [47, 53, 55, 57] times, using care not to twist, ch 1, join in first ch of beg ch-3. *(46 [50, 54, 56, 58] hdc)*

Rnd 2: Ch 2, 2 hdc in same ch as joining, [2 hdc in side edge of next hdc of rnd 1] around, join in top of beg ch-2, turn. *(94 [102, 110, 114, 118] hdc)*

Rnd 3: Ch 2, hdc in Pattern Stitch in each st around, join in top of beg ch-2, turn.

Rnds 4–10 [4–12, 4–14, 4–16, 4–18]: Rep rnd 3.

Rnd 11 [13, 15, 17, 19]: With B, rep rnd 3.

Rnd 12 [14, 16, 18, 20]: With MC, rep rnd 3.

Rnd 13 [15, 17, 19, 21]: With snow, rep rnd 3.

Rnd 14 [16, 18, 20, 22]: With MC, rep rnd 3.

Rnd 15 [17, 19, 21, 23]: With B, rep rnd 3.

Rnds 16–18 [18–20, 20–22, 22–24, 24–26]: With MC, rep rnd 3.

Rnd 19 [21, 23, 25, 27]: Sl st in each st around, fasten off.

Sew rnd 1 of Girl's Overskirt to rnd 25 [27, 29, 32, 33] of Body. ●

Dolman Sweater Set

DESIGNS BY DARLENE DALE FOR CARON INTERNATIONAL

INTERMEDIATE

Finished Sizes

Instructions given fit child's
size 2; changes for child's
size 4 and child's size 6 are
in [ ].

Finished Garment Measurements

Chest: 22¼ inches *(size 2)* [24
inches *(size 4)*, 25¾ inches
(size 6)]

Note: Chest measurement does
not include border overlap.

Hat: 14 inches in
circumference *(size 2)* [16
inches in circumference
(size 4), 18 inches in
circumference *(size 6)*]

Gauge

Size F hook: 4 sc = 1 inch; 5 sc rows = 1 inch
Size G hook: 15 sc = 4 inches; 4 sc rows = 1 inch
Size H hook: 7 sc = 2 inches; 7 rows = 2 inches

Materials

- Caron Simply
  Soft medium
  (worsted) weight yarn (6
  oz/315 yds/170g per skein):
    2 [2, 3] skeins #9717
    orchid *(MC)*
- Caron Simply Soft Baby
  medium (worsted) weight
  yarn (2 oz/95 yds/57g
  per skein):
    2 [2, 3] skeins #0008
    sweet orchid *(CC)*
- Sizes F/5/3.75mm *(size 2)*
  G/6/4mm *(size 4)* and H/8/
  5mm *(size 6)* crochet hooks
  or sizes needed to obtain
  gauge
- Tapestry needle
- Sewing needle and
  matching sewing thread
- ¾-inch button

Pattern Notes

Weave in loose ends as work progresses.
Join rounds with a slip stitch unless otherwise stated.

Special Stitch

Popcorn (pc): 5 sc in indicated st, draw up a lp, remove hook, insert hook in first sc of 5-sc group, pick
up dropped lp, draw through st on hook.

HAT

Front

Row 1: Starting a bottom edge of Hat band, with
size F [G, H] hook and CC, ch 28, sc in 2nd ch from
hook, sc in each rem ch across, turn. *(27 sc)*

Row 2: Ch 1, sc in each sc across, turn.

Row 3: Ch 1, sc in first sc, [ch 1, sk next sc, sc in next
sc] 13 times, turn. *(14 sc, 13 ch-1 sps)*

Row 4: Ch 1, sc in first sc, sc in next ch-1 sp, [ch 1,
sk next sc, sc in next ch-1 sp] 12 times, sc in next sc,
turn. *(15 sc, 12 ch-1 sps)*

Row 5: Ch 1, sc in first sc, [ch 1, sc in next ch-1 sp] 12
times, ch 1, sc in last sc, turn. *(14 sc, 13 ch-1 sps)*

Rows 6 & 7: Rep rows 4 and 5.

Row 8: Rep row 4, fasten off CC, turn.

Row 9: With size F [G, H] hook, attach MC with sl st in
first st, ch 1, 2 sc in first st, sc in each sc and each ch-
1 sp across to last sc, 2 sc in last sc, turn. *(29 sc)*

Row 10: Ch 1, sc in each st across, turn.

Row 11: Ch 1, sc in each of next 2 sc, [**pc** *(see Special Stitch)* in next sc, sc in each of next 5 sc, **fphdc** *(see Stitch Guide)* in next st 1 row below, sk sc directly behind post st, sc in each of next 5 sc] twice, pc in next sc, sc in each of next 2 sc, turn. *(24 sc, 3 pc, 2 fphdc)*

Row 12: Rep row 10.

Row 13: Ch 1, sc in each of next 2 sc, [pc in next sc, sc in each of next 5 sc, fphdc in next fphdc directly below, sk sc directly behind post st, sc in each of next 5 sc] twice, pc in next sc, sc in each of next 2 sc, turn.

Row 14: Rep row 10.

Row 15: Rep row 13.

Row 16: Rep row 10.

Row 17: Ch 1, sc in each of next 2 sc, [fphdc in top of pc directly below, sc in each of next 5 sc, pc in next sc directly above fphdc, sc in each of next 5 sc] twice, fphdc in top of pc directly below, sc in each of next 2 sc, turn. *(24 sc, 3 fphdc sts, 2 pc)*

Row 18: Rep row 10.

Row 19: Ch 1, sc in each of next 2 sc, [fphdc in next fphdc, sk sc directly behind post st, sc in each of next 5 sc, pc in next sc, sc in each of next 5 sc] twice, sc in each of next 2 sc, turn.

Row 20: Rep row 10.

Row 21: Rep row 19.

Row 22: Rep row 10.

Rows 23–28: Rep rows 11–16.

Row 29: Ch 1, sc in each st across, fasten off.

Back

Rows 1–29: Rep rows 1–29 of Front.

Finishing

Sew Front and Back tog across each side and top edge.

Bottom Trim

Rnd 1 (RS): With size F [G, H] hook, attach MC with sl st in side seam, ch 1, **reverse sc** *(Fig. 1)*

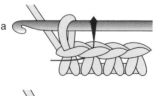

Reverse Single Crochet
Fig. 1

in each st around, join in beg sc, fasten off.

Pompom

With CC, make 2 Pompoms, each 2 inches in diameter. Attach 1 Pompom to each top corner of Hat.

SWEATER

Back Bottom Border

Row 1: Beg at bottom edge, with size F [G, H] hook and CC, ch 46, sc in 2nd ch from hook, sc in each rem ch across, turn. *(45 sc)*

Row 2: Ch 1, sc in each st across, turn.

Row 3: Ch 1, sc in first sc, [ch 1, sk next sc, sc in next sc] 22 times, turn. *(23 sc, 22 ch-1 sps)*

Row 4: Ch 1, sc in first sc, sc in next ch-1 sp, [ch 1, sk next sc, sc in next ch-1 sp] 21 times, sc in next sc, turn. *(24 sc, 21 ch-1 sps)*

Row 5: Ch 1, sc in first sc, [ch 1, sk next sc, sc in next ch-1 sp] 21 times, ch 1, sk next sc, sc in next sc, turn. *(23 sc, 22 ch-1 sps)*

Rows 6 & 7: Rep rows 4 and 5.

Row 8: Rep row 4, fasten off CC, turn.

Back Body

Row 1: Attach MC with sl st in first st, ch 1, sc in each st across, turn. *(45 sc)*

Row 2: Ch 1, sc in each st across, turn.

Row 3: Ch 1, sc in first st, ***pc** *(see Special Stitch)* in next st, sc in each of next 5 sts, **fphdc** *(see Stitch Guide)* in next st 1 row below, sk st directly behind post st**, sc in each of next 5 sts, rep from * across, ending last rep at **, sc in next st, turn. *(37 sc, 4 pc, 4 fphdc)*

Row 4: Rep row 2.

Row 5: Ch 1, sc in first st, *pc in next pc, sc in each of next 5 sc, fphdc around fphdc directly below**, sc in each of next 5 sc, rep from * across, ending last rep at **, sc in next st, turn.

Row 6: Rep row 2.

Row 7: Rep row 5.

Row 8: Rep row 2.

Row 9: Ch 1, 2 sc in first st, *fphdc in top of pc, sc in each of next 5 sts, pc in next st directly above fphdc**, sc in each of next 5 sts, rep from * across, ending last rep at **, 2 sc in next st, turn. *(39 sc, 4 fphdc, 4 pc)*

Row 10: Rep row 2.

Row 11: Ch 1, 2 sc in first st, sc in next st, *fphdc in next fphdc, sk sc directly behind post st, sc in each of next 5 sts, pc in next st**, sc in each of next 5 sts, rep from * across, ending last rep at **, sc in next st, 2 sc in last st, turn. *(41 sc, 4 fphdc, 4 pc)*

Row 12: Rep row 2.

Row 13: Inc 1 st at beg and end of row, rep row 11. *(43 sc, 4 fphdc, 4 pc)*

Row 14: Rep row 2.

Rows 15–38: Continue in pattern of rows 3–14, inc 1 st at beg and end of each RS row *(odd-numbered row)* maintaining post st and pc pat between sc sts. *(75 sts)*

Rows 39–42: Continue in pat of rows 3–6, inc 1 st at beg and end of each RS row *(odd-numbered row)* maintaining post st and pc pat between sc sts. Back Body will measures approximately 8¾ [9¾, 10¾] inches. *(67 sc, 6 pc, 6 fphdc)*

Work even in pat until Back Body measures 10 [11½, 13] inches, ending with a WS row, turn.

Work in pat across 32 sts of right shoulder, fasten off, sk next 15 sts, attach MC with sl st in next st, ch 1, work in pat across rem 32 sts for left shoulder, turn.

Left Front

Maintaining pat, work on 32 sts for 3 rows, then inc 1 st at neckline edge every RS row. *(35 sts)* Continue in pat until armhole edge measures 6 [7, 8] inches. Working across Left Front, **sc dec** *(see Stitch Guide)* a st at armhole edge every RS row 14 times. *(21 sts)* Maintaining pat on 21 sts on Left Front until length

measures the same as Back Body, ending with a RS row, fasten off.

Front Bottom Border

Row 1: Attach CC in first sc with sl st, ch 1, sc in same st as beg ch-1, [ch 1, sk next st, sc in next st] across, turn. *(11 sc, 10 ch-1 sps)*

Row 2: Ch 1, sc in first sc, sc in next ch-1 sp, [sk next sc, ch 1, sc in next ch-1 sp] across, sc in last sc, turn. *(12 sc, 9 ch-1 sps)*

Row 3: Ch 1, sc in first sc, [ch 1, sk next sc, sc in next ch-1 sp] across, ending with, ch 1, sk next sc, sc in last sc, turn. *(11 sc, 10 ch-1 sps)*

Rows 4 & 5: Rep rows 2 and 3.

Row 6: Rep row 2.

Row 7: Ch 1, sc in each sc and each ch-1 sp across, turn.

Right Front

With WS facing, attach MC in first st of right shoulder at neck edge, ch 1, sc in each st across, turn. *(32 sc)* Rep the same as Left Front, inc and dec sts as indicated.

Sweater Cuff

Make 2.

Row 1 (RS): With size F [G, H] hook, attach CC with a sl st at cuff edge, ch 1, work 29 sc evenly spaced across, turn. *(29 sc)*

Row 2: Ch 1, sc in each sc across, turn.

Row 3: Ch 1, sc in first sc, [ch 1, sk next sc, sc in next sc] across, turn.

Row 4: Ch 1, sc in first sc, sc in next ch-1 sp, [sk next sc, ch 1, sc in next ch-1 sp] across, sc in last sc, turn.

Row 5: Ch 1, sc in first sc, [ch 1, sk next sc, sc in next ch-1 sp] across, ending with ch 1, sk next sc, sc in last sc, turn.

Rows 6–11: [Rep rows 4 and 5 alternately] 3 times. At the end of row 11, **do not turn.**

Row 12: Ch 1, **reverse sc** *(see Fig. 1 on page 140)* in each sc across, leaving a 24-inch length of yarn, fasten off.

Sew underarm and side seam.

CONTINUED ON PAGE 140

Bear Blanket Buddy

DESIGN BY DARLA SIMS

INTERMEDIATE

Finished Size

38 x 38 inches

Gauge

Size G hook: 3 V-sts = 3 inches
Size H hook: [Shell, ch 3] twice = 4 inches; rows 1–5 = 2½ inches

Pattern Notes

Weave in loose ends as work progresses.
Join rounds with a slip stitch unless otherwise stated.
All rows are worked with right side facing.

Materials

4 MEDIUM

- Red Heart Baby Econo medium (worsted) weight yarn (6 oz/460 yds/170g per skein):
  2 skeins #0001 white *(A)*
  1 skein each #1046 carousel print *(B)* and #1680 pastel green *(C)*
- Sizes G/6/4mm and H/8/5mm crochet hooks or sizes needed to obtain gauge
- Tapestry needle
- 12-inch tall teddy bear
- 1¼-inch-wide pink ribbon: 1½ yds

Do not turn at end of rows—fasten off at the end of each row.

Special Stitches

Shell: 5 dc in st indicated.
V-stitch (V-st): (Dc, ch 1, dc) in indicated st.

BLANKET

Row 1 (RS): With size H hook and B, ch 112, 2 dc in 4th ch from hook *(first 3 sk chs count as first dc)*, *sk next 5 chs, **shell** *(see Special Stitches)* in next ch, ch 3, rep from * 18 times, sk next 5 chs, 3 dc in last ch, fasten off. *(18 shells)*

Row 2: Attach A with sc in top of beg ch-3, *ch 2, dc in 2nd sk ch of sk ch-5 sp below, ch 1, dc in 4th sk ch of same ch-5 sp, ch 2, sc in 3rd dc of next shell, rep from * 18 times, ch 2, sc in top of last dc, fasten off.

Row 3: Attach C with sc in first sc of row 2, ch 3, *shell in next ch-1 sp, ch 3, rep from * 18 times, ch 3, shell in next ch-1 sp, ch 3, sc in last dc, fasten off.

Row 4: Attach A in top of first sc of previous row, ch 3 *(counts as first dc)*, dc in next ch-1 sp, *ch 2, sc in 3rd dc of next shell, ch 2, sc over both ch lengths below to right of sc between ch lengths below, ch 1, sc over both ch lengths below to left of same sc, rep from * 18 times, ch 2, sc in 3rd dc of last shell, ch 1, dc in next ch-1 sp, dc in last st, fasten off.

Row 5: Attach B in sp between last dc and ending

CONTINUED ON PAGE 140

Flower Patch Afghan

DESIGN BY ELAINE BARTLETT

INTERMEDIATE

Finished Size

31½ x 36½ inches

Materials

3 LIGHT

- TLC Baby light (light worsted) weight yarn (Solids: 6 oz/490 yds/170g, Multis: 5 oz/360 yds/141g per skein):

  5 skeins #7624 lime

  2 skeins #7959 giggle multi

- Size G/6/4mm crochet hook or size needed to obtain gauge
- Tapestry needle
- Stitch markers

Gauge

Motif = 3¾ inches; 7 dc = 1½ inches; rnds 1 & 2 = 2 inches

Pattern Notes

Weave in loose ends as work progresses.

Join rounds with a slip stitch unless otherwise stated.

Chain-3 at beginning of double crochet row or round counts as first double crochet unless otherwise stated.

Special Stitches

3-double crochet cluster (3-dc cl): [Yo, insert hook in indicated st, yo, draw up a lp, yo, draw through 2 lps on hook] 3 times in same st, yo, draw through all 4 lps on hook.

Beginning 3-double crochet cluster (beg 3-dc cl): Ch 2 *(counts as first dc of cluster)*, [yo hook, insert hook in indicated st, yo, draw up a lp, yo, draw through 2 lps on hook] twice in same st as beg ch-2, yo, draw through all 3 lps on hook.

MOTIF

Make 72.

Rnd 1 (RS): With giggle multi, ch 4, join in first ch to form a ring, ch 1, 12 sc in ring, join in beg sc. *(12 sc)*

Rnd 2: Beg 3-dc cl *(see Special Stitches)* in same sc as joining, ch 1, [**3-dc cl** *(see Special Stitches)* in next sc, ch 1] around, join in top of beg 3-dc cl, fasten off. *(12 cls, 12 ch-1 sps)*

Rnd 3: Attach lime with sc, ch 1 *(counts as first hdc)* in any ch-1 sp between cls, *(2 dc, ch 2, 2 dc) in next ch-1 sp *(for corner)*, hdc in next ch-1 sp, ch 2**, hdc in next ch-1 sp, rep from * around, ending last rep at **, join in first ch-1. *(16 dc, 8 hdc, 8 ch-2 sps)*

Rnd 4: Sl st in each st across to next corner ch-2 sp, ch 3 *(counts as first dc)*, (2 dc, ch 2, 3 dc) in same corner ch-2 sp, *ch 1, 3 dc in next ch-2 sp, ch 1**, (3 dc, ch 2, 3 dc) in next corner ch-2 sp, rep from * around, ending last rep at **, join in 3rd ch of beg ch-3. *(36 dc, 8 ch-1 sps, 4 ch-2 sps)*

Rnd 5: Ch 3, dc in each of next 2 dc, *(2 dc, ch 2,

CONTINUED ON PAGE 141

Car Seat Blankie

DESIGN BY MARY ANN SIPES

INTERMEDIATE

Finished Size

25 x 36 inches

Gauge

5 sc = 3 inches; sc and dc rows = 2 inches

Pattern Notes

Weave in loose ends as work progresses.

Join rounds with a slip stitch unless otherwise stated.

BLANKIE

Row 1 (RS): Ch 42, sc in 2nd ch from hook, sc in each rem ch across, turn. *(41 sc)*

Row 2: Ch 3 *(counts as first dc)*, [sk next sc, 3 dc in next sc, sk next sc, dc in next sc] 10 times, turn. *(10 groups 3-dc, 11 dc)*

Materials

- Red Heart Baby Clouds super bulky (super chunky) weight yarn (6 oz/140 yds/170g per skein):
  4 skeins #9549 orchid
- Size M/13/9mm crochet hook or size needed to obtain gauge
- Yarn needle

Row 3: Ch 1, sc in each st across, turn. *(41 sc)*

Row 4: Ch 1, sc in each of next 2 sc, tr in next sc, [sc in each of next 3 sc, tr in next sc] 9 times, sc in each of last 2 sc, turn.

Note: As work progresses, push tr sts to right side.

Row 5: Rep row 3.

Rows 6–49: [Rep rows 2–5 consecutively] 11 times.

Rows 50 & 51: Rep rows 2 and 3. At the end of row 51, fasten off.

Border

Rnd 1 (RS): Attach yarn with sl st in lower right corner, ch 1, 3 sc in same corner st, working across end of rows, sc in each sc row and 2 sc in each dc row, 3 sc in corner st, sc in each st to next corner, 3 sc in corner st, sc in each sc row and 2 sc in each dc row, 3 sc in corner st, working across opposite side of foundation ch, sc in each ch across, join in beg sc, turn.

Rnd 2: Ch 1, sc in same st as beg ch-1, *[tr in next sc, sc in next sc] across to center corner sc, (tr, sc, tr) in center corner sc, rep from * around, join in beg sc, turn.

Rnd 3: Ch 1, sc in each st around, working 3 sc in each center corner st, join in beg sc, fasten off. ●

Welcome Baby

DESIGNS BY MARIA NAGY

INTERMEDIATE

Finished Sizes
Afghan: 29 x 29 inches
Hat: 6–9 months

Finished Garment Measurement
Hat: 8 inches in diameter

Materials
- Bernat Baby Coordinates light (light worsted) weight yarn (6 oz/431 yds/160g per skein):

  3 LIGHT

    2 skeins #01008 baby pink
    1 skein #01000 white
- Sizes F/5/3.75mm and G/6/4mm crochet hooks or sizes needed to obtain gauge
- Tapestry needle
- ⅝-inch-wide white ribbon: 38 inches

Gauge
Afghan: rnds 1–3 = 3½ inches; Motif = 5 inches square
Hat: 3 dc = 1 inch; 2 dc rnds = 1 inch

Pattern Notes
Weave in loose ends as work progresses.
Join rounds with a slip stitch unless otherwise stated.

Special Stitch
Puff stitch (puff st): Yo, insert hook in indicated st, yo, draw up a 1-inch lp, [yo, insert hook in same st, yo, draw up a 1-inch lp] twice, yo, draw through all 7 lps on hook, ch 1 to lock.

AFGHAN

Motif
Make 25.
Rnd 1: With size F hook and baby pink, ch 5, sl st in first ch to form a ring, ch 1, 12 sc in ring, join in beg sc. *(12 sc)*
Rnd 2: Ch 1, 2 sc in each sc around, join in beg sc, fasten off. *(24 sc)*
Rnd 3: Working over rnd 2 and into sc sts of rnd 1, attach white with sl st in first st, ch 1, **puff st** *(see Special Stitch)* in same st as beg ch-1, ch 3, [puff st in next sc of rnd 1, ch 3] around, join in beg st, fasten off. *(12 puff sts)*
Rnd 4: Attach baby pink with a sl st in any ch-3 sp, ch 1, [(2 sc, ch 3, 2 sc) in same ch-3 sp for corner, 2 sc in each of next 2 ch-3 sps] around, join in beg sc, fasten off. *(32 sc, 4 corner ch-3 sps)*
Rnd 5: Attach white in any corner ch-3 sp with a sc, *ch 4 *(counts as tr)*, tr in same ch-3 sp, [sk next st, sc in next st, ch 4, tr in same st] 4 times**, sc in next corner ch-3 sp, rep from * around, ending last rep at **, join in beg sc, fasten off. *(20 each ch-4 sps, tr and sc)*
Rnd 6: Attach baby pink with sl st around vertical post of last tr of previous rnd, ch 4 *(counts as first tr)*, 2 tr around vertical post of same tr, *ch 3, 3 tr around vertical post of next tr, [ch 1, 2 tr around vertical post of next tr] 3 times, ch 1**, 3 tr around vertical post of next tr, rep from * around, ending last rep at **, join in top of beg ch-4, fasten off. *(48 tr, 16 ch-1 sps, 4 ch-3 sps)*

Assembly

With tapestry needle and length of baby pink yarn, working in **back lps** (see Stitch Guide) of each Motif, whipstitch Motifs tog in 5 rows of 5 Motifs. Sew 5 rows of Motifs tog.

Border

Rnd 1: With size F hook, attach baby pink in center corner ch-5 sp with a sc, *ch 5, sc in next tr, [ch 5, sk next 2 tr, sc in next ch-1 sp] 4 times, ch 5, sk next 2 tr, sc in next tr, ch 5, sc in junction of joining, rep from * across to next corner ch-3 sp**, instead of working sc in junction of joining, sc in next corner ch-3 sp, rep from * around, ending last rep at **, ch 5, join in beg sc at first corner, fasten off.

Rnd 2: Attach white with sl st in first sc of previous rnd, ch 1, puff st in same st as beg ch-1, ch 3, [puff st in next sc, ch 3] around, join in beg puff st.

Rnd 3: Ch 1, sc in top of puff st, ch 4, tr in same sc, [sc in top of next puff st, ch 4, tr in same puff st] around, join in beg sc, fasten off.

Rnd 4: Working behind sts of rnd 3, attach baby pink with sl st in any ch-3 sp of rnd 2, ch 4, 2 tr in same ch-3 sp as beg ch-4, ch 3, [3 tr in next ch-3 sp of rnd 2, ch 3] around, join in 4th ch of beg ch-4.

Rnd 5: Sl st in 3rd tr of 3-tr group, ch 1, sc in same tr as beg ch-1, ch 5, **dtr** (see Stitch Guide) in same tr, [sk next ch-3 sp and next 2 tr, sc in next tr, ch 5, dtr in same tr] around, ending with join in beg sc, fasten off.

HAI

Rnds 1–3: With size G hook, rep rnds 1–3 of Motif for Afghan. (12 puff sts)

Rnd 4: Attach baby pink with sl st in any ch-3 sp, ch 3 (counts as first dc), 2 dc in same ch-3 sp, ch 1, [3 dc in next ch-3 sp, ch 1] around, join in 3rd ch of beg ch-3. (36 dc)

Rnd 5: Ch 3, dc in each of next 2 dc, dc in next ch-1 sp, [dc in each of next 3 dc, dc in next ch-1 sp] around, join in 3rd ch of beg ch-4. (48 dc)

Rnds 6–11: Ch 3, dc in each dc around, join in 3rd ch of beg ch-3.

Rnd 12: Ch 1, sc in same st as beg ch-1, ch 3, sk 2 dc, [sc in next dc, ch 3, sk next 2 dc] around, join in beg sc.

Rnd 13: Sl st into ch-3 sp, ch 5 (counts as first dtr), 3 dtr in same ch-3 sp, sk next sc, [4 dtr in next ch-3 sp, sk next sc] around, join in 5th ch of beg ch-5.

Rnd 14: Ch 1, (sc, ch 4, tr) in same dtr, sk next 3 dtr, [(sc, ch 4, tr) in next dtr, sk next 3 dtr] around, join in beg sc.

Rnd 15: Sl st into ch-4 sp, ch 1, (sc, ch 4, tr) in same ch-4 sp, [(sc, ch 4, tr) in next ch-4 sp] around, join in beg sc, fasten off.

Rnd 16: With RS facing working around the posts of sc sts of rnd 12, attach white with sl st, ch 1, sc around same sc post as beg ch-1, ch 4, tr around same sc as previous sc, sk next ch-3 sp, [(sc, ch 4, tr) around the post of next sc of rnd 12, sk next ch-3 sp] around, join in beg sc, fasten off.

Ribbon Weave

Weave ribbon through dtr sts of rnd 13, weaving over 4 sts, under 4 sts around, tie ends in a bow. ●

Pretty in Pink Sweater

DESIGN BY CATHERINE COSTA

EASY

Finished Size

Instructions given for child's
size 6; changes for sizes 12,
18 months are in [ ].

Finished Garment Measurement

Chest: 19 [20, 21½] inches

Materials

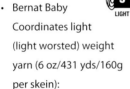

- Bernat Baby
  Coordinates light
  (light worsted) weight
  yarn (6 oz/431 yds/160g
  per skein):
    2 skeins #01008 baby
      pink
    30 yds #01005 sky
- Size J/10/6mm crochet
  hook or size needed to
  obtain gauge
- Tapestry needle
- Stitch markers
- 15mm buttons: 3 matching

Gauge

With 2 strands of yarn held tog: 5 sc = 2 inches;
5 rows = 1½ inches

Pattern Notes

Weave in loose ends as work progresses.
Join rounds with a slip stitch unless otherwise stated.

SWEATER

Back

Row 1: Starting at bottom edge with 2 strands of
baby pink held tog, ch 26 [29, 31] sc in 2nd ch from
hook, sc in each rem ch across, turn. *(25 [28, 30] sc)*
Row 2: Ch 1, sc in each sc across, turn.
Rep row 2 until Back measures 6½ [7, 7½] inches from
beg. For **underarm**, place st marker at each edge.
Rep row 2 until Back measures 9½ [10¾, 11½] inches
from beg.

Left Shoulder Shaping
Row 1: Ch 1, sc in each of next 9 [10, 11] sc, turn.
Row 2: Ch 1, sc in each sc across, turn.
Rep row 2 until Left Shoulder measures 1½ inches,
fasten off.

Right Shoulder Shaping
Row 1: With finished Left Shoulder to the right, sk
next 7 [8, 8] sc of last row of Back, attach 2 strands of
baby pink in next sc, ch 1, sc in same sc as beg ch-1,
sc in each of next 8 [9, 10] sc, turn. *(9 [10, 11] sc)*
Row 2: Ch 1, sc in each sc across, turn.
Rep row 2 until Right Shoulder measures 1½ inches,
fasten off.

Front

Row 1: Starting at bottom edge with 2 strands of
baby pink, ch 26 [29, 31] sc in 2nd ch from hook, sc
in each rem ch across, turn. *(25 [28, 30] sc)*
Row 2: Ch 1, sc in each sc across, turn.
Rep row 2 until Front from beg measures 6½ [7, 7½]
inches. For underarm, place st marker at each edge.

Rep row 2 until Front from beg measures 7½ [8½, 9] inches.

Left Neck & Shoulder Shaping
Row 1: Ch 1, sc in each of next 9 [10, 11] sc, turn.
Row 2: Ch 1, sc in each sc across, turn.
Rep row 2 until Left Neck and Shoulder Shaping measures 3½ [3¾, 4] inches, then work one extra row as buttonhole row as follows.
Buttonhole row: Ch 1, sc in 1 [2, 2] sc, ch 1, sk next sc, [sc in each of next 2 sc, ch 1, sk next sc] twice, sc in next 1 [1, 2] sc st(s), turn. *(3 buttonholes)*
Next row: Ch 1, sc in each st across, fasten off.

Right Shoulder Shaping
Row 1: With finished Left Shoulder to the right, sk next 7 [8, 8] sc of last row of Front, attach 2 strands of baby pink in next sc, ch 1, sc in same sc as beg ch-1, sc in each of next 8 [9, 10] sc, turn. *(9 [10, 11] sc)*
Row 2: Ch 1, sc in each sc across, turn.
Rep row 2 until Right Shoulder measures 3½ [3¾, 4] inches, fasten off.

Sleeve
Make 2.
Row 1: Starting at wrist area of Sleeve, with 2 strands of baby pink, ch 18 [19, 21], sc in 2nd ch from hook, sc in each rem ch across, turn. *(17 [18, 20] sc)*
Row 2: Ch 1, sc in each sc across, turn.
Row 3: Ch 1, 2 sc in first sc, sc in each rem sc across, turn.
Next rows: [Rep rows 2 and 3 alternately] 4 [7, 7] times. *(22 [26, 28] sc)*
Rep row 2 until total length of Sleeve is 6½ [7¼, 8] inches, fasten off.

Finishing
With RS facing, whipstitch right shoulder closed.

Position buttons on Back Left Shoulder and sew in place opposite buttonholes. Button shoulder buttons and tack ends of overlapped rows of button and buttonhole placket.
Sew sleeves into armhole openings, sew sleeve and side seams.

Neckline Trim
Attach 2 strands baby pink at right shoulder seam, ch 1, sc evenly spaced around Neckline opening, join in beg sc, fasten off.

Top Stitching
Working between rows 1 and 2 of Sweater bottom edge, holding 2 strands of sky tog on WS of Sweater at seam and leaving a 2-inch length, beg on RS, insert hook RS to WS, draw up a lp of yarn and draw through from WS to RS, [insert hook RS to WS in next st to the right, yo, draw up a lp from WS to RS draw through lp on hook] around bottom edge of Sweater, ending with last st in same st as beg st, leaving a 2-inch length, fasten off. With all ends on WS, knot ends tog, weave ends in on underside of ch, fasten off rem pieces.
Rep Top Stitching between rows 1 and 2 of each Sleeve. ●

Pastel Shells Afghan

DESIGN BY KATHERINE ENG

EASY

Finished Size
29 x 40 inches

Materials

- Bernat Baby Coordinates light (light worsted) weight yarn (6 oz/431 yds/160g per skein):
    1 skein each #01009 soft blue, #01010 soft mauve, #01008 baby pink and #01011 lemon custard
- Size I/9/5.5mm crochet hook or size needed to obtain gauge
- Tapestry needle

Gauge
3 shells and 4 sc = 4 inches; rows 1–4 = 2½ inches

Pattern Notes
Weave in loose ends as work progresses.
Join rounds with a slip stitch unless otherwise stated.

Special Stitches
Small shell: 3 dc in indicated st.
Large shell: 5 dc in indicated st.

AFGHAN
Row 1 (RS): With soft blue, ch 134, sc in 2nd ch from hook, [sk next ch, **small shell** *(see Special Stitches)* in next ch, sk next ch, sc in next ch] across, turn. *(33 shells)*

Row 2: Ch 3 *(counts as first dc)*, dc in same st as beg ch-3, [sc in center dc of next small shell, small shell in next sc] across, ending with 2 dc in last sc, turn.

Row 3: Ch 1, sc in first sc, [small shell in next sc, sc in center dc of next small shell] across, ending with sc in last dc, turn.

Row 4: Rep row 2, fasten off.

Row 5: Attach soft mauve with sl st in first dc, rep row 3.

Row 6: Rep row 2, fasten off.

Row 7: Attach lemon custard with sl st in first dc, rep row 3.

Row 8: Rep row 2, fasten off.

Row 9: Attach baby pink with sl st in first dc, rep row 3.

Row 10: Rep row 2, fasten off.

Row 11: Attach soft blue with sl st in first dc, rep row 3.

Rows 12 & 13: Rep rows 2 and 3.

Row 14: Rep row 2, fasten off.

Rows 15–64: [Rep rows 5–14 consecutively] 5 times. At the end of row 64, **do not fasten off**, turn.

Row 65: Ch 1, sc in each dc and dc in each sc across, fasten off.

Border
Rnd 1: Attach lemon custard with sl st in first sc of row 65, ch 1, (sc, ch 2, sc) in same sc as beg ch-1,

CONTINUED ON PAGE 141

Toddler's Tote

DESIGN BY RHONDA DODDS

EASY

Finished Size

18 inches wide x 9 inches deep x 11 inches high, excluding Handle

Materials

- Red Heart Super Saver medium (worsted) weight yarn (7 oz/364 yds/198g per skein):

  7 skeins #356 amethyst

  1 skein each #368 paddy green, #324 bright yellow, #254 pumpkin and #319 cherry red
- Sizes H/8/5mm and K/10½/6.5mm crochet hooks or sizes needed to obtain gauge
- Tapestry needle
- Stitch markers
- Multicolored ¾-inch buttons: 2
- Red 1-inch buttons: 2

Gauge

Size H hook: 3 sc = 1 inch
Size K hook & 3 strands held tog: 5 sc = 2 inches; 4 rows = 1½ inches

Pattern Notes

Weave in loose ends as work progresses.
Use 3 strands of yarn held together unless otherwise stated.

TOTE

Ends & Base

Row 1 (RS): Beg at top edge of end, with size K hook and 3 strands amethyst held tog, ch 20, sc in 2nd ch from hook, sc in each rem ch across, turn. *(19 sc)*
Rows 2–96: Ch 1, sc in each sc across, turn.

Handle

Row 97: Sl st in each of next 8 sc, ch 1, sc in same sc as last sl st, sc in each of next 4 sc, leaving rem 7 sts unworked, turn. *(5 sc)*
Rows 98–164: Ch 1, sc in each of next 5 sc, turn. At the end of row 164, leaving a 12-inch length of yarn, fasten off.

Front

Row 1: With WS facing and size K hook, attach 3 strands amethyst in 28th row of Base with sl st, ch 1, sc in same row as beg ch-1, sc in each of next 39 rows, turn. *(40 sc)*
Rows 2–28: Ch 1, sc in each sc across, turn. At the end of row 28, fasten off.

Back & Closure Flap

Row 1: With WS facing and size K hook, attach 3 strands amethyst on opposite side of Base in 67th row with sl st, ch 1, sc in same row as beg ch-1, sc in each of next 39 rows, turn. *(40 sc)*
Rows 2–48: Rep row 2 of Front.
Row 49 (WS): Ch 1, **fpsc** *(see Stitch Guide)* in each sc across, turn.

Rows 50–55: Ch 1, sc in each sc across, turn.

Row 56: Ch 1, sc in each of next 6 sc, ch 2, sk next 2 sts (buttonhole), sc in each of next 24 sc, ch 2, sk next 2 sc (buttonhole), sc in each of next 6 sc, turn.

Row 57: Ch 1, sc in each of next 6 sc, sc in each of next 2 chs, sc in each of next 24 sc, sc in each of next 2 chs, sc in each of next 6 sc, turn. (40 sc)

Rows 58–60: Ch 1, sc in each sc across, turn. At the end of row 60, fasten off.

Assembly

With rem length from Handle, sew last row of Handle centered on opposite side of foundation ch of End. With size K hook, matching rows and working through both thicknesses with right end of Tote facing (Front to left, Back to right), working on the bottom right edge, attach 3 strands of bright

yellow with sl st, ch 1, sc evenly spaced up right edge, around outer edge of Closure Flap and down left edge of left end of Tote, fasten off.

With size K hook, attach 3 strands with a sl st in right

Side Pocket

Make 1 each paddy green, bright yellow, cherry red and pumpkin.

Row 1 (RS): With size K hook and 3 strands of yarn, ch 13, sc in 2nd ch from hook, sc in each rem ch across, turn. *(12 sc)*

Rows 2–15: Ch 1, sc in each sc across, turn.

Rnd 16: Now working in rnds around edge of Pocket, ch 1, [3 sc in corner st, sc evenly spaced across edge] around, join in beg sc, leaving a 24-inch length of yarn, fasten off.

Sew a Side Pocket to outside and inside of each End of Tote.

Large Pocket

Make 1 each cherry red and pumpkin.

Row 1 (RS): Ch 31, sc in 2nd ch from hook, sc in each rem ch across, turn. *(30 sc)*

Rows 2–20: Ch 1, sc in each sc across, turn.

Rnd 21: Rep rnd 16 of Side Pocket, leaving a 36-inch length of yarn, fasten off.

Sew cherry red Large Pocket to center Back outside Tote.

Sew pumpkin Large Pocket to center Front inside Tote.

Button Strap

Make 1 each paddy green and pumpkin.

Row 1 (RS): With size H hook and 1 strand yarn, ch 21, sc in 2nd ch from hook, sc in each rem ch across, turn. *(20 sc)*

Row 2: Ch 1, sc in each of next 16 sc, ch 1, sk next sc *(buttonhole)*, sc in each of next 3 sc, turn.

Row 3: Ch 1, sc in each of next 3 sc, sc in next ch-1 sp, sc in each of next 16 sc, leaving an 8-inch length of yarn, fasten off.

Sew multicolored button centered to end opposite buttonhole; with button facing, sew same end at top edge next to Side Pocket. Fold buttonhole end upward and button. Rep on opposite end with rem Button Strap. ●

end in side edge of row 96, ch 1, sc in same sc as beg ch-1, sc in each of next 6 sc, working on Handle, sc in each row across, sc in opposite side of foundation ch of first End, sc in each of next 7 sts, fasten off. With size K hook, attach 3 strands of bright yellow in bottom left edge *(Front to right, Back to left)* and working through both thicknesses, sc evenly spaced up side edge, working in opposite side of foundation ch of end, sc in each of next 7 chs, sc in each row across opposite side of Handle, across rem 7 sts of row 96 and through both thicknesses of right end and front to bottom edge, fasten off.

Sew red buttons to Tote Front opposite buttonholes.

Pink Poodle

DESIGN BY SHEILA LESLIE

EASY

Finished Size

11 inches tall

Materials

- Bernat Super Value medium (worsted) weight yarn (7 oz/382 yds/197g per skein): **4 MEDIUM**
    1 skein #07438 baby pink
    2 yds #07421 black
- Bernat Softee Baby light (light worsted) weight yarn (5 oz/455 yds/140g per ball): **3 LIGHT**
    1 ball #30301 baby pink marl
- Bernat Eye Lash super bulky (super chunky) weight yarn (1¾ oz/77 yds/50g per skein): **6 SUPER BULKY**
    1 skein #35415 kiss
- Sizes I/9/5.5mm and J/10/6mm crochet hooks or sizes needed to obtain gauge
- Yarn needle
- Fiberfill
- Black 12mm shank buttons: 2
- ⅜-inch-wide pink ribbon: 57 inches
- Stitch marker

Gauge

Size J hook and 1 strand each light pink and light pink marl held tog: 3 sc = 1 inch; 3 sc rnds = 1 inch

Pattern Notes

Weave in loose ends as work progresses.

Do not join rounds unless otherwise stated.

Use a stitch marker to mark rounds.

For children under 3 years old, omit buttons and embroider eyes with black yarn.

POODLE

Head

Rnd 1: Starting at top of Head with size J hook and 1 strand baby pink and kiss held tog, ch 2, 6 sc in 2nd ch from hook, **do not join**, place st marker *(see Pattern Notes)*. *(6 sc)*

Rnd 2: 2 sc in each sc around. *(12 sc)*

Rnd 3: [Sc in next sc, 2 sc in next sc] around. *(18 sc)*

Rnd 4: [Sc in each of next 2 sc, 2 sc in next sc] around. *(24 sc)*

Rnd 5: [Sc in each of next 3 sc, 2 sc in next sc] around. *(30 sc)*

Rnds 6–8: Sc in each sc around. At the end of rnd 8,

sl st in next sc, fasten off, turn piece so that WS is facing outward.

Rnd 9: With size I hook, attach baby pink and baby pink marl with sc in sl st of previous rnd, sc in each rem sc around. *(30 sc)*

Rnds 10–15: Sc in each sc around.

Rnd 16: [Sc in each of next 3 sts, **sc dec** *(see Stitch Guide)* in next 2 sts] around, stuff Head with fiberfill. *(24 sc)*

Rnd 17: [Sc in next st, sc dec in next 2 sts] around. *(16 sc)*

Rnds 18 & 19: [Sc dec in next 2 sts] around. *(4 sc at end of last rnd)*

At the end of rnd 19, sl st in next st, leaving 12-inch length of yarn, fasten off.

Snout

Rnd 1: With size I hook and 1 strand baby pink and baby pink marl held tog, ch 2, 6 sc in 2nd ch from hook. *(6 sc)*

Rnd 2: Sc in each st around.

Rnd 3: [Sc in next st, 2 sc in next st] around. *(9 sc)*

Rnds 4 & 5: [Sc in each of next 2 sts, 2 sc in next st] around. *(16 sc)*

Rnd 6: [2 sc in next st, sc in each of next 3 sts] around. *(20 sc)*

Rnd 7: [Sc in each of next 4 sts, 2 sc in next st] around. *(24 sc)*

Rnd 8: Sc in each st around, sl st in next st, leaving 8-inch length of yarn, fasten off. Stuff Snout with fiberfill and sew over rnds 11–17 of Head. With ¾ inch between eyes, sew buttons to rnd 10 above Snout. With length of black, using satin stitch, embroider Nose and using straight stitch, embroider Mouth centered directly below Nose.

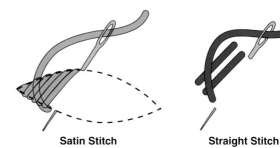

Satin Stitch   Straight Stitch

Ear
Make 2.

Row 1: With size J hook and 1 strand baby pink and kiss held tog, ch 11, sc in 2nd ch from hook, sc in each of next 2 chs, hdc in each of next 6 chs, 5 dc in last ch; working on opposite side of foundation ch, hdc in each of next 6 chs, sc in each of next 3 chs, turn. *(23 sts)*

Row 2: Ch 1, sc in each of next 11 sts, 3 sc in next st, sc in each of next 11 sts, turn. *(25 sc)*

Row 3: Ch 1, sl st in each of next 2 sts, sc in each of next 9 sts, 2 sc in next st, sc in next st, 2 sc in next st, sc in each of next 9 sts, sl st in next 2 sts, leaving 8-inch length of yarn, fasten off.

Sew an Ear to each side of Head over Rnd 7.

Body

Rnds 1–4: Rep rnds 1–4 of Head. *(24 sc)*

Rnd 5: [2 sc in next st, sc in each of next 3 sts] around. *(30 sc)*

Rnds 6 & 7: Sc in each st around.

Rnd 8: [Sc in each of next 4 sts, 2 sc in next st] around. *(36 sc)*

Rnds 9–21: Sc in each st around. At the end of rnd 21, stuff Body with fiberfill, continue stuffing as work progresses.

Rnd 22: [Sc in each of next 4 sts, sc dec in next 2 sts] around. *(30 sc)*

Rnd 23: [Sc in each of next 3 sts, sc dec in next 2 sts] around. *(24 sc)*

Rnd 24: [Sc in each of next 2 sts, sc dec in next 2 sts] around. *(18 sc)*

Rnd 25: [Sc in next st, sc dec in next 2 sts] around. *(12 sc)*

Rnd 26: [Sc dec in next 2 sts] around, sl st in next st, leaving 8-inch length of yarn, fasten off, sew opening closed. *(6 sc)*

Sew Head to rnds 4–9 of Body.

Leg

Make 4.

Rnd 1: With size I hook and 1 strand baby pink and baby pink marl held tog, ch 2, 6 sc in 2nd ch from hook. *(6 sc)*

Rnd 2: 2 sc in each sc around.

Rnd 3: [Sc in next st, 2 sc in next st] around. *(18 sc)*

Rnds 4 & 5: Sc in each st around. At the end of rnd 5, sl st in next st, fasten off, turn piece inside out so that WS is temporarily on the outside.

Rnd 6: With size J hook and 1 strand baby pink and kiss held tog, attach with sc in last sl st of previous rnd, sc in each rem st around. *(18 sc)*

Rnds 7 & 8: Sc in each st around. At the end of rnd 8, sl st in next st, fasten off. Turn inside out again so that the fuzzier WS will be on the outside.

Rnd 9: With size I hook and 1 strand baby pink and baby pink marl held tog, attach with sc in last sl st of previous rnd, sc in each of next 6 sts, sc dec in next 2 sts, sc in each of next 7 sts, sc dec in next 2 sts. *(16 sc)*

Rnds 10–14: Sc in each st around. At the end of rnd 14, sl st in next st, leaving a 12-inch length, fasten off. Stuff Legs with fiberfill and sew to underside of Body.

Tail

Rnd 1: With size J hook and 1 strand baby pink and kiss held tog, ch 2, 7 sc in 2nd ch from hook. *(7 sc)*

Rnd 2: 2 sc in each st around. *(14 sc)*

Rnds 3 & 4: Sc in each st around.

Rnd 5: [Sc dec in next 2 sts] around, sl st in next st, fasten off, turn Tail inside out. *(7 sc)*

Rnd 6: With size I hook and 1 strand baby pink and baby pink marl held tog, attach with sc in sl st of previous rnd, sc in each rem st around. *(7 sc)*

Rnds 7–10: Sc in each sc around. At the end of rnd 10, sl st in next st, leaving 6-inch length of yarn, fasten off. Stuff Tail with fiberfill and sew to top of back of Body.

Finishing

Cut 2 lengths of ribbon each 17 inches long, tie a length around top edge of Ear, tie ends in a bow. Tie 2nd length around opposite Ear. Tie rem 23 inches in a bow around neckline. ●

Tiny Trendsetter

DESIGN BY LORI LEIGH SANFRATELLO

INTERMEDIATE

Finished Sizes

Instructions given fit child's size 2–3 (small); changes for 4–5 (medium) and 6–7 (large) are in [ ].

Finished Garment Measurements

Bolero chest: 20 inches (small) [21 inches (medium), 22 inches (large)]

Bolero length (not including sleeves): 8 inches (small) [9 inches (medium), 10 inches (large)]

Hat: 5 inches in diameter (small) [5½ inches in diameter (medium), 5½ inches in diameter (large)]

Materials

- Caron Simply Soft medium (worsted) weight yarn (6 oz/330 yds/170g per skein):
  1 skein #9701 white
- Hobby Lobby Yarn Bee Frosting bulky (chunky) weight yarn (4 oz/140 yds/113g per ball):
  1 ball #22 Baltic cream
- Sizes J/10/6mm, K/10½/6.5mm and N/13/9mm crochet hooks or size needed to obtain gauge
- Tapestry needle
- 2 barrette backings
- Fabric glue

Gauge

Size N hook and white: 2 dc = 1 inch; 1 dc row = 1 inch

BOLERO

Body

Row 1: Beg at neckline, with size K hook and Baltic cream, ch 58 [61, 64], sc in 2nd ch from hook and in each ch across, turn. (57 [60, 63] sc)

Rows 2 & 3: Ch 1, sc in each st across, turn. At end of row 3, fasten off.

Row 4: With size N hook, attach white with sl st in first st, ch 3 (counts as first dc), dc in each st across, turn.

Rows 5 & 6 [5 & 6, 5–7]: Ch 3, dc in each st across, turn. At end of last row, fasten off.

Row 7 [7, 8]: With size K hook, attach Baltic cream with sc between first 2 dc, sc in between each dc across, turn. Fasten off. (56 [59, 62] sc)

Row 8 [8, 9]: With size N hook, attach white with sl st in first st, ch 3, dc in next st, [2 dc in next st, dc in each of next 2 sts] across, turn. (74 [78, 82] dc)

Rows 9 & 10 [9–11, 10–12]: Ch 3, dc in each st across, turn. At end of last row, fasten off.

Row 11 [12, 13]: With size K hook, attach Baltic cream with sc between first 2 dc, sc in between each dc across, turn, fasten off. (73 [77, 81] sc)

First Sleeve

Rnd 1: With size N hook, attach white with sl st in 11th [12th, 13th] st, ch 3, 2 dc in next st, [dc in each of next 2 sts, 2 dc in next st] 5 times, leaving rem sts unworked, join with sl st in 3rd ch of beg ch-3. (23 [23, 23] dc)

Rnds 2 & 3 [2 & 3, 2–4]: Ch 3, dc in each st around, join with sl st in 3rd ch of beg ch-3. At end of last rnd, fasten off.

Rnd 4 [4, 5]: With size K hook, attach Baltic cream with sc between first 2 dc, sc in between each dc around, join with sl st in beg sc, fasten off.

Rnd 5 [5, 6]: With size N hook, attach white with sl st in first st, ch 3, dc in each st around, join with sl st in

next ch sp] around, join with sl st in 3rd ch of beg h-4. At end of last row, fasten off.

Rnd 13: With size K hook, attach Baltic cream with sc in any ch-1 sp, sc in each ch-1 sp around, join with sl st in beg sc. Fasten off.

Rnd 14: With size N hook, attach white with sc in first st, sc in same st, 2 sc in each st around, **do not join**. *(48 sc)*

Rnd 15: [Sc in each of next 2 sts, 2 sc in next st] around. *(64 sc)*

Rnd 16: [Sc in each of next 3 sts, 2 sc in next st] around. *(80 sc)*

Rnds 17–19 or to 1 inch shorter than desired brim length: Sc in each st around. At end of last rnd, fasten off.

Rnd 20: With size K hook, attach Baltic cream with sc in any st, sc in each st around, join with sl st in beg sc. Fasten off.

FLOWER

Make 2.

Rnd 1: With size J hook and white, ch 4, sl st in first ch to form ring, [sc in ring, ch 4] 6 times, join with sl st in beg sc.

Rnd 2: Sl st in ch-4 sp, ch 1, (sc, ch 1, {dc, ch 1} 4 times, sc, ch 1) in same ch sp and in each ch sp around, join with sl st in sc on rnd 1 between last and first petal.

Rnd 3: Working in front of petals, [ch 3, sl st in sc on rnd 1 between petals] around, ch 3, join with sl st in joining sl st on last rnd.

Rnd 4: Ch 1, (sc, ch 1, {dc, ch 1} 3 times, sc, ch 1) in each ch-3 sp around, join with sl st in sc on rnd 3 between petals.

Rnd 5: Working around sc on rnd 1, attach Baltic cream with sl st around any sc, ch 2, [sl st around next sc, ch 2] around, join with sl st in beg sl st.

Rnd 6: Ch 1, (sc, 2 dc, sc) in each ch-1 sp around, join with sl st in beg sc, fasten off.

Glue 1 barrette to back of each Flower.

Pin Flower to Bolero to close.

Fold brim on Hat up and place barrette to hold in place. ●

3rd ch of beg ch-3.

Rnds 6 & 7 [6–8, 7–9]: Ch 3, dc in each st around, join with sl st in 3rd ch of beg ch-3. At end of last rnd, fasten off.

Rnd 8 [9, 10]: With size K hook, attach Baltic cream with sc between first 2 dc, sc in between each dc around, join with sl st in beg sc, fasten off.

2nd Sleeve

Counting from other edge, work same as First Sleeve.

HAT

Rnd 1: With size J hook for small size, or size K hook for medium and large sizes, with white, ch 4, sl st in first ch to form ring, ch 1, 8 sc in ring, **do not join**. *(8 sc)*

Rnds 2 & 3: 2 sc in each st around. *(32 sc)*

Rnds 4–6: Sc in each st around.

Rnd 7: [2 sc in next st, sc in next st] around. *(48 sc)*

Rnd 8: Ch 4 *(counts as first dc and ch-1)*, sk next st, [dc in next st, ch 1, sk next st] around, join with sl st in 3rd ch of beg ch-4.

Rnds 9–12 or to 1 inch shorter than desired brim length: Ch 4, sk next ch sp, [dc in next st, ch 1, sk

Little Cowgirl

DESIGNS BY CINDY CARLSON

INTERMEDIATE

Finished Sizes
Instructions given fit child's size 2; changes for sizes 4, 6, 8 are in [ ].

Finished Garment Measurements
Chest: 22 [24, 26, 28] inches
Vest length: 9 [10, 12, 14] inches
Hip: 22¾ [24, 25½, 26¾] inches
Skirt length: 9 [10½, 12, 14] inches

Gauge
Size J hook and lake blue: Sc row and slant st row = 1 inch; 3 dc = 1 inch

Pattern Notes
Weave in loose ends as work progresses.
Join rounds with a slip stitch unless otherwise stated.

Materials

- TLC Amore medium (worsted) weight yarn (6 oz/278 yds/170g per skein): 1 [2, 2, 3] skeins #3823 lake blue
- Red Heart LusterSheen fine (sport) weight yarn (4 oz/335 yds/113g per skein): 1 skein #0001 white
- Sizes D/3/3.25mm and J/10/6mm crochet hooks or sizes needed to obtain gauge
- Yarn needle
- Sewing needle and thread
- Silver ⅞-inch star-shaped shank buttons: 4
- ¾-inch-wide elastic: 22 [24, 26, 28] inches

Use size D hook for Fringe only.
Chain-3 at beginning of double crochet row or round counts as first double crochet unless otherwise stated.

Special Stitches
Slant stitch (slant st): Sk next st, dc in each of next 3 sts, dc in sk st.
Cross-stitch (cross-st): Sk next st, dc in next st, dc in skipped st.

VEST

Front
Make 2.
Row 1: Starting at bottom edge with size J hook and lake blue, ch 17 [21, 25, 29], sc in 2nd ch from hook, sc in each rem ch across, turn. *(16 [20, 24, 28] sc)*
Row 2: Ch 3 *(counts as first dc)*, dc in next st, **slant st** *(see Special Stitches)* across to last 2 sts, dc in each of next 2 sts, turn. *(3 [4, 5, 6] slant sts, 4 dc)*
Row 3: Ch 1, sc in each st across, turn. *(16 [20, 24, 28] sc)*
Row 4: Ch 3, dc in next st, slant st across to last 2 sts, dc in each of next 2 sts, turn. *(3 [4, 5, 6] slant sts, 4 dc)*
Rows 5–10 [5–12, 5–14, 5–16]: [Rep rows 3 and 4 alternately] 3 [4, 5, 6] times, turn.
Row 11 [13, 15, 17]: Rep row 3.
Row 12 [14, 16, 18]: Sl st in each of next 3 sts, ch 1, sc in same st as last sl st, sc in each of next 11 [15, 19, 23] sts, leaving rem 2 sts unworked, turn. *(12 [16, 20, 24] sc)*

Row 13 [15, 17, 19]: Ch 1, sc in each of next 11 [13, 15, 17] sts, leaving last st unworked, turn.

Row 14 [16, 18, 20]: Sk first st, sc in each of next 10 [12, 14, 16] sts, turn.

Row 15 [17, 19, 21]: Ch 1, sc in each st across, turn.

Row 16 [18, 20, 22]: Sk first st, sc in each of next 9 [11, 13, 15] sts, turn.

Row 17 [19, 21, 23]: Ch 1, sc in each st across, turn.

Row 18 [20, 22, 24]: Sk first st, sc in each of next 8 [10, 12, 14] sts, turn.

Row 19 [21, 23, 25]: Ch 1, sc in each st across, turn.

Row 20 [22, 24, 26]: Sk first st, sc in each of next 7 [9, 11, 13] sts, turn.

Row 21 [23, 25, 27]: Ch 1, sc in each st across, fasten off. *(7 [9, 11, 13] sc)*

Back

Row 1: Starting at bottom edge with size J hook and lake blue, ch 35 [39, 43, 47] sc in 2nd ch from hook, sc in each rem ch across, turn. *(34 [38, 42, 46] sc)*

Row 2: Ch 3, **cross-st** *(see Special Stitches)* in each st across to last st, dc in last st, turn. *(16 [18, 20, 22] cross-sts, 2 dc)*

Row 3: Ch 1, sc in each st across, turn.

Row 4: Ch 3, cross-st in each st across to last st, dc in last st, turn.

Rows 5–10 [5–12, 5–14, 5–16]: [Rep rows 3 and 4 alternately] 3 [4, 5, 6] times, turn.

Row 11 [13, 15, 17]: Rep row 3.

Row 12 [14, 16, 18]: Sl st in each of next 6 sts, ch 1, sc in same st as last sl st, sc in each of next 23 [27, 31, 33] sts, leaving last 5 sts unworked, turn. *(24 [28, 32, 34] sc)*

Rows 13–20 [15–22, 17–24, 19–26]: Ch 1, sc in each st across, turn. *(24 [28, 32, 34] sc)*

First Shoulder Shaping

Row 21 [23, 25, 27]: Ch 1, sc in each of next 7 [9, 11, 13] sts, fasten off.

2nd Shoulder Shaping

Row 21 [23, 25, 27]: With finished Shoulder Shaping to the right, sk next 10 sts *(all sizes)*, attach lake blue

in next st with a sl st, ch 1, sc in same st as beg ch-1, sc in each of next 6 [8, 10, 12] sts, fasten off. *(7 [9, 11, 13] sts)*

Finishing

Using care that slant of slant sts points towards the center of front, with yarn needle and length of lake blue, sew side and shoulder seams.

Edging

Rnd 1 (RS): Attach lake blue at side seam, ch 1, **reverse sc** *(see Fig. 1)* in each st around entire outer edge of Vest, join in beg sc, fasten off.

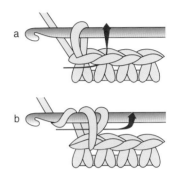

Reverse Single Crochet
Fig. 1

Fringe

Working around post of sts of row 12 [14, 16, 18] of each Front and Back, sk first and last st of each section, work 10 [14, 18, 22] on each Front and 22 [26, 30, 32] on Back.

Cut 138 [162, 186, 204] lengths of white, each 4 inches long. [With RS facing, hold 3 strands of white tog, fold strands in half, insert size D hook around the vertical post of sc, draw strands through at fold to form a lp on hook, draw cut ends *(6 strands)* through lp on hook, pull ends gently to secure], rep until each Fringe is completed.

SKIRT

Row 1: Beg at bottom edge of Skirt, with size J hook and lake blue, ch 69 [73, 77, 81], sc in 2nd ch from hook, sc in each rem ch across, turn. *(68 [72, 76, 80] sc)*

Row 2: Ch 3, dc in next st, **slant st** *(see Special Stitches)* in each st across to last 2 sts, dc in each of next 2 sts, turn. *(16 [17, 18, 19] slant sts, 4 dc)*

Row 3: Ch 1, sc in each st across, turn. *(68 [72, 76, 80] sc)*

Row 4: Ch 3, slant st in each st across to last 2 sts,

dc in each of next 2 sts, turn.

Rows 5–10 [5–12, 5–14, 5–16]: [Rep rows 3 and 4 alternately] 3 [4, 5, 6] times.

Row 11 [13, 15, 17]: Rep row 3.

Rows 12–23 [14–25, 16–27, 18–29]: Ch 1, sc in each st across, turn. At the end of last rep, fasten off.

Bottom Trim

Row 1 (RS): With size J hook, attach lake blue with sl st in opposite side of foundation ch, ch 1, sc in same ch as beg ch-1, sc in next ch, [dc in each of next 2 chs, sc in each of next 2 chs] across, fasten off.

Finishing

With yarn needle and a length of lake blue, sew center back seam of Skirt.

For **waistband casing**, turn 3 rows at top of Skirt to WS, sew around leaving approximately 2 inches unsewn, **do not fasten off.**

Pass elastic through casing and with sewing needle and thread, sew ends of elastic tog and then sew rem casing closed, secure and fasten off.

Fringe

Cut 204 [216, 228, 240] lengths of white, each 4 inches long, work around posts of sts of row 12 [14, 16, 18] of Skirt.

[With RS facing, hold 3 strands of white tog, fold strands in half, insert size D hook around the vertical post of sc, draw strands through at fold to form a lp on hook, draw cut ends *(6 strands)* through lp on hook, pull ends gently to secure] rep until each Fringe is completed. ●

Dolman Baby Sweater & Hat continued from page 113

Front Edges & Neckline Trim

Row 1 (RS): With Size F [G, H] hook, attach CC with sl st in bottom edge of Front Bottom Border, ch 1, sc evenly sp up right front, around neckline and down Left Front ending with an odd number of sts, turn.

Rows 2–7: Rep rows 2–7 of Sweater Cuff.

Row 8: Ch 1, sc in each sc and each ch-1 sp across, turn.

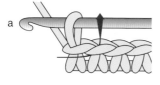

**Reverse Single Crochet
Fig. 1**

Row 9: Ch 1, sc in each sc across, **do not turn.**

Rnd 10: Now working in rnds, ch 1, working around entire outer edge of Sweater, reverse sc in each st around, join in beg sc, fasten off.

Button Loop

With size F [G, H] hook and CC, ch 10, sl st to join in first ch, leaving a 6-inch length, fasten off.

Sew Button Loop to Right Front approximately 5 inches down from shoulder and ½-inch in from edge. Sew button to Left Front opposite Button Loop ½-inch in from edge. ●

Bear Blanket Buddy continued from page 115

turning ch from previous row, ch 3, 2 dc in same sp, *ch 3, shell in next ch-1 sp, rep from * 18 times, ch 2, sc in top of last dc, fasten off.

Rep rows 2–5 consecutively until Blanket measures approximately 35 inches ending with row 2 or row 4, fasten off.

Border

Rnd 1 (RS): With size G hook, attach A with sc in first st of last row of Blanket, sc in same st as first sc, *work 109 sc across to next corner, 3 sc in corner st, 110 sc across to next corner**, 3 sc in next corner, rep from * around, ending last rep at **, sc in same st as beg 2-sc group, join in beg sc.

Rnd 2: Ch 4 *(counts as first dc, ch-1)*, dc in same st as beg ch-4, *sk next 2 sc, **V-st** *(see Special Stitches)* in next sc, rep from * around, join in 3rd ch of beg ch-4.

Rnd 3: Sl st in ch-1 sp of same V-st, ch 3, (ch 1, dc) 4 times in same ch-1 sp, [dc in next ch-1 sp of next V-st, (ch 1, dc) 4 times in same ch-1 sp of V-st] around, join in 3rd ch of beg ch-3, fasten off.

Finishing

Cut ends of ribbon on diagonal. Weave ribbon through gaps between sts of last row of Blanket. Draw ribbon to fit around Bear's underarms meeting at center front. Tie tightly and knot ends, tie ends in a bow. ●

Flower Patch Afghan continued from page 116

2 dc) in next corner ch-2 sp, [dc in each of next 3 dc, dc in next ch-1 sp] twice**, dc in each of next 3 dc, rep from * around, ending last rep at**, join in 3rd ch of beg ch-3, fasten off. *(60 dc, 4 ch-2 sps)*

Assembly

With tapestry needle and lime, holding Motifs flat with RS facing, working through both lps of each st on each edge of both Motifs, whipstitch Motifs tog in 9 rows of 8 Motifs, then whipstitch the 9 rows tog.

Border

Rnd 1 (RS): Attach lime with sl st in any corner ch-2 sp, ch 3, 2 dc in same corner ch-2 sp, [dc in each dc across edge of Motif to joining of 2 Motifs, dc in next ch-2 sp, **dc dec** *(see Stitch Guide)* in same ch-2 sp and in next ch-2 sp, dc in same ch-2 sp as last portion of dc dec] around, working 3 dc in each rem corner ch-2 sps, join in 3rd ch of beg ch-3, fasten off. *(582 dc, 30 dc dec)*

Rnd 2: Attach giggle with sc in 2nd dc after a 3-dc corner group, *[sk next 2 dc, 5 dc in next dc, sk next 2 dc, sc in next dc] across to next corner, sk next dc, 3 dc in each of next 3 dc of corner group, sk next dc**, sc in next dc, rep from * around, ending last rep at **, join in beg sc, fasten off. *(102 sc, 98 groups 5-dc, 12 groups 3-dc)* ●

Pastel Shells Afghan continued from page 127

*sk next 2 sts, **large shell** *(see Special Stitches)* in next st, sk next 2 sts**, sc in next st, rep from * across, ending last rep at **, (sc, ch 2, sc) in last sc; working in ends of rows, sc evenly spaced across, (sc, ch 2, sc) in first ch of opposite side of foundation ch, rep from * across, ending last rep at **, (sc, ch 2, sc) in last st; working in ends of rows, sc in each st across, join in beg sc.

Rnd 2: Sl st in first ch-2 sp, ch 1, (sc, ch 2, sc, ch 3, sc, ch 2, sc) in corner ch-2 sp, *ch 4, (sc, ch 3, sc) in center dc of next large shell, ch 4**, sc in next sc, rep from * across edge, ending last rep at **, (sc, ch 2, sc, ch 3, sc, ch 2, sc) in corner ch-2 sp, working across sc edge, ch 4, sk next 2 sc, [sl st in next sc, ch 4, sk next 2 sc] across to next corner ch-2 sp, (sc, ch 2, sc, ch 3, sc, ch 2, sc) in corner ch-2 sp, rep from * across, ending last rep at **, (sc, ch 2, sc, ch 3, sc, ch 2, sc) in corner ch-2 sp, ch 4, sk next 2 sc, [sl st in next sc, ch 4, sk next 2 sc] across edge, join in beg sc, fasten off. ●

Home Accents
in a Hurry

Dress up your home with our great selection of contemporary accessories including afghans, pillows, table accents, kitchen items and beyond.

Watermelon Print Throw

DESIGN BY KATHERINE ENG

EASY

Finished Size
44 x 66 inches

Gauge
Rows 1 & 2 = 1¾ inches at points; 4 dc groups across = 4 inches

Pattern Note
Weave in loose ends as work progresses.

THROW

First Half
Row 1 (RS): Starting at center with pink multi, ch 160, 2 dc in 4th ch from hook, [sk next 3 chs, (sl st, ch 3, 2 dc) in next ch] across to last 4 chs, sk next 3 chs, sc in last ch, turn. *(39 dc groups)*

Row 2: Ch 3 *(counts as first ch-3 sp of row)*, 2 dc in first sc, [(sl st, ch 3, 2 dc) in next ch-3 sp] across, ending

Materials
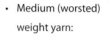
- Medium (worsted) weight yarn:

    32 oz/1600 yds/907g pink multi

    6 oz/300 yds/170g pink
- Size K/10½/6.5mm crochet hook or size needed to obtain gauge
- Tapestry needle

with sc in last ch-3 sp, turn.

Rows 3–30: Rep row 2. At the end of row 30, fasten off.

Row 31 (RS): Attach pink in sc, ch 3, 2 dc in first sc, [(sl st, ch 3, 2 dc) in next ch-3 sp] across, ending with sc in last ch-3 sp, turn.

Rows 32–35: Rep row 2. At the end of row 35, fasten off.

2nd Half
Row 1 (RS): With RS of First Half facing and working in opposite side of foundation ch, attach pink multi in first ch, ch 3, 2 dc in same ch as beg ch-3, [sk next 3 chs, (sl st, ch 3, 2 dc) in next ch] across to last 4 chs, sk next 3 chs, sc in last ch, turn. *(39 dc groups)*

Rows 2–30: Rep row 2 of First Half.

Rows 31–35: Rep rows 31–35 of First Half.

Border
Row 1 (RS): Working in side edge of rows, attach pink with sl st in side edge of end sc of row 35, ch 1, sc in same st as beg ch-1, [(sc, ch 3, sc) in side edge of each ch-3 sp, sc in end of each sc row] across entire edge of Throw, working a sc in center foundation ch, fasten off.

Rep row 1 of Border on opposite side edge of rows of Throw. ●

Classy Cables Pillow

DESIGN BY DARLA SIMS

INTERMEDIATE

Finished Sizes

18 x 18 inches

Gauge

Size G hook: 4 sc = 1 inch
Size H hook: 7 hdc = 2 inches

Pattern Notes

Weave in loose ends as work progresses.
Join rounds with a slip stitch unless otherwise stated.
Pillow cover is smaller than actual pillow form and is necessary for cover to fit snuggly and stay in place.

PILLOW

Front

Row 1: Starting at bottom edge with size H hook,

Materials

- TLC Essentials medium (worsted) weight yarn (6 oz/312 yds/170g per skein):
    4 skeins #2615 light celery
- Sizes G/6/4mm and H/8/5mm crochet hooks or sizes needed to obtain gauge
- Yarn needle
- Stitch markers
- 18 x 18-inch pillow form

4 MEDIUM

ch 53, hdc in 3rd ch from hook *(2 sk chs count as first hdc)*, hdc in each rem ch across, turn. *(52 hdc)*

Row 2: Ch 2 *(counts as first hdc)*, hdc in each st across, turn. *(52 hdc)*

Row 3: Ch 2, hdc in next st, *sk next st, [**fpdc** *(see Stitch Guide)* in next hdc of row 1, sk st directly behind post st] twice, fpdc in hdc directly below sk hdc, hdc in each of next 2 hdc, rep from * across, turn. *(10 cables, 22 hdc)*

Row 4: Rep row 2.

Row 5: Ch 2, hdc in next hdc, [fpdc in each of next 3 fpdc, hdc in each of next 2 hdc] 10 times, turn.

Row 6: Rep row 2.

Row 7: Ch 2, hdc in next hdc, *sk next fpdc, fpdc in each of next 2 fpdc, fpdc in sk fpdc, hdc in each of next 2 hdc, rep from * across, turn. *(10 cables, 22 hdc)*

Rows 8–47: [Rep rows 4–7 consecutively] 10 times. At the end of row 47, fasten off.

Back

Rows 1–47: Rep rows 1–47 of Front. At the end of row 47, turn, **do not fasten off**.

Flap

Row 1: With size H hook, ch 1, **hdc dec** *(see Stitch Guide)* in next 2 sts, hdc in each st across to last 2 sts, hdc dec in last 2 sts, turn. *(50 hdc)*

Row 2: Ch 1, hdc dec in next 2 sts, hdc in each st

CONTINUED ON PAGE 172

Pocket Place Mat Set

DESIGNS BY JOYCE BRAGG

EASY

Finished Sizes
Place Mat: 18 x 12 inches
Flatware Pocket: 3¾ x 8½
 inches
Napkin Ring: 1¾ x 3 inches in
 diameter

Materials
- TLC Cotton
 Plus medium
 (worsted) weight yarn (3½
 oz/178 yds/100g per skein):
  2 skeins #3001 white
  1 skein each #3252
   tangerine, #3643 kiwi
   and #3222 yellow
- Sizes G/6/4mm and
 H/8/5mm crochet hooks
 or sizes needed to obtain
 gauge
- Tapestry needle

Gauge
Size G hook: 5 sc = 1 inch
Size H hook: 9 dc = 2 inches

Pattern Notes
Weave in loose ends as work progresses.
Join rounds with a slip stitch unless otherwise
stated.

PLACE MAT
Row 1: With size H hook and white, ch 74, sc in 2nd
ch from hook, sc in each rem ch across, turn. *(73 sc)*
Row 2: Ch 1, working in **front lps** *(see Stitch Guide)*
for this row only, sc in each st across, turn.

Row 3: Ch 1, sc in each sc across, turn.
Row 4: Rep row 2.
Row 5: Ch 3 *(counts as first dc)*, dc in each st
across, turn.
Rows 6 & 7: Rep row 3.
Rows 8–43: [Rep rows 2–7 consecutively] 6 times.
Rows 44 & 45: Rep rows 2 and 3.
Row 46: Rep row 2.
Row 47: Working across side edge of rows, ch 1, sc in
end of each sc row, 2 sc in end of each dc row, fasten
off. *(53 sc)*
Row 48: Working across opposite side edge of rows,
join white with sc in end of first sc row, sc in end of
each sc row, 2 sc in side edge of each dc row, fasten
off. *(53 sc)*
Row 49 (RS): With size G hook, attach yellow with sc
in first sc of row 47, sc in each of next 4 sc, [sk next
sc, (sc, hdc, 3 dc, hdc, sc) in next sc, sk next sc, sc in
each of next 5 sc] 6 times, fasten off.
Row 50: With size G hook, attach kiwi with sl st in
first sc of previous row, ch 1, sc in same sc as beg ch-
1, sc in each rem st across, fasten off.
Row 51: With size G hook, attach tangerine in **back
lp** *(see Stitch Guide)* of first sc of row 50 with sl st, sl st
in back lp of each sc across, fasten off.
Rows 52–54: Rep rows 49–51 on opposite edge of
Place Mat.

Rose

Make 1.

Rnd 1 (RS): With size H hook and tangerine, ch 2, 5 sc in 2nd ch from hook, **do not join**. *(5 sc)*

Rnd 2: [(Sc, hdc, 3 dc, hdc, sc) in next sc] 5 times. *(5 petals)*

Rnd 3: [Ch 3, sl st in sc between next 2 petals] 5 times.

Rnd 4: [(Sc, hdc, 5 dc, hdc, sc) in next ch-3 sp] 5 times, join in beg sc, fasten off. *(5 petals)*

Star Flower

Make 1.

Rnd 1: With size H hook and kiwi, ch 2, 5 sc in 2nd ch from hook, sl st in next st, fasten off. *(5 sc)*

Rnd 2: Attach yellow in sc with a sl st, ch 1, 2 sc in same sc as beg ch-1, 2 sc in each rem sc around, join in beg sc. *(10 sc)*

Rnd 3: Ch 1, sc in next sc, *(sc, hdc, 3 dc, hdc, sc) in next sc**, sc in next sc, rep from * around, ending last rep at **, join in beg sc, fasten off. *(5 petals)*

Viola

Make 1.

Rnd 1: With size H hook and yellow, ch 2, 6 sc in 2nd ch from hook, join in beg sc, **do not fasten off**. *(6 sc)*

Rnd 2: Attach kiwi in next sc with a sl st, ch 1, sc in same sc as beg ch-1, *(sc, hdc, 3 dc, hdc, sc) in next sc**, sc in next sc, rep from * around, ending last rep at **, join in beg sc, draw up a lp of yellow, fasten off kiwi, turn. *(3 petals)*

Rnd 3: With yellow, [ch 3, sl st in next sc between petals] twice, turn.

Rnd 4: [(Sc, hdc, 5 dc, hdc, sc) in next ch-3 sp] twice, sl st in next sc of previous rnd, fasten off. Attach the 3 Flowers to upper left corner of Place Mat.

FLATWARE POCKET

Rnd 1: With size H hook and white, ch 35, join with sl st in first ch, ch 1, sc in each sc around, join in beg sc. *(35 sc)*

Rnd 2: Ch 1, working in back lps of each st only, sc in each st around, join in beg sc.

Rnd 3: Ch 1, sc in each st around, join in beg sc.

Rnd 4: Rep rnd 2.

Rnd 5: Ch 3 *(counts as first dc)*, dc in each st around, join in 3rd ch of beg ch-3.

Rnd 6: Rep rnd 3.

Rnds 7–16: [Rep rnds 2–6 consecutively] twice.

Rnd 17: Rep rnd 2.

Row 18: Now working in rows, ch 3, dc in each of next 16 sts, turn. *(17 dc)*

Row 19: Ch 1, sc in each of next 17 sts, turn.

Row 20: Rep row 19.

Row 21: Ch 1, working in **front lps** *(see Stitch Guide)* only, sc in each st across, turn.

Row 22: Rep row 19.

Row 23: Rep row 21.

Row 24: Rep row 18.

Rows 25 & 26: Rep row 19.

Row 27: Rep row 21, fasten off, turn.

Row 28: Attach kiwi with sl st in first sc, ch 1, sc in same sc as beg ch-1, sc in each rem sc across, fasten off, **do not turn**.

Row 29: Attach tangerine in **back lp** *(see Stitch Guide)* of first sc with sl st, sl st in each st across, fasten off.

Row 30: For **Flatware divider**, with front facing and size H hook, attach yellow with sc in first sc of rnd 17, sc in each of next 4 sc, sl st between 5th and 6th dc of row 18 of back, sc in each of next 7 sc, sl st between the 11th and 12th dc of row 18 of back, sc in each of next 6 sc, fasten off.

Bottom Edging

Row 1: With size G hook, working through both thicknesses of opposite side of foundation ch, fold piece flat, attach yellow with sl st, ch 1, sc in same st as beg ch-1, sc in each of next 2 sts, sk next st, (sc, hdc, 3 dc, hdc, sc) in next st, sk next st, sc in each of next 5 sts, sk next st, (sc, hdc, 3 dc, hdc, sc) in next st, sk next st, sc in each of next 3 sts, fasten off.

Row 2: Attach kiwi with sl st in first sc of row, ch 1, sc in each sc across, fasten off.

Row 3: Working in back lps only, attach tangerine with a sl st, sl st in each back lp across, fasten off.

CONTINUED ON PAGE 172

Kitchen Set

DESIGNS BY ELAINE BARTLETT

EASY

Finished Sizes

Dishcloth: 9 inches in
diameter
Scrubbie Dishcloth: 6½ inches
in diameter
Towel Hanger: 2 x 8¼ inches,
excluding Flower Button

Materials

- Bernat Organic
cotton medium
(worsted) weight yarn
(1¾/87 yds/50g per ball):
2 balls #43116 mineral
spring
- Size H/8/5mm crochet
hook or size needed to
obtain gauge
- Tapestry needle
- Stitch markers
- 3½ inches in diameter
scrubbie
- Elastic ponytail holder

Gauge

4 dc = 1 inch; 2 dc rows = 1 inch

Pattern Notes

Weave in loose ends as work progresses.
Join rounds with a slip stitch unless otherwise stated.

DISHCLOTH

Rnd 1 (RS): Starting at center, leaving a 2-inch
length at beg, ch 2, 12 sc in 2nd ch from hook, join in
beg sc. Pull beg length tightly and secure. *(12 sc)*
Rnd 2: Ch 2 *(counts as first dc)*, dc in same st as beg
ch-2, 2 dc in each sc around, join in 3rd ch of beg
ch-3. *(24 dc)*
Rnd 3: Ch 1, sc in each dc around, join in beg sc.
Rnds 4 & 5: Rep rnds 2 and 3. *(48 sts at end of last rnd)*

Rnd 6: Ch 2, dc in same st as beg ch-2, *dc in each of
next 3 sts**, 2 dc in next st, rep from * around, ending last rep at **, join in beg ch-2. *(60 dc)*
Rnd 7: Rep rnd 3.
Rnd 8: Ch 2, dc in same st as beg ch-2, *dc in each of
next 5 sts**, 2 dc in next st, rep from * around, ending last rep at **, join in beg ch-2. *(70 dc)*
Rnd 9: Rep rnd 3.
Rnd 10: Ch 2, dc in same st as beg ch-2, *dc in each
of next 5 sts**, 2 dc in next st, rep from * around,
ending last rep at **, join in beg ch-2. *(82 dc)*
Rnd 11: Rep rnd 3.

Flower Button

Rnds 1 & 2: Leaving an 18-inch length at beg, rep rnds 1–3 of Dishcloth. *(24 dc)*

Rnd 4: Ch 1, 2 sc in same sc as beg ch-1, sc in next sc, [2 sc in next sc, sc in next sc] around, join in beg sc, fasten off. *(36 sc)*

With beg length from rnd 1; sew Flower Button to center of WS of row 13 of Strap. ●

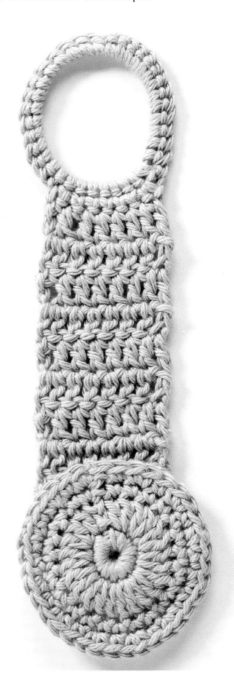

Rnd 12: Ch 2, dc in same st, *dc in each of next 4 sts**, 2 dc in next st, rep from * around, ending last rep at **, join in beg ch-2. *(99 dc)*

Rnd 13: Rep rnd 3, fasten off.

SCRUBBIE DISHCLOTH

Rnd 1 (RS): Attach yarn with sc through mesh along side of Scrubbie, work 39 more sc, join in beg sc. *(40 sc)*

Rnd 2: Ch 2 *(counts as first dc)*, dc in same st, *dc in next st**, 2 dc in next st, rep from * around, ending last rep at **, join in beg ch-2. *(60 dc)*

Rnd 3: Ch 1, sc in each st around, join in beg sc.

Rnds 4 & 5: Rep rnds 2 and 3, fasten off at end of last rnd. *(90 sts)*

TOWEL HANGER

Strap

Rnd 1 (RS): Join yarn to ponytail holder with a sc, work 34 more sc around elastic, join in beg sc. *(35 sc)*

Row 2: Now working in rows, ch 1, sc in same sc as beg ch-1, sc in each of next 7 sc, turn. *(8 sc)*

Row 3: Place a st marker in row for RS, ch 2 *(counts as first dc)*, dc in each of next 7 sts, turn. *(8 dc)*

Rows 4–13: Ch 2, dc in each dc across, turn.

Row 14: Ch 1, sc in each dc across, fasten off.

Woodland Throw

DESIGN BY DORA OHRENSTEIN

BEGINNER

Finished Size
39 x 41 inches

Materials

- Moda Dea Metro bulky (chunky) weight yarn (3½ oz/124 yds/100g per ball):
    - 5 balls #9863 mocha latte *(A)*
    - 3 balls #9340 chocolate *(B)*
- Size I/9/5.5mm crochet hook or size needed to obtain gauge
- Tapestry needle

Gauge
5 hdc = 2 inches; 4 hdc rows = 2 inches

Pattern Notes
Weave in loose ends as work progresses.
Join rounds with a slip stitch unless otherwise stated.

THROW
Row 1: Starting at bottom with A, ch 106, hdc in 3rd ch from hook *(2 sk chs count as first hdc)*, hdc in each rem ch across, turn. *(105 hdc)*

Row 2: Ch 2 *(counts as first hdc)*, hdc in each hdc across, turn.

Row 3: Ch 2, hdc in each hdc across, **change color** *(see Stitch Guide)* to B, turn.

Row 4: Ch 2, hdc in each hdc across, change color to A, turn.

Rows 5 & 6: Rep row 2.

Row 7: Rep row 3.

Rows 8–75: [Rep rows 4–7 consecutively] 17 times. At the end of row 75, change color to B, fasten off A.

Border
Rnd 76: With B, ch 1, sc in each st evenly spaced around outer edge of Throw, working 3 sc in each corner, join in beg sc.

Rnd 77: Ch 1, sc in each sc around, working 3 sc in center corner sc of each corner, join in beg sc, fasten off. ●

Woven Shell Table Runner

DESIGN BY TERRY DAY

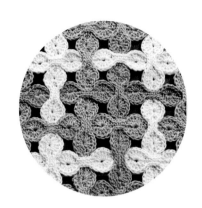

EASY

Finished Size

14 x 45 inches

Materials

- TLC Cotton Plus medium (worsted) weight yarn (3½ oz/178 yds/100g per skein): 2 skeins each #3100 cream, #3303 tan and #3503 spruce
- Size F/5/3.75mm crochet hook or size needed to obtain gauge
- Tapestry needle
- Washable fabric glue
- Steam iron

Gauge

4 sc = 1 inch; 12 dc in ch = 1½ inches in diameter

Pattern Notes

Weave in loose ends as work progresses.
Join with a slip stitch unless otherwise stated.

RUNNER

7-Shell Strip

Make 7 each cream, tan and spruce.
Row 1: Ch 57, 5 dc in 3rd ch from hook (*2 sk chs count as first dc)*, [sk next 2 chs, sl st in each of next 4 chs, sk next 2 chs, 6 dc in next ch] across to last ch, 12 dc in last ch, working on opposite side of foundation ch, [sk next 2 chs, sc in each of next 4 chs (*these 4 sc will be directly opposite 4 sl sts on opposite side of ch)*, sk next 2 chs, 6 dc in next ch (*these 6 dc will be opposite 6 dc on opposite side of ch)*] across, join in beg dc, fasten off.

22-Shell Strip

Make 2 each cream, tan and spruce.
Row 1: Ch 192, 5 dc in 3rd ch from hook, [sk next 2 chs, sl st in each of next 4 chs, sk next 2 chs, 6 dc in next ch] across to last ch, 12 dc in last ch, working on opposite side of foundation ch, [sk next 2 chs, sc in each of next 4 chs, sk next 2 chs, 6 dc in next ch] across, join in beg dc, fasten off.

Finishing

Using photo as a guide, lay out 7-Shell Strips alternating colors. Alternating colors, weave 22-Shell Strips over and under the 7-Shell Strips. Press pieces with a steam iron so that they lay nice and flat. Place a dot of fabric glue where pieces intersect at straight portion of strip making sure that shells all along outside edges are lined up evenly. Press down firmly on all glued areas to assure good adhesion. Do not move Runner until completely dry. ●

Simply Sweet Doilies

DESIGN BY KATHERINE ENG

EASY

Finished Size

7½ inches in diameter

Gauge

Rnds 1–3 = 1¾ inches in diameter; [dc, ch 2] 3 times = 1 inch

Pattern Notes

Weave in loose ends as work progresses.

Join rounds with a slip stitch unless otherwise stated.

Special Stitches

Small shell: 3 dc in st indicated.

Large shell: 5 dc in indicated st.

V-stitch (V-st): (Dc, ch 2, dc) in indicated st.

DOILY

Rnd 1: Starting at center, with white, ch 5, sl st to

Materials

- Aunt Lydia's Classic size 10 crochet cotton (white & ecru: 400 yds per ball; solids: 350 yds per ball):
    150 yds #1 white
    10 yds each #493 French rose and #479 bridal blue
- Size B/1/2.25mm crochet hook or size needed to obtain gauge
- Tapestry needle

join in first ch to form a ring, ch 1, 12 sc in ring, join in beg sc. *(12 sc)*

Rnd 2: Ch 4 *(counts as first dc, ch-1)*, dc in same st as beg ch-4, ch 1, [(dc, ch 1, dc) in next sc, ch 1] around, join in 3rd ch of beg ch-4. *(24 dc)*

Rnd 3: Sl st in next ch-1 sp, ch 1, sc in same ch-1 sp as beg ch-1, *small shell *(see Special Stitches)* in next ch-1 sp**, sc in next ch-1 sp, rep from * around, ending last rep at **, join in beg sc. *(12 small shells, 12 sc)*

Rnd 4: Ch 5 *(counts as first dc, ch-2)*, sc in center dc of small shell, ch 2, [dc in next sc, ch 2, sc in center dc of small shell, ch 2] around, join in 3rd ch of beg ch-5. *(12 dc, 12 sc)*

Rnd 5: Ch 5, sk next ch-2 sp, dc in next sc, ch 2, [dc in next dc, ch 2, dc in next sc, ch 2] around, join in 3rd ch of beg ch-5. *(24 dc)*

Rnd 6: Ch 1, sc in same dc as beg ch-1, *large shell *(see Special Stitches)* in next dc**, sc in next dc, rep from * around, ending last rep at **, join in beg sc. *(12 large shells, 12 sc)*

Rnd 7: Ch 5, dc in same sc as beg ch-5, ch 2, *sc in center dc of large shell, ch 2**, V-st *(see Special Stitches)* in next sc, ch 2, rep from * around, ending last rep at **, join in 3rd ch of beg ch-5. *(12 V-sts, 12 sc)*

Rnd 8: Ch 5, *dc in next dc, ch 2**, dc in next sc, ch 2, dc in next dc, ch 2, rep from * around, ending last rep at **, join in 3rd ch of beg ch-5. *(36 dc)*

Rnd 9: Rep rnd 6. *(18 large shells, 18 sc)*

CONTINUED ON PAGE 173

Puffy Flowers Throw

DESIGN BY NANCY NEHRING

INTERMEDIATE

Finished Size

45 x 55 inches

Gauge

4 sc = 3 inches; 4 sc rows = 3 inches

Pattern Note

Weave in loose ends as work progresses.

Special Stitches

Beginning puff stitch (beg puff st): Ch 1, insert hook in next sc, yo, draw up a lp, [yo, insert hook in same sc, yo, draw up a lp] 3 times *(8 lps on hook)*, sk next sc, insert hook in next sc, yo, draw up a lp, [yo, insert hook in same sc, yo, draw up a lp] 3 times, yo, draw through all 13 lps on hook, ch 1 to lock.

Ending puff stitch (ending puff st): Sk ch-1 locking st, insert hook in top of puff st of previous row, yo, draw up a lp, [yo, insert hook in same puff st of previous row, yo, draw up a lp] 3 times, yo, draw through

Materials

SUPER BULKY 6

- Lion Brand Romance super bulky (super chunky) weight yarn (8 oz/480 yds/224g per ball):
  2 balls #100 snowdrop
- Size P/15/10mm crochet hook or size needed to obtain gauge
- Tapestry needle

all 8 lps on hook, ch 1 to lock, ch 1, insert hook in same puff st of previous row, yo, draw up a lp, [yo, insert hook in same puff st of previous row, yo, draw up a lp] 3 times, yo, draw through all 8 lps on hook, ch 1 to lock, sk next ch-1.

THROW

Row 1: Starting at bottom edge, ch 64, sc in 2nd ch from hook, sc in each rem ch across, turn. *(63 sc)*

Row 2: Ch 1, sc in each sc across, turn.

Row 3: Rep row 2.

Row 4: Ch 1, sc in each of next 2 sc, [work **beg puff st** *(see Special Stitches)*, sc in each of next 5 sc] 7 times, work beg puff st, sc in each of next 2 sc, turn. *(8 beg puff sts, 39 sc)*

Row 5: Ch 1, sc in each of next 2 sc, [work **ending puff st** *(see Special Stitches)*, sc in each of next 5 sc] 7 times, work ending puff st, sc in each of next 2 sc, turn. *(8 ending puff sts, 39 sc)*

Row 6: Ch 1, sc in each of next 2 sc, [sc in top of puff st, sc in ch-1 sp between puff sts, sc in top of next puff st, sc in each of next 5 sc] 7 times, sc in top of next puff st, sc in ch-1 sp between puff sts, sc in top of next puff st, sc in each of next 2 sc, turn. *(63 sc)*

Rows 7–10: Rep row 2.

Row 11: Ch 1, sc in each of next 6 sc, [beg puff st, sc in each of next 5 sc] 7 times, sc in last sc, turn.

Row 12: Ch 1, sc in each of next 6 sc, [ending puff st,

CONTINUED ON PAGE 173

Patchwork Bolster Pillow

DESIGN BY DORA OHRENSTEIN

EASY

Finished Size
9 x 22-inch Bolster

Gauge
10 dc = 2 inches; 5 dc rows = 2 inches

Pattern Notes
Weave in loose ends as work progresses.
Join rounds with a slip stitch unless otherwise stated.
The Bolster cover is crocheted in 5 vertical panels sewn together after all are completed. The patchwork

Materials
- Senso Wool Cotton size 3 (150 yds per ball):
  - 4 balls #1308 plum *(A)*
  - 2 balls each #1303 mossy green *(B)*, #1305 granite *(C)*, #1306 slate blue *(D)* and #1307 deep purple *(E)*
- Size B/1/2.25mm crochet hook or size needed to obtain gauge
- Tapestry needle
- Sewing needle and matching thread
- 1½ yds lightweight charcoal gray fabric for lining
- 9 x 22-inch bolster pillow form

results from repeating a Stripe Scheme 3 times in each panel with minor variations.

Stripe Scheme
For Stripe Scheme work 6 rows, 3 rows, 1 row, 3 rows, 5 rows, 1 row and 4 rows.

PILLOW

Basic Panel
Row 1: Ch 27, dc in 4th ch from hook *(3 sk chs count as first dc)*, dc in each rem ch across, turn. *(25 dc)*
Row 2: Ch 3 *(counts as first dc)*, dc in each dc across, turn.
Row 3: Ch 1, sc in each sc, turn.
Rep row 2, following the Stripe Scheme for each panel. Fasten off each color when the last row of a stripe is completed.

Panel No. 1
Make 2.
Work Stripe Scheme 3 times in the following color sequence:
A, B, C, B, D, A, E, C, A, B, A, C, D, A, E, C, A, C, B, C, A, then add 6 rows of D and 1 row C.

Panel No. 2
Make 2.
Beg with 4 rows of B, and then work Stripe Scheme

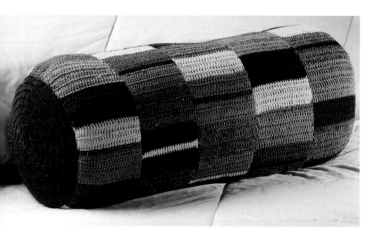

3 times in the following color sequence:
D, A, E, A, C, D, A, B, D, A, D, E, C, B, A, E, C, E, D, B, C,
then work 3 rows of E.

Panel No. 3

Make 1.

Sk first 6 rows of Stripe Scheme, then continue with
rem of Stripe Scheme in the following color scheme:
C, A, C, E, A, D, now work 2 complete Stripe Schemes
in the following color scheme: B, D, E, D, A, B, E, C, E,
D, E, B, D, C, then continue with 6 rows of A, 3 rows
of B, 1 row of E, 3 rows of B, fasten off.

Joining Panels

Arrange strips from left as follows, Panel 2 with first
row at top, Panel 1 with first row at top, Panel 3 with
first row at top, Panel 2 with last row on top and
Panel 1 with last row on top.

Using tapestry needle and C, sew panels tog. With
WS facing, sew opposite side of foundation chs to
last rows of Panels along edge.

End Panel

Make 2.

Rnd 1: With A, ch 4 *(counts as first dc, ch-1)*, 15 dc in
first ch of ch-4, join in top of beg ch-4. *(16 dc)*

Rnd 2: Ch 3 *(counts as first dc)*, dc in same st as beg
ch-3, 2 dc in each dc around, join in 3rd ch of beg
ch-3. *(32 dc)*

Rnd 3: Ch 3, dc in same st as beg ch-3, dc in next dc,
[2 dc in next dc, dc in next dc] around, join in 3rd ch
of beg ch-3. *(48 dc)*

Rnd 4: Ch 3, dc in same st as beg ch-3, dc in each of
next 2 dc, [2 dc in next dc, dc in each of next 2 dc]
around, join in 3rd ch of beg ch-3. *(64 dc)*

Rnd 5: Ch 3, dc in same st as beg ch-3, dc in each of
next 3 dc, [2 dc in next dc, dc in each of next 3 dc]
around, join in 3rd ch of beg ch-3. *(80 dc)*

Rnd 6: Ch 3, dc in same st as beg ch-3, dc in each of
next 4 dc, [2 dc in next dc, dc in each of next 4 dc]
around, join in 3rd ch of beg ch-3. *(96 dc)*

Rnd 7: Ch 3, dc in same st as beg ch-3, dc in each of
next 5 dc, [2 dc in next dc, dc in each of next 5 dc]
around, join in 3rd ch of beg ch-3. *(112 dc)*

Rnd 8: Ch 3, dc in same st as beg ch-3, dc in each of
next 6 dc, [2 dc in next dc, dc in each of next 6 dc]
around, join in 3rd ch of beg ch-3. *(128 dc)*

Rnd 9: Ch 3, dc in same st as beg ch-3, dc in each of
next 7 dc, [2 dc in next dc, dc in each of next 7 dc]
around, join in 3rd ch of beg ch-3, fasten off. *(144 dc)*

Bolster Lining

Cut fabric to match width of Bolster cover, plus 1
inch longer in length. Place around Bolster insert
with 1 long edge overlapping the other and sew in
place. Cut 2 circles approximately 1 inch larger in circumference than side panels. Tuck these into lining
and sew the lining securely over the edges.

Finishing

Place Bolster cover on pillow form. Make sure all
Panels are lined up and even looking—cover can be
gently tugged to correct any misalignments. Holding
Bolster on its end like a drum, place 1 side panel
on top. Edges of side panel will not meet edges of
Bolster cover until sewn. With safety pins, attach
End Panel to Bolster cover at 4 points. With A and
tapestry needle, sew End Panel to cover, picking up
outermost strands of each rnd. Sew 2nd End Panel to
opposite end of Bolster. ●

Retro Place Mat Set

DESIGNS BY MARY ANN SIPES

INTERMEDIATE

Finished Sizes

Place Mat: 12 x 15 inches

Trivet: 6¼ x 7¼ inches

Coaster: 3¾ x 5¼ inches

Materials

- Lion Brand Microspun light (light worsted) weight yarn (2½ oz/168 yds/70g per ball):

  3 balls each #100 lily white and #153 ebony
- Size H/8/5mm crochet hook or size needed to obtain gauge
- Tapestry needle

Gauge

4 dc = 1 inch; sc and dc rnd = 1 inch

Pattern Notes

Weave in loose ends as work progresses.

Join rounds with a slip stitch unless otherwise stated.

Materials listed make 4 of each of the following: Place Mats, Trivets and Coasters.

Special Stitches

Beginning scallop (beg scallop): Ch 3, 4 dc in st indicated.

Small scallop: 5 dc in indicated st.

Large scallop: 7 dc in indicated st.

PLACE MAT

Rnd 1 (RS): Starting at center with ebony, ch 19, 3 sc in 2nd ch from hook, 2 sc in next ch, sc in each of next 14 chs, 2 sc in next ch, 3 sc in next ch, working on opposite side of foundation ch, 2 sc in next ch, sc in each of next 14 chs, 2 sc in last ch, join in sl st in **back lp** (see Stitch Guide) of beg sc. (42 sc)

Rnd 2: Working in back lps, ch 3 (counts as first dc), dc in same st as beg ch-3, 2 dc in each of next 4 sts, dc in each of next 14 sts, 2 dc in each of next 7 sts, dc in each of next 14 sts, 2 dc in each of next 2 sts, join in beg ch-3, fasten off. (56 dc)

Rnd 3: Attach lily white with sl st in back lp of first dc,

working in back lps, ch 1, sc in same st as joining, *sk next dc, **small scallop** (see Special Stitches) in next st, sk next st**, sc in next st, rep from * around, ending last rep at **, join in beg sc, fasten off. (14 small scallops)

Rnd 4: Attach ebony with sl st in back lp of first sc, ch 4 (counts as first dc, ch-1), working in back lps only, (dc, ch 1, dc) in same sc as beg ch-4, sk next 2 dc, sc in next dc, *sk next 2 dc, dc in next sc, (ch 1, dc) twice in same sc, sk next 2 dc**, sc in next dc, rep from * around, ending last rep at **, join in 3rd ch of beg ch-4, fasten off. (14 dc groups)

Rnd 5: Attach lily white with sl st in back lp of center dc of dc group, working in back lps only, ch 1, sc in same dc, *small scallop in next sc**, sc in center dc of dc group, rep from * around, ending last rep at **, join in beg sc, fasten off. (14 small scallops)

Rnd 6: Attach ebony with sl st in back lp of first sc, working in back lps only, ch 3, dc in each of next 3 sts, [2 dc in each of next 2 sts, 3 dc in next st, 2 dc in each of next 2 sts, dc in each of next 34 sts] twice, dc in each of next 2 sts, join in beg ch-3. (96 dc)

Rnd 7: Working in back lps only, ch 3, dc in each st around, join in 3rd ch of beg ch-3, fasten off.

Rnd 8: Attach lily white with sl st in back lp of first dc, working in back lps only, ch 1, sc in same st as beg ch-1, *sk next st, small scallop in next st, sk next st**, sc in next st, rep from * around, ending last rep at **, join in beg sc, fasten off. (24 small scallops)

Rnd 9: Attach ebony with sl st in back lp of first sc, working in back lps only, ch 4, (dc, ch 1) twice and dc in same st as beg ch-4, sk next 2 dc, sc in next dc, *sk next 2 sts, dc in next sc, (ch 1, dc) 3 times in same sc, sk next 2 dc**, sc in next dc, rep from * around, ending last rep at **, join in 3rd ch of beg ch-4, fasten off.

Rnd 10: Attach lily white with sl st in back lp of center ch-1 sp, working in back lps only, *large scallop (see Special Stitches) in next sc, sk next ch-1 sp**, sl st in center ch-1 sp, rep from * around, ending last rep at **, join in beg sl st, fasten off, turn. (24 large scallops)

Rnd 11: With WS facing, attach ebony in **front lp** (see Stitch Guide) only, sl st in front lp of each st around, fasten off.

TRIVET

Rnd 1 (RS): With ebony, ch 11, 3 sc in 2nd ch from hook, 2 sc in next ch, sc in each of next 6 chs, 2 sc in next ch, 3 sc in last ch, working on opposite side of foundation ch, 2 sc in next ch, sc in each of next 6 chs, 2 sc in next ch, join with sl st in **back lp** (see Stitch Guide) only. (26 sc)

Rnd 2: Working in back lps only, ch 3 (counts as first dc), dc in same st as joining, 2 dc in each of next 4 sts, dc in each of next 6 sts, 2 dc in each of next 7 sts, dc in each of next 6 sts, 2 dc in each of next 2 sts, join in 3rd ch of beg ch-3, fasten off. (40 dc)

Rnd 3: Attach lily white with sl st in back lp of first dc, working in back lps only, ch 1, sc in same st as beg ch-1, *sk next dc, **small scallop** (see Special Stitches) in next dc, sk next dc**, sc in next dc, rep from * around, ending last rep at **, join in beg sc, fasten off. (10 small scallops)

Rnd 4: Attach ebony with sl st in back lp of sc, ch 4 (counts as first dc, ch 1), working in back lps only, (dc, ch 1) twice and dc in same st as beg ch-4, *sk 2 dc, sc in next dc, sk 2 dc**, dc in next sc, (ch 1, dc) 3 times in same sc, sk next 2 dc, rep from * around, ending last rep at **, join in 3rd ch of beg ch-4, fasten off. (10 dc groups)

Rnd 5: Attach lily white with sl st in back lp of center ch-1 sp, *large scallop (see Special Stitches) in next sc**, sl st in center ch-1 sp, rep from * around, join, fasten off. (10 large scallops)

Joining

Rnd 6: Holding WS of Trivets tog and working through back lps, attach ebony with sl st, sl st in each st around, fasten off.

COASTER

Rnds 1–3: Rep rnds 1–3 of Trivet.

Rnd 4: With WS facing, attach ebony with sl st in **front lp** (see Stitch Guide), sl st in front lp of each st around, fasten off. ●

Tranquil Moments Afghan

DESIGN BY TRUDY ATTEBERRY

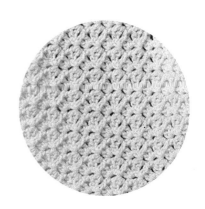

EASY

Finished Size

52 x 68½ inches

Gauge

7 shells = 8 inches; 7 shell rows = 4 inches

Pattern Notes

Weave in loose ends as work progresses.
Afghan is crocheted vertically.

Special Stitch

Shell: (2 dc, ch 2, sc) in indicated st.

Materials

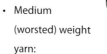

- Medium (worsted) weight yarn:
  65 oz/3250 yds/1843g off-white
- Size K/10½/6.5mm crochet hook or size needed to obtain gauge
- Tapestry needle

AFGHAN

Row 1: Ch 239, **shell** *(see Special Stitch)* in 3rd ch from hook, [sk next 3 chs, shell in next ch] across, turn. *(60 shells)*

Row 2: Ch 2 *(does **not** count as a st)*, shell in ch-2 sp of each shell across, turn.

Rows 3–90: Rep row 2. At the end of row 90, fasten off.

Row 91: Working on opposite side of foundation ch, with WS of row 1 facing, attach yarn with sc in first ch, (ch 2, 2 dc) in same ch as beg sc, sk next 3 chs, [(sc, ch 2, 2 dc) in next ch, sk next 3 chs] across to last ch, (sc, ch 2, 2 dc, ch 2, sl st) in last ch, fasten off.

Fringe

Fringe is attached in beg ch-2 sp of each row.
For each Fringe, cut 8 strands each 17 inches long. Fold strands in half, insert hook in ch-2 sp at end of row, draw fold through to form a lp on hook, draw all loose ends through lp on hook, tighten. Trim ends. ●

Blue Skies Throw

DESIGN BY ELAINE BARTLETT

EASY

Finished Size
45 x 59 inches

Materials

4 MEDIUM

- Red Heart Plush medium (worsted) weight yarn (6 oz/278 yds/170g per skein):
    5 skeins #9822 bluebird
    2 skeins #9103 cream
- Size K/10½/6.5mm crochet hook or size needed to obtain gauge
- Tapestry needle
- Stitch markers

Gauge
Rnds 1 and 2 of motif = 3 inches; motif = 7 inches square

Pattern Notes
Weave in loose ends as work progresses.
Join rounds with a slip stitch unless otherwise stated.

THROW

Motif
Make 48.

Rnd 1: With cream, ch 4, join in first ch to form a ring, ch 3 *(counts as first dc, ch-1)*, (dc in ring, ch 1) 11 times, join in 2nd ch of beg ch-3, fasten off. *(12 dc, 12 ch-1 sps)*

Rnd 2: Attach bluebird in any ch-1 sp with sc, ch 1 *(sc, ch-1 counts as first dc)*, *(2 dc, ch 2, 2 dc) in next ch-1 sp, dc in next ch-1 sp, ch 1**, dc in next ch-1 sp, rep from * around, ending last rep at **, join in beg ch-1. *(24 dc, 4 ch-1 sps, 4 ch-2 sps)*

Rnd 3: Sl st in ch-2 sp, ch 3 *(counts as first dc)*, (2 dc, ch 2, 3 dc) in same ch-2 sp as beg ch-3, *ch 1, 3 dc in next ch-1 sp, ch 1**, (3 dc, ch 2, 3 dc) in next ch-2 sp, rep from * around, ending last rep at **, join in 3rd ch of beg ch-3. *(36 dc, 8 ch-1 sps, 4 ch-2 sps)*

Rnd 4: Sl st into ch-2 sp, ch 3, (2 dc, ch 2, 3 dc) in same ch-2 sp, *[ch 1, 3 dc in next ch-1 sp] twice, ch 1**, (3 dc, ch 2, 3 dc) in next ch-2 sp, rep from * around, ending last rep at **, join in 3rd ch of beg ch-3, fasten off. *(48 dc, 12 ch-1 sps, 4 ch-2 sps)*

Rnd 5: Attach cream with sc in any st, sc in each dc and each ch-1 sp around working (2 sc, ch 2, 2 sc) in each ch-2 sp, join in beg sc, fasten off. *(76 sc, 4 ch-2 sps)*

Rnd 6: Attach bluebird with sc in any sc, sc in each sc around working (sc, ch 2, sc) in each ch-2 sp, join in beg sc, fasten off. *(84 sc, 4 ch-2 sps)*

With RS facing and bluebird, whipstitch Motifs tog working through both lps. Make 8 rows of 6 motifs and then whipstitch the 8 rows tog.

Edging

Rnd 1: Attach bluebird with a sc in any sc, sc in each sc and each ch sp of joining, working 3 sc in each of the 4 corner ch-2 sps, join in beg sc, fasten off. *(560 sc)*

Rnd 2: Attach cream with sc in any sc, ch 1 *(counts as first dc)*, dc in same sc, 2 dc in each sc around, join in top of beg ch-1, fasten off. *(1120 dc)*

Rnd 3: Attach bluebird with a sc in any dc, sc in each dc around, join in beg sc, fasten off. ●

Classy Cables Pillow continued from page 147

across to last 2 sts, hdc dec in last 2 sts, turn. *(48 hdc)*
Rows 3–25: Rep row 2. *(2 hdc)*
Row 26: Ch 1, hdc dec in next 2 sts, fasten off. *(1 hdc)*

Flap Edging
Row 1 (RS): With size G hook, attach yarn with sc in side edge of row 1 of Flap, work 42 sc across side edge to row 26, 3 sc in hdc of row 26, work 43 sc across opposite edge of Flap.
Row 2: Ch 1, **reverse sc** *(see Fig. 1)* in each sc of row 1 of Flap Edging, fasten off.

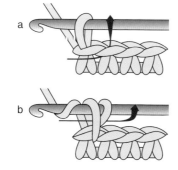

**Reverse Single Crochet
Fig. 1**

FROG

Loop Piece

With size G hook, make a ch approximately 18 inches

in length, sl st in 2nd ch from hook, sl st in each ch across, leaving a 12-inch length of yarn, fasten off. Using photo as a guide, form lp first, then frog, securing as you go with yarn threaded into yarn needle inserting needle between sts as you tack into place, form rem 2 lps.

Button Piece

With size G hook, make a ch approximately 18 inches in length, sl st in 2nd ch from hook, sl st in each ch across, leaving a 12-inch length of yarn, fasten off. Using photo as a guide, beg with double knot at end for button closure, shape and sew rem 3 lps as for Loop Piece.

Finishing

With long length of yarn, sew Front and Back tog on sides and bottom edge, leaving Flap free, insert pillow form. Working through top lps of Front and ridge on WS of last cable row of Back, whipstitch opening closed. Sew Frog to front of Flap. ●

Pocket Place Mat Set continued from page 150

Rose

Rnds 1–4: Rep rnds 1–4 of Rose for Place Mat.
Sew Rose to center front of Flatware Pocket.

NAPKIN RING

Rnd 1 (RS): With size H hook and white, ch 29, sl st to join in beg ch to form a ring, ch 1, sc in each ch around, join in beg sc. *(29 sc)*
Rnd 2: Ch 1, working in **back lps** *(see Stitch Guide)* only, sc in each st around, join in beg sc.
Rnd 3: Ch 3 *(counts as first dc)*, dc in each sc around, join in 3rd ch of beg ch-3.
Rnd 4: Rep rnd 2, fasten off.
Rnd 5: Attach kiwi in first sc with sl st, ch 1, sc in same

sc as beg ch-1, sc in each sc around, join in beg sc, fasten off.
Rnd 6: Working in back lps only, attach tangerine with sl st, sl st in back lp of each st around, fasten off.
Rnd 7: Working in opposite side of foundation ch, attach kiwi with a sc, sc in each ch around, join in beg sc, fasten off.
Rnd 8: Working in back lps only, attach yellow with sl st, sl st in back lp of each st around, fasten off.

Rose

Rnds 1–4: Rep rnds 1–4 of Rose for Place Mat.
Sew Rose to center of Napkin Ring. ●

Simply Sweet Doilies continued from page 158

Rnd 10: Rep rnd 7. *(18 V-sts, 18 sc)*

Rnd 11: Rep rnd 8. *(54 dc)*

Rnd 12: Ch 5, [dc in next dc, ch 2] around, join in 3rd ch of beg ch-5.

Rnd 13: Rep rnd 6, fasten off. *(27 large shells, 27 sc)*

Rnd 14: Attach French rose *(bridal blue)* with sl st in any sc between large shells, ch 1, [sc in sc between large shells, sc in each of next 2 dc, 3 sc in next dc, sc in each of next 2 dc] around, join in beg sc, fasten off. *(224 sc)*

Rnd 15: Attach white with sl st in same sc as beg of previous rnd, ch 1, sc in same sc as beg ch-1, *ch 1, sk next 2 sc, (sc, ch 2, sc) in next sc, (sc, ch 3, sc) in next sc, (sc, ch 2, sc) in next sc, ch 1, sk next 2 sc**, sc in next sc, rep from * around, ending last rep at **, join in beg sc, fasten off. *(189 sc, 27 ch-3 sps, 54 ch-2 sps)* ●

Puffy Flowers Throw continued from page 161

sc in each of next 5 sc] 7 times, sc in last sc, turn.

Row 13: Ch 1, sc in each of next 6 sc, [sc in top of next puff st, sc in ch-1 sp between puff sts, sc in top of next puff st, sc in each of next 5 sc] 7 times, sc in next sc, turn. *(63 sc)*

Rows 14–17: Rep row 2.

Rows 18–73: [Rep rows 4–17 consecutively] 4 times.

Row 74–78: Rep rows 4–8. ●

General Instructions

Please review the following information before working the projects in this book. Important details about the abbreviations and symbols used are included.

Hooks

Crochet hooks are sized for different weights of yarn and thread. For thread crochet, you will usually use a steel crochet hook. Steel crochet-hook sizes range from size 00 to 14. The higher the number of the hook, the smaller your stitches will be. For example, a size 1 steel crochet hook will give you much larger stitches than a size 9 steel crochet hook. Keep in mind that the sizes given with the pattern instructions were obtained by working with the size of thread or yarn and hook given in the materials list. If you work with a smaller hook, depending on your gauge, your finished project size will be smaller; if you work with a larger hook, your finished project size will be larger.

Gauge

Gauge is determined by the tightness or looseness of your stitches and affects the finished size of your project. If you are concerned about the finished size of the project matching the size given, take time to crochet a small section of the pattern and then check your gauge. For example, if the gauge called for is 10 dc = 1 inch, and your gauge is 12 dc to the inch, you should switch to a larger hook. On the other hand, if your gauge is only 8 dc to the inch, you should switch to a smaller hook.

If the gauge given in the pattern is for an entire motif, work one motif and then check your gauge.

Understanding Symbols

As you work through a pattern, you'll quickly notice several symbols in the instructions. These symbols are used to clarify the pattern for you: brackets [ ], curlicue braces { }, parentheses ( ) and asterisks *.

Brackets [ ] are used to set off a group of instructions worked a specific number of times. For example, "[ch 3, sc in next ch-3 sp] 7 times" means to work the instructions inside the [ ] seven times.

Occasionally, a set of instructions inside a set of brackets needs to be repeated, too. In this case, the text within the brackets to be repeated will be set off with curlicue braces { }. For example, "[dc in each of next 3 sts, ch 1, {shell in next ch-1 sp} 3 times, ch 1] 4 times." In this case, in each of the four times you work the instructions included in the brackets, you will work the section included in the curlicue braces three times.

Parentheses ( ) are used to set off a group of stitches to be worked all in one stitch, space or loop. For example, the parentheses ( ) in this set of instructions, "Sk 3 sc, (3 dc, ch 1, 3 dc) in next st" indicate that after skipping 3 sc, you will work 3 dc, ch 1 and 3 more dc all in the next stitch.

Single asterisks * are also used when a group of instructions is repeated. For example, "*Sc in each of the next 5 sc, 2 sc in next sc, rep from * around, join with a sl st in beg sc" simply means you will work the instructions from the first * around the entire round.

Double asterisks ** are used to indicate when a partial set of repeat instructions are to be worked. For example, "*Ch 3, (sc, ch 3, sc) in next ch-2 sp, ch 3**, shell in next dc, rep from * 3 times, ending last rep at **" means that on the third repeat of the single asterisk instructions, you stop at the double asterisks.

Stitch Guide

ABBREVIATIONS

beg	begin/beginning
bpdc	back post double crochet
bpsc	back post single crochet
bptr	back post treble crochet
CC	contrasting color
ch	chain stitch
ch-	refers to chain or space previously made (i.e., ch-1 space)
ch sp	chain space
cl	cluster
cm	centimeter(s)
dc	double crochet
dec	decrease/decreases/decreasing
dtr	double treble crochet
fpdc	front post double crochet
fpsc	front post single crochet
fptr	front post treble crochet
g	gram(s)
hdc	half double crochet
inc	increase/increases/increasing
lp(s)	loop(s)
MC	main color
mm	millimeter(s)
oz	ounce(s)
pc	popcorn
rem	remain/remaining
rep	repeat(s)
rnd(s)	round(s)
RS	right side
sc	single crochet
sk	skip(ped)
sl st	slip stitch
sp(s)	space(s)
st(s)	stitch(es)
tog	together
tr	treble crochet
trtr	triple treble
WS	wrong side
yd(s)	yard(s)
yo	yarn over

Chain—ch: Yo, pull through lp on hook.

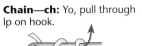

Slip stitch—sl st: Insert hook in st, yo, pull through both lps on hook.

Single crochet—sc: Insert hook in st, yo, pull through st, yo, pull through both lps on hook.

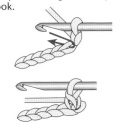

Front loop—front lp
Back loop—back lp

Front Loop   Back Loop

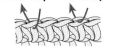

Front post stitch—fp:
Back post stitch—bp: When working post st, insert hook from right to left around post st on previous row.

Back   Front

Post of Stitch

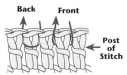

Half double crochet—hdc: Yo, insert hook in st, yo, pull through st, yo, pull through all 3 lps on hook.

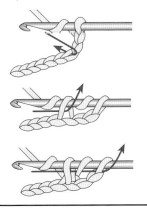

Double crochet—dc: Yo, insert hook in st, yo, pull through st, [yo, pull through 2 lps] twice.

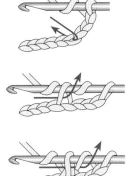

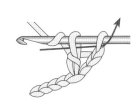

Change colors: Drop first color; with 2nd color, pull through last 2 lps of st.

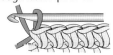

Treble crochet—tr: Yo 2 times, insert hook in st, yo, pull through st, [yo, pull through 2 lps] 3 times.

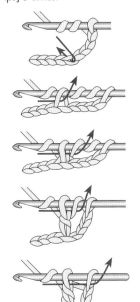

Double treble crochet—dtr: Yo 3 times, insert hook in st, yo, pull through st, [yo, pull through 2 lps] 4 times.

Single crochet decrease (sc dec): (Insert hook, yo, draw up a lp) in each of the sts indicated, yo, draw through all lps on hook.

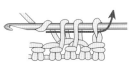

Example of 2-sc dec

Half double crochet decrease (hdc dec): (Yo, insert hook, yo, draw lp through) in each of the sts indicated, yo, draw through all lps on hook.

Example of 2-hdc dec

Double crochet decrease (dc dec): (Yo, insert hook, yo, draw lp through, yo, draw through 2 lps on hook) in each of the sts indicated, yo, draw through all lps on hook.

Example of 2-dc dec

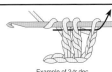

Example of 2-tr dec

Treble crochet decrease (tr dec): Holding back last lp of each st, tr in each of the sts indicated, yo, pull through all lps on hook.

US		UK
sl st (slip stitch)	=	sc (single crochet)
sc (single crochet)	=	dc (double crochet)
hdc (half double crochet)	=	htr (half treble crochet)
dc (double crochet)	=	tr (treble crochet)
tr (treble crochet)	=	dtr (double treble crochet)
dtr (double treble crochet)	=	ttr (triple treble crochet)
skip	=	miss

Special Thanks

Trudy Atteberry
Tranquil Moments Afghan

Svetlana Avrakh
Floral Cluster Skirt

Renee' Barnes
Blue Hawaii Jacket

Elaine Bartlett
Blue Skies Throw, Flower
Patch Afghan, Kitchen Set,
Spa Set

Joyce Bragg
Bride's Bag, Chic & Classy
Laptop Bag, Glitzy Cell
Phone Pouch, Kimono
Jacket, Pocket Place Mat Set

Raynelda Calderon
Edelweiss Scarf

Cindy Carlson
Little Cowgirl

Belinda "Bendy" Carter
Linen Straps

Catherine Costa
Pretty in Pink Sweater

Michelle Crean
Medallion Bookmarks

**Darlene Dale for Caron
International**
Dolman Sweater Set

Terry Day
Woven Shell Table Runner

Rhonda Dodds
Toddler's Tote

Katherine Eng
Cozy Evening Slippers,
Pastel Shells Afghan, Simply
Sweet Doilies, Watermelon
Print Throw, Wear Anywhere
Skirt

Mary Ann Frits
Jazzy Diamonds

Ferosa Harold
Wedding Favor Bags

Rosalie Johnston
Denim Vest

Jenny King
Autumn Wrap

Jewdy Lambert
Fabulous Felted Tote

Sheila Leslie
Classic in Copper Hat &
Scarf, Pink Poodle

Alexandra Lockhart
Posh Purse

Jo Ann Maxwell
Glass Slippers

Maria Nagy
Welcome Baby

Nancy Nehring
Puffy Flowers Throw

Joyce Nordstrom
Oro Valley Scarf, Square
Deal Shrug

Dora Ohrenstein
Patchwork Bolster Pillow,
Woodland Throw

Ann Parnell
Ravishing in Red Top

Sue Penrod
Teddy Bear Magnet

Lori Leigh Sanfratello
Tiny Trendsetter

Nanette Seale
Baby His & Her Onesies,
Baby His & Her Sailor Suits

Darla Sims
Bear Blanket Buddy,
Classy Cables Pillow, Easy
Summer Vest or Top, Hot
Spots Top

Mary Ann Sipes
Car Seat Blankie, Retro Place
Mat Set

Diane Stone
Blushing Rose Sachet

Michele Maks Thompson
Winter Warmers

**Margret Willson for Caron
International**
Hairpin Lace Shawl

Buyer's Guide

**Spinrite Yarns
(Bernat & Patons)**
320 Livingstone Ave. South
Listowell, ON
Canada
N4W 3H3
(888) 368-8401
www.bernat.com
www.patonsyarns.com

Caron International Inc.
Customer Service
P.O. Box 222
Washington, NC 27889
www.caron.com

**Coats & Clark
(Aunt Lydia's, Moda Dea,
Red Heart, TLC)**
Consumer Services
P.O. Box 12229
Greenville, SC 29612-0229
(800) 648-1479
www.coatsandclark.com
www.modadea.com

DMC Corp.
77 South Hackensack Ave.
Bldg 10F
South Kearny, NJ 07032
(973) 589-0606
www.dmc-usa.com

Ecolution
P.O. Box 697
Santa Cruz, CA 95061
(800) 973-HEMP (4367)
www.ecolution.com

Erdal
333 Northern Blvd. #5
Great Neck, NY 11021
(800) 237-6594
www.erdal.com

Hobby Lobby
Crafts, Etc.®
Customer Service
7717 SW 44th Street
Oklahoma City, OK 73179
(800) 888-0321 Ext. 1275
www.craftsetc.com

Kreinik Mfg. Co., Inc.
1708 Gihon Rd.
Parkersburg, WV 26102
(800) 537-2166
www.kreinik.com

Lion Brand
135 Kero Road
Carlstadt, NJ 07072
(800) 258-YARN (9276)
www.lionbrand.com

Plymouth
500 Lafayette St.
Bristol, PA 19007
(215) 788-0459
www.plymouthyarn.com

RYC
Green Lane Mill
Holmfirth
HD9 2BR
England
(603) 886-5041
www.ryclassic.com